Basic Beaded Bobby Pin
PG 8

3-Bead Basic
PG 14

Scalloped Edge
PG 18

Decorated Tips
PG 22

Bobby Pin Designs

The Twist
PG 24

The Daisy
PG 28

Grapes
PG 34

Dragonfly
PG 40

WHAT COMES WITH THIS BOOK

This book comes with all the materials you need to make beaded bobby pins. Included are beads (assortment may vary from what is pictured here), 28-gauge wire, and an assortment of small and large bobby pins.

Faceted crystal beads

E beads

Decorative beads

Bugle beads

Seed beads

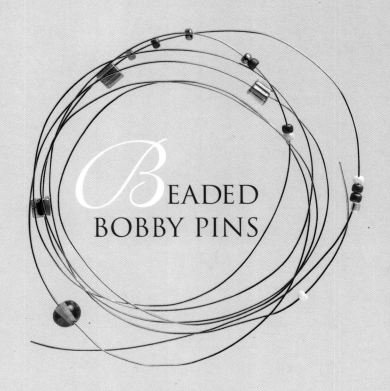

Beaded Bobby Pins

by Marilyn Green

KLUTZ.

KLUTZ

KLUTZ® is a kids' company staffed entirely by real human beings. We began our corporate life in 1977 in an office we shared with a Chevrolet Impala. Today we've outgrown our founding garage, but Palo Alto, California, remains Klutz galactic headquarters. For those of you who collect corporate mission statements, here's ours:

- Create wonderful things.
- Be good.
- Have fun.

Write Us
We would love to hear your comments regarding this or any of our books. We have many!

KLUTZ.®

455 Portage Avenue
Palo Alto, California 94306
Visit us  **KLUTZ**.com

N E L V A N A
Klutz is a Nelvana Company

Do You Teach?
We offer a classroom set of make-your-own Klutz books. E-mail bookfactory@klutz.com, write, or visit our website for details.

Additional Copies and More Supplies
For the location of your nearest Klutz retailer, call (650) 857-0888. Should they be tragically out of stock, additional copies of this book, extra sets of bobby pins, beads, and wire, and the entire library of 100% Klutz certified books are available in our mail order catalog. See back page.

Book printed in Korea; beads made in Czech Republic; wire and bobby pins, Taiwan.
© 1999 Klutz, Inc. All rights reserved.
Klutz® is a registered trademark of Klutz, Inc.

ISBN 1-57054-401-8

4 1 5 8 5

Setting Up

Choose a well-lighted spot with a flat surface on which to set your beads. In addition to the supplies provided, you'll need a ruler or tape measure, fingernail clippers for cutting the wire, and a white china plate on which to spread your beads. If you want to keep beads separated by color, use several small, shallow saucers. Placing your beading plate(s) on a towel helps keep beads from bouncing onto the table and floor. A light-colored towel is best for bead visibility.

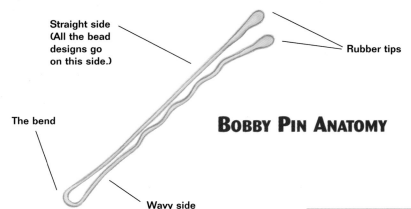

Straight side (All the bead designs go on this side.)

Rubber tips

The bend

Wavy side

BOBBY PIN ANATOMY

TAMING YOUR WIRE

You use wire to attach beads to the bobby pins. We provide 28-gauge wire because it threads easily through the tiny holes of seed beads. Cut wire with fingernail clippers; do not use your good scissors. Here are two tips for working with wire:

Keep the wire in an open loop to avoid kinks.

Kinks can be removed by rubbing wire up and down against the side of an old table — not your mom's best table.

However, repeated straightening will weaken the wire eventually, causing it to break. If your wire is badly kinked, it is better to cut a new piece and start over.

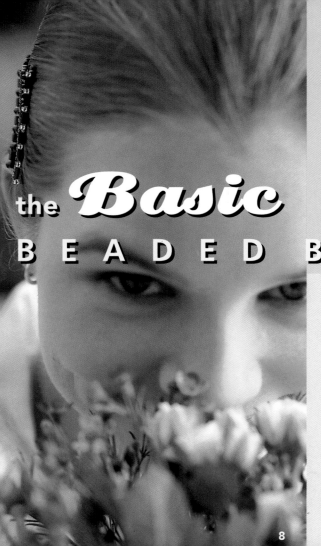

the *Basic*
BEADED BOBBY

You have to learn the Basic. You can make an incredible variety of beaded bobby pins with this simple technique.

Once you've made a simple pin, experiment with different bead sizes and color combinations. See page 22 for inspiration.

YOU WILL NEED

A small bobby pin

25–28 seed beads

18–20 inches
of 28-gauge wire

fingernail clippers

1 Hold the bobby pin with the straight side facing you. Place the center of the length of wire over the straight side of the bobby pin near the bend.

2 Hold the center point of the wire against the bobby pin with your thumb. Now grasp the wire to the right of the bobby pin and slide it through the rubber tips and up to the bend in the bobby pin.

Wrap this half of the wire over the bobby pin to the right. End up looking like this.

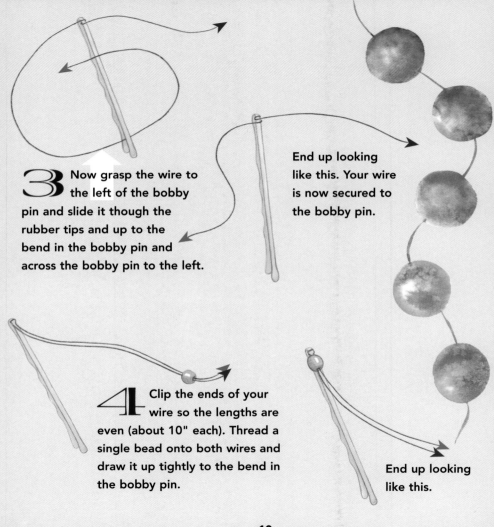

3 Now grasp the wire to the left of the bobby pin and slide it though the rubber tips and up to the bend in the bobby pin and across the bobby pin to the left.

End up looking like this. Your wire is now secured to the bobby pin.

4 Clip the ends of your wire so the lengths are even (about 10" each). Thread a single bead onto both wires and draw it up tightly to the bend in the bobby pin.

End up looking like this.

5 Wrap wires as in illustration, pulling the wire tightly against the bead to secure it.

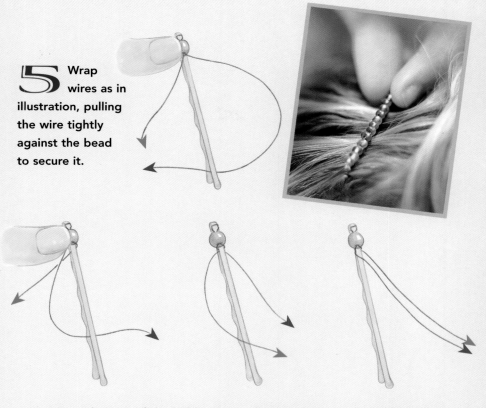

Here's a side view of the bobby pin to show you what it should look like... and to remind you not to wrap your wire around the whole bobby pin. Be sure to wrap around the flat side only.

End up looking like this.

Side view

6 Continue threading on beads and wrapping until you come to the rubber tips of the bobby pin.

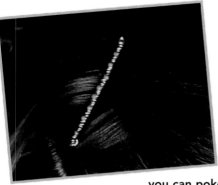

Finishing Off

Now wrap each wire end around the bobby pin tightly several times to secure it. If the hole in your bead is large enough, you can poke the wire ends inside to hide them as shown at right.

If your beads are tiny, wrap wire around the bobby pin as shown in the illustrations below and clip off excess wire. Wrapping wire **here** rather than at the rubber **tip** will prevent the wire ends from poking you when you place the bobby pin in your hair. If you're using tiny beads you won't be able to go back through your last bead to finish. Instead, wrap three times above and below the last bead.

Finishing with big beads

Thread back through blue bead

Clip here to finish

End up like this

Finishing with tiny beads

Clip here to finish

Clip here to finish

1
2
3

THREE-BEADS-AT-A-TIME

BASIC BOBBY PIN

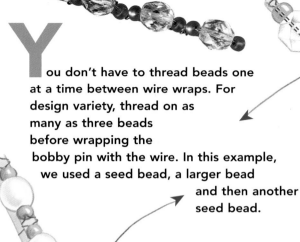

You don't have to thread beads one at a time between wire wraps. For design variety, thread on as many as three beads before wrapping the bobby pin with the wire. In this example, we used a seed bead, a larger bead and then another seed bead.

Start like this — three beads, then a wrap.

Finish by first wrapping three times at the tip...

...then bring your wires up and wrap three times here.

Clip here to finish

Clip here to finish

With just this basic technique you can make an incredible variety of designs by varying your colors and bead choices.

THE Scalloped VARIATION

1 For this variation, you need a longer length of wire. For a small bobby pin, 27 inches is plenty. Follow the directions for making the three-beads-at-a-time bobby pin just described (page 14).

When you reach the rubber tips, wrap each length of wire around the bobby pin several times to secure your beads.

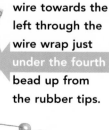

2 Thread six seed beads on the wire to the right.

Now thread that wire towards the left through the wire wrap just under the fourth bead up from the rubber tips.

4th bead

Detail

19

3 Continue making six-bead scallops from side to side until you reach the bend of the bobby pin.

4 When you reach the bend in the bobby pin wrap the wire around the bend several times to secure it. Clip off excess wire.

5 Return your attention to the rubber tip end of the bobby pin. Repeat all the steps you just finished. Thread six seed beads onto the wire to the left of the bobby and then thread that wire towards the right through the wire wrap just above the third bead up from the rubber tips.

Finish as in step 3.

YOU CAN MAKE

ALL OF THESE

the twist

The twisted bobby pin is probably the fastest project in this book. It works best with small beads.

1 Attach wire to the bobby pin as in the basic bobby (page 8). Thread an equal number of beads on each wire until each beaded section is as long as the bobby pin. A short bobby pin is about 25 to 30 seed beads long, depending upon the width of your beads from hole to hole.

2 Now hold the bobby pin in one hand and the wire with the other hand. Twist the wire three or four times.

3 Wrap each wire twice around the rubber-tipped end of the bobby pin to secure.

4 Now "sew" the excess wire around the underside of the twist and the flat side of the bobby pin to secure the beaded twist to the pin. "Sew" with the right wire first and then with the left, wrapping until you reach the curved end of the bobby pin with each wire. Wrap wires around the curve in the bobby pin to secure. Clip excess wire.

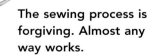

The sewing process is forgiving. Almost any way works.

27

the Daisy

For a small bobby pin with five flowers

YOU WILL NEED

A small bobby pin

40 seed beads

20 inches of 28-gauge wire

1 Cut 20" of 28-gauge wire. Start this bobby pin by securing your wire and attaching a seed bead as in the basic bobby pin.

2 Thread six beads onto the left wire. Push the beads up the wire as far as they will go.

Take this wire...

...back through the first bead.

Now hold your pin like this.

3 Pull the wire tight, forming a loop. *Important:* Use a finger to hold the line of six beads as far up the wire toward the bobby pin as possible.

6
5
4
3 2
1

Detail

Note the numbered beads in the illustration.

4 Pull the loop tight.

End up like this.

Pull tight.

Thread a contrasting bead onto the same wire. This bead forms the center of the flower.

5 Look at the illustration carefully to identify the numbered beads on your flower. Push the contrasting bead into the center of the flower and thread the wire down through the fourth flower bead as shown. To avoid kinks, pull the wire carefully, always keeping it in a loop or U shape.

Pull the wire tight.

6 Wrap the wires around the bobby as shown and pull to secure your flower.

Pull tight.

Pull tight.

7 Add a separator bead to the bobby pin as in step 1.

8 Continue making daisies to cover the bobby pin. Wrap and snip to finish as usual.

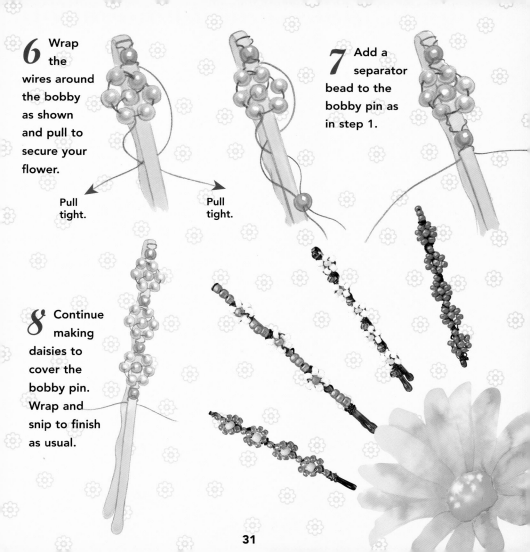

Adding Leaves

For a small bobby pin with
a single daisy and two leaves

YOU WILL NEED

A small bobby pin, 39 seed beads,

20 inches of 28-gauge wire,

fingernail clippers

1 Cover a
bobby pin
with a daisy and
several seed beads
for the stem as
in illustration.

See page 28
for how to
make a daisy.

2 Thread eight
beads onto
the right wire.

3 Thread this wire back through the first bead on this wire as indicated...

4 ...then pull it tight to form the first leaf and wrap the wire around the bobby to secure.

5 Make another leaf on the left wire.

Cover the rest of the bobby pin with seed beads and finish as in the basic bobby pin.

GRAPES

You can start this project on either end of the bobby pin, depending upon how you want the grapes to appear in your hair.

1 Cut 20" of 28-gauge wire. Attach a single bead to the curved end of the bobby pin as in steps 1–6 of the basic bobby.

2 Thread two green beads on the right wire.

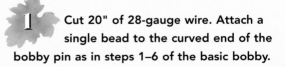

3 Thread the right wire back through the first of the two beads. Keep the loop open to avoid kinking.

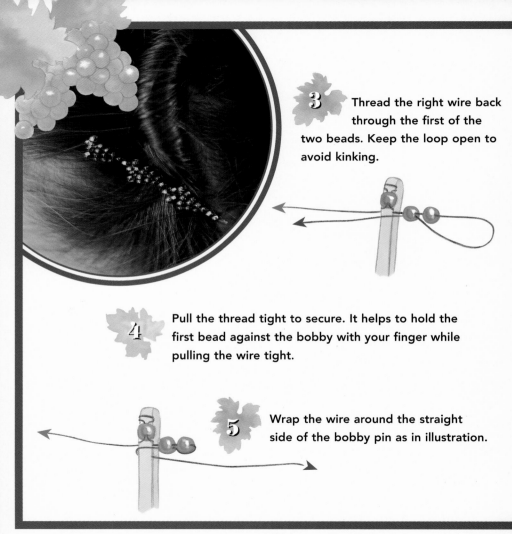

4 Pull the thread tight to secure. It helps to hold the first bead against the bobby with your finger while pulling the wire tight.

5 Wrap the wire around the straight side of the bobby pin as in illustration.

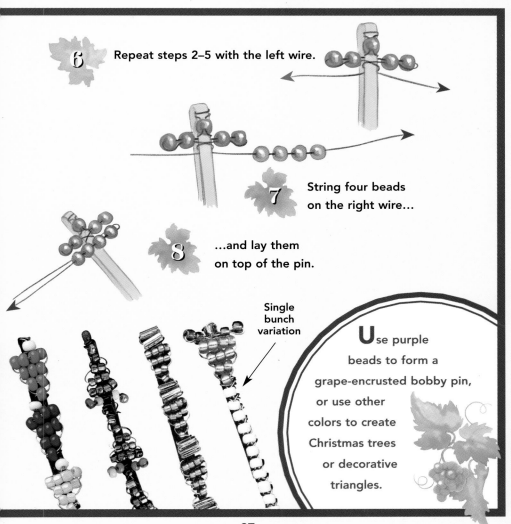

6 Repeat steps 2–5 with the left wire.

7 String four beads on the right wire...

8 ...and lay them on top of the pin.

Single bunch variation

Use purple beads to form a grape-encrusted bobby pin, or use other colors to create Christmas trees or decorative triangles.

9 Now thread the green wire back through all four beads. Pull the two wires tight.

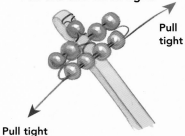

Pull tight

Pull tight

10 Repeat step 8 with a row of three beads. Next do a row of two beads. End your grape cluster with a single bead — also attached as in step 8.

11 Wrap wires around the bobby to secure the grape cluster.

12 Add a green bead to the bobby as in step 1. Then add a second bead also as in step 1.

Grape leaves

13 Make another pair of grape leaves. Then make an additional bunch of grapes. Continue this process until the bobby pin is covered. Finish as in the basic bobby pin. Wrap and clip at the end as usual.

39

YOU WILL NEED

A small bobby pin

83 seed beads

3 E beads

27 inches of
28-gauge wire

1 faceted crystal bead

fingernail clippers

dragonfly

40

Cut 27" of wire and secure it to the bobby pin as in steps 1–3 of the basic bobby pin (page 9). We started at the curved end of the bobby pin, so the insect sits on the tips of the pin. You can start your project at either end of the bobby pin — depending on where you want the dragonfly.

41

2

Make a row of 14 beads, attaching them as in steps 4–6 of the basic bobby pin (page 9).

3

Add an E bead and wrap.

E bead

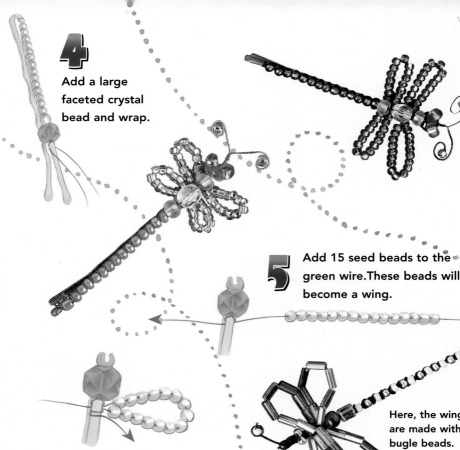

4 Add a large faceted crystal bead and wrap.

5 Add 15 seed beads to the green wire. These beads will become a wing.

Here, the wings are made with bugle beads.

6 Wrap the wire around the flat side of the bobby pin as indicated in the illustration to secure the wing.

43

7 Grab the entire wing between your fingers and give it a twist as in the illustration.

8 Repeat steps 4–6 on the left wire to form the second wing.

9 Thread on a seed bead and wrap.

10 Repeat steps 5–7, threading on 18 seed beads this time to create another set of wings.

11

Bring wires up from the underside of the bobby. Thread an E bead on each wire to form the dragonfly's eyes.

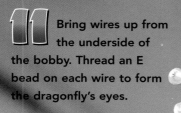 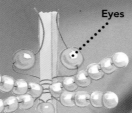 **Eyes**

Antennae

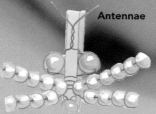

Bring the wires to meet in the center of the bobby. Twist the wire a few times as in the illustration. The long ends form the antennae.

Clip here.

12

Loop the "antennae" through two beads. Pull tight and clip.

45

Credits & Acknowledgments

Project Designers
Marilyn Green
Sherri Haab
Jacqueline Lee
Ann Tevepaugh Mitchell
Laura Torres

Book Design
Kevin Plottner

Illustrations
Sara Boore

Photographers
Peter Fox
Mark Gottlieb
Thomas Heinser
Jock McDonald

Hair and Makeup
Annaliese & Bernadine
Bibianol/Artists Untied,
Erin Gallager, Jenny
Hwang Ikeda,
Jasmine Manders,
David Searle

Model Casting
Corie Thompson
THS Casting
Sheila Wolfson

Models
Bernadette Alverio, Jerylyn Andrews,
Corie Au, Jennifer Austin, Laura Bellini,
Samantha Blattels, Nicole Brandt-Young,
Katie Chou, Molly Anne Coogan,
Kelly Curran, Molly Daly, Kathleen Marie
Diggins, Robin Easterbrook, Stephanie
Evans, Amber Henard, Kelsey Jessup,
Kalona Patrice Johnson, Gladie Kirkman,
Mai Komoriya, Gaile Lai,
Emilie Louie, Erica
Martinez, Molly
McAndrew, Sarah
McIntyre, Polivia Ponsart,
Nadine Rumble, Tiffany
Simon, Catherine
Spence, Megan Staats,
Blair Thomson-Levin,
Laura Wolfson,
Mickey the Poodle

Testers
Mary Beth Arago,
Laurie Campbell,
Molly Coogan,
Molly Daly, Anna
Ferrari, Rachel &
Michelle Haab, Paula
Hannigan, Elizabeth
Jackson, Connie
Kuge, Christy Lynn,
Patty Morris, Ronda Rosner, Kristin
Schaller, Maria Seamans, Bridget
Stolee, Kathy Wang, Sheila Wolfson

Arbiter of Good Taste
MaryEllen Podgorski

Picky, Picky, Picky
John Cassidy

Write us for a free catalog
in five easy steps

Klutz Catalog! You can order the entire library of 100% Klutz certified books, extra sets of bobby pins, beads, and wire, and a diverse collection of other things we happen to like from The Klutz Catalog. It is, in all modesty, unlike any other catalog — and it's yours for the asking.

1 Cut out.　**2** Fill in.　**3** Add stamp.　**4** Mail (important).　**5** Wait impatiently.　We'll take care of the rest.

Who Are You?

Name: _____

Age: _____ ❏ Too high to count　　❏ Boy ❏ Girl

Address: _____

City: _____ State: _____ Zip: _____

My Bright Ideas!

Tell us what you think of this book. _____

_____

What would you like us to write a book about? _____

_____

_____

❏ Check this box if you want us to send you **The Klutz Catalog**.

If you're a grown-up who'd like to hear about new Klutz stuff, give us your e-mail address and we'll stay in touch.

E-mail address: _____

BEADED BOBBY PINS

More Great Books from KLUTZ

Bead Rings

Beadlings: How to Make Beaded Creatures & Creations

Beads: A Book of Ideas & Instructions

Create Anything with Clay

Hair: A Book of Braiding & Styles

Hair Wraps

Hemp Bracelets

KLUTZ®

455 Portage Avenue
Palo Alto, CA 94306

Attn: Fi Fi

Why Do You Need This New Edition?

This edition of *The Writer's FAQs* differs from the previous edition in several key ways. Here are five that make this book indispensable:

1. **Expanded research section.** This edition offers a **new chapter on plagiarism** to help you understand how and why not only to avoid it, but how to define and recognize it. There is also an **expanded chapter on evaluating sources** to keep you up-to-date on new practices and technologies.

2. **New chapters on common assignments, with expanded coverage of argument.** The **new chapter on argument** includes coverage on using logical, ethical, and emotional appeals. It also explains, with examples, the importance of visual rhetoric. You will also find an expanded **thesis section offering more examples** on narrowing and revising your claims. Sections on **writing about literature** and **portfolios** have been expanded into stand-alone chapters, and a **new chapter on multimodal projects** provides tips on how to format and organize your materials.

3. **Updated and more complete documentation section.** You'll find new **Paper Format Quick Guides** in all four styles, **new student paper excerpts,** and **more documentation examples than ever before. New annotated images of sources** and **Quick Guides for Works Cited (MLA) and References entries (APA)** offer you easy-to-use guidelines for source documentation. In addition, the **CSE chapter has been significantly expanded** to include twice the number of citation samples featuring all three citation options.

4. **An enhanced focus on FAQs.** New **FAQ boxes** throughout the text offer you ways to proceed and answers for your frequently asked questions. You can also refer to the **Question & Correct pages** at the beginning of each section.

5. **Even more student-friendly features than ever before.** A **Detailed Table of Contents** has been added, and **learning outcomes** on each part opener provide an overview of the key topics in each section of the book. This edition's **color-coded highlighting system** for documentation styles and its distinctive **colored on-page tabs with correction symbols** make it even more user-friendly for writers and researchers.

PEARSON

The Writer's FAQs

A POCKET HANDBOOK

FIFTH EDITION

MURIEL HARRIS
Purdue University

JENNIFER L. KUNKA
Francis Marion University

PEARSON

Boston Columbus Indianapolis New York San Francisco Upper Saddle River
Amsterdam Cape Town Dubai London Madrid Milan Munich Paris
Montreal Toronto Delhi Mexico City Sao Paulo Sydney Hong Kong
Seoul Singapore Taipei Tokyo

Senior Sponsoring Editor:
Katharine Glynn
Assistant Editor: Rebecca Gilpin
Director of Development:
Mary Ellen Curley
Development Editor:
Anne Stameshkin
Executive Marketing Manager:
Tom DeMarco
Executive Digital Producer:
Stefanie Snajder
Digital Project Manager:
Janell Lantana
Digital Editor: Sara Gordus

Production/Project Manager:
Eric Jorgensen
**Project Coordination, Text
Design, and Electronic Page
Makeup:** Laserwords Maine
Senior Cover Design Manager:
John Callahan
Cover Image: cobalt88/Shutterstock
Senior Manufacturing Buyer:
Roy Pickering
Printer/Binder: RR Donnelley &
Sons/Crawfordsville
Cover Printer: Lehigh-Phoenix
Color/Hagerstown

Credits and acknowledgments borrowed from other sources and reproduced, with permission, in this textbook appear on the appropriate page within text [or on page 288].

Library of Congress Control Number: 2012031631

1 2 3 4 5 6 7 8 9 10—DOC—15 14 13 12

www.pearsonhighered.com

ISBN 10:   0-321-85752-6
ISBN 13: 978-0-321-85752-1

How to Use This Book

- **Need to know what's in this book?** Check the Detailed Contents inside the back cover of the book. The beginning of each major section also lists what's covered there.

- **Have a question this book can answer?** On pp. vi–viii you'll find a list of questions that writers often ask and the page numbers to turn to for answers. And there are more questions to help you at the beginning of each part.

- **What can you learn in each chapter?** There are Learning Objectives listing the skills and processes covered in the pages that follow.

- **What are FAQ and Try This boxes?** Throughout the book, you'll find FAQ boxes that answer "frequently asked questions" about writing. The Try This boxes have suggestions for you to use when planning, researching, revising, and editing.

- **Do you have questions about words such as *affect/ effect* or *fewer/less* that are confusing?** Look through the Glossary of Usage, on pp. 279–283, to see if the words you want to check are listed there.

- **Do you want to know the meaning of some grammatical term?** On pp. 283–288 are the definitions of the most commonly used grammatical terms.

- **Is there an index for looking up the information I need?** On pp. 289–294 is an alphabetical list of topics covered in this book.

- **Do you want to know what some correction symbols refer to?** On the inside back cover is a list of correction symbols some instructors use, and there are page numbers to go to in this book to explain them.

We hope you find this book easy to use and so helpful that it becomes a writing friend to keep nearby as you write. We offer special thanks to the student writers who shared their writing in this book: Jennifer Coker, Sydney Cumbie, and Staci Poston. We are deeply indebted to our faithful in-house support team members, Sam Harris (and family) and Andrew Kunka.

Muriel Harris
Jennifer L. Kunka

Question and Correct

Research   p. 135

Documentation   p. 179

I

Composing, Conversing, Collaborating

Contents of this section

Question and Correct

	SECTION	PAGE
LEARNING OBJECTIVE: Defining global issues and higher-order concerns (HOCs)		
✦ What are global issues or higher-order concerns (HOCs), and why are they important?	1	4
LEARNING OBJECTIVE: Understanding the relationship between purpose, audience, and topic		
✦ What are some different purposes for writing, and why should I think about them?	1a	4
✦ Why is it important to think about the audience of my paper?	1b	5
✦ How can I come up with a topic to write about?	1c	5

1

Global Issues/Higher-Order Concerns (HOCs)

This chapter covers the **global issues** of writing, the **higher-order concerns**, or **HOCs**.

1a Purpose

The purpose of writing is the goal we want to achieve when we write for others. We write to convey information, to persuade others to believe or act in certain ways, to help them remember, to help them learn more about the topic they are writing about, and to explore more fully what is on our minds. You too can plan your writing by asking yourself what you want your audience to know, believe, or do after reading your paper. And checking that your purpose fits your assignment will keep the writing effective. For example, if a writer is asked to review a movie and offer an evaluation, but writes a plot summary instead, the paper will not be effective because it doesn't fulfill the assignment.

FAQ

What are common purposes for writing?
- **Summarizing.** Stating concisely the main points of a piece of writing
- **Defining.** Explaining the meaning of a word or concept
- **Analyzing.** Breaking the topic into parts and examining how these parts work
- **Persuading.** Offering convincing support for a point of view
- **Reporting.** Examining evidence and data on a subject and presenting an objective overview
- **Evaluating.** Setting up and explaining criteria for evaluation and judging the quality or importance of what is being evaluated
- **Discussing or examining.** Considering main points, implications, and relationships to other topics

- **Interpreting.** Explaining the meaning or implications of a topic
- **Exploring.** Considering a topic by putting mental notions into written form

1b Audience

Is the audience you are writing to appropriate for your assignment and purpose? The information you include, your tone, and your assumptions about your readers' level of interest or knowledge of a subject will shape your writing.

TRY THIS

Defining Your Audience

Ask yourself the following questions:

- **Who is my audience?** Peers? A potential boss? A teacher? Readers of a particular publication? People who are likely to agree or disagree?
- **What information should be included?** What do your readers already know about the subject? What will they need to know to understand your topic and point of view?
- **What is the audience's attitude?** Are readers interested in the subject, or will you need to create interest? Are they sympathetic, neutral, or inclined to disagree? How might you convince those who don't agree?
- **What is the audience's background?** What is their education, specialized knowledge, religion, race, cultural heritage, political views, occupation, and age?

1c Topic

The topic of a piece of writing may be something the writer chooses, or it may be assigned. To choose a topic, try one or more of the strategies suggested here.

TRY THIS

Finding a Topic

- What is a problem you'd like to solve?
  _____ is a problem, and I think we should _____.
- What is something that pleases, puzzles, irritates, or bothers you?
  _____ annoys (or pleases) me because _____.

- What is something you'd like to convince others of?
  I think that _____ because _____.

- What is something that seems to contradict what you read or see around you?
  Why does _____? (or) I've noticed that _____, but _____.

- What is something you'd like to learn more about?
  I wonder how _____.

- What is something you know about that others may not know?
  I'd like to tell you about _____.

1d Thesis

A thesis statement is the main idea or subject of your paper. It's the promise you make to your readers: if they read the paper, this is what they'll read about. In an informative paper, your thesis statement summarizes your discussion about your topic. In an argumentative paper, your thesis communicates your primary position, solution, or interpretation to your audience. Thesis statements are often written as a single, concise sentence. For longer or more complex works, your thesis might be written in two or three sentences or even a short paragraph.

FAQ

How do I write an effective thesis statement?

There are two parts to an effective thesis statement: the **topic** and a **comment** that makes an important point about the topic.

Topic	Comment
Effective document design	helps technical writers present complex material more clearly.
Twitter	has become a popular social networking tool that provides users with a simple way to keep up with friends and interact with celebrities, politicians, and people who share common interests.

An effective thesis statement should have a topic that interests your readers, is as specific as possible, and is limited enough to make it manageable.

Once you have drafted a thesis statement, review and revise it, if necessary, to make sure it is focused and clearly written.

Narrow thesis statements that are too general

If a thesis statement is too general, it will be very difficult for you to decide what to write about. Consider this thesis statement:

Thesis statement: Education in the United States needs to improve.

To narrow your thesis, think about journalists' questions. **Who** *should be responsible for improving education, and* **for whom** *should it be improved?* **What** *should be improved, and* **why?** **How** *should it be improved? Think about all the ways education could be improved. Music education? Financial education? More funding for teachers? Smaller class sizes? Alternative curriculum strategies? Consider this revision:*

Revised thesis statement: To meet the global marketplace's demand for civil engineers, American high schools should offer college-prep courses that include hands-on training in engineering.

This thesis statement now states **who** *should take action* (American high schools), **what** *should be done* (offer hands-on training in engineering), **how** (through college prep courses), *and* **why** (to meet the global marketplace's demand for civil engineers). *With these specifics, the writer will be able to provide a more focused argument.*

Strengthen thesis statements that are too vague

Thesis statements that are too vague can leave too much to the readers' interpretation. Consider this thesis:

Thesis statement: Homeowners who help the environment should receive federal tax credits.

What kind of "help" is covered here? Homeowners who recycle a few aluminum cans each year? Who plant a tree each year? More specifics are needed to define what kind of "help" deserves a tax credit.

Consider this revision:

Revised thesis statement: Homeowners who install solar panels or other energy-producing equipment on their houses should receive a one-time federal tax credit up to $5000.

This thesis now defines "help" as the homeowner installing energy-producing equipment. This thesis also explains how much of a tax credit this writer believes homeowners should receive.

Add qualifying statements to your thesis when appropriate

A qualifier can limit how much your thesis covers. Often, qualifying words or statements help prove your argument more effectively. Consider the following:

Thesis statement: Increased drilling for oil on the Intercontinental Shelf will solve the United States' dependence on foreign oil.

Will this single solution "solve" the problem? Critics could point out that increased drilling on the Intercontinental Shelf will take time and may not yield enough oil to meet Americans' needs. If the entire problem cannot be solved *with this solution, words like* reduce *and* lessen *would offer a more manageable thesis statement.*

Consider the revision:

Revised thesis statement: Increasing drilling for oil on the Intercontinental Shelf will reduce the United States' dependence on foreign oil.

This thesis statement allows the writer to continue with the argument without having to solve *the entire problem—just* reduce *it.*

1e Organization

As you read over your draft, check to see if your topic sentences clearly communicate the central idea of each paragraph. Then ask yourself if each paragraph contributes to the thesis in some way and if each paragraph leads logically to the next one. With any organizational strategy, you want to avoid jumps in the development of your thesis that might confuse your reader. For suggestions on how to organize your paragraphs and whole papers, see 1f.

For some—but not all—writers, creating an **outline**, either before or after drafting, can be useful because it helps group related ideas together and rearrange material into the best logical structure. Informal outlines are often written as simple lists, sometimes called "working outlines," and it's easy to revise as you progress. For formal outlines, choose sentences, words, or phrases that show how items are related. Use Roman numerals for main headings, capital letters for major subheads, and lowercase letters for minor subheads. If you find that some idea or subtopic doesn't seem to fit, it may not belong in the paper.

I. Show Need for More Donated Food for Local
    Homeless ← ─────────────────────────── Main idea

    A. Current level of homeless
        in the community ← ─────────────── Subheading

        1. Homeless shelters overcrowded ⎫
        2. Food banks empty by end   ⎬ Supporting ideas
            of the month   ⎭

    B. Donations not keeping up with demand

    C. Major local donor (restaurant) out of business

    D. Projections for future unemployment when auto
        parts plant closes

II. Offer Solutions

    A. Local media (newspapers, TV) used to present
        problem

    B. Requests for donations sent to local churches and
        synagogues

    C. New commercial sources sought
        1. Local supermarkets
        2. College residence hall cafeterias
        3. Restaurants

    D. Volunteer food collectors and distributors sought

1f Paragraph development

A paragraph is well developed when it has enough details, examples, specifics, supporting evidence, and information to back up your thesis. You may need to delete material that is no longer relevant or add material to strengthen your thesis and help you achieve your purpose. Try to read your paper as an uninformed reader would, and ask yourself what else you'd need to know.

Consider these strategies for organizing your ideas as you develop your paragraphs:

- **Chronological order.** Show historical development or explain a process

- **General-to-specific order.** Provide basic information before giving specific details and examples

- **Cause-and-effect order.** Describe how someone or something affects someone or something else

- **Compare-and-contrast.** Discuss similarities and differences between groups

1g   Transitions

Every paragraph should be written so that each sentence flows smoothly into the next. If your ideas, sentences, and details fit together clearly, your readers can follow along easily and not get lost. To help your reader, try repeating key terms and phrases and using synonyms, pronouns, and transitional devices between sentences and paragraphs. (See Chapter 15 for a list of transition words and phrases.) Also check for missing information that causes a break in your explanation or argument.

FAQ

How can I connect ideas between paragraphs?

To create a transition between paragraphs on two different subjects, try creating a sentence at the beginning of the next paragraph with 1) an introductory phrase or clause referring back to the topic of the previous paragraph, and 2) an independent clause introducing the topic of the following paragraph.

1h   Introductions

The introduction brings the reader into your world, builds interest in your subject, and announces topics. Think of an introduction as a plan or map: by the end of it, your readers should have a clear sense of what your topic is and how the paper will be organized. Try one or more of the following strategies for writing an introduction:

- Introduce a relevant quotation from a credible source.
- Cite an interesting statistic.
- Offer a concrete example.
- Provide a vivid description.
- Pose a question.
- Relate an anecdote.
- Suggest a future possibility (something that hasn't happened yet but could reasonably occur)

1i   Conclusions

The conclusion signals that the paper is ending and helps put the whole paper in perspective. It is your opportunity to summarize your major points and make a memorable or persuasive final statement. Consider the following strategies as you write your conclusion.

Look backward through your paper. If the paper has a complex discussion, try any of the following:

* *Summarize the main points* to remind the reader of what was discussed.

* *Emphasize points* you don't want the reader to forget.

* *Refer to something in the introduction*, thus coming full circle.

Look forward to the future implications of your topic. If the paper is short or doesn't need a summary, try the following:

* *Pose a question* for the reader to consider.

* *Offer advice.*

* *Call for action* the reader can take.

* *Consider possible outcomes and effects* of your topic.

1j Revision

An important part of writing is revising—re-seeing how effectively the paper communicates your ideas and checking that the ideas and paragraphs are ordered appropriately. Spending time on revision can make your writing more effective, persuasive, and interesting. As you write, consider these questions to revise for global issues or Higher-Order Concerns (HOCs).

Purpose.   What is the purpose of this paper? Have you achieved the purpose? If not, what's needed?

Audience.   Who is the audience for this paper? What assumptions have you made about your audience members? Did you tell them what they already know? Did you leave out anything your audience needs to know?

Topic.   Is your topic narrowed down sufficiently so you can discuss it effectively, given the expected length of your assignment?

Thesis.   Is the thesis clearly stated? Has it been narrowed sufficiently? Is it appropriate for the assignment? Can you summarize your thesis?

Organization.   What is the central idea of each paragraph? Does that idea contribute to the thesis? Do the paragraphs progress in an organized, logical way?

Development. Are there paragraphs where more details, examples, or specifics would help? Are there irrelevant details that should be omitted?

Transitions. Are there places where the paper doesn't flow? Are there sentence or paragraph gaps where transitions may be needed?

Introduction. Does your introduction grab the reader's attention and introduce your topic? Would another introduction strategy be more effective?

Conclusion. Does the conclusion bring together the ideas of the paper? Would looking ahead to the future of your topic help to wrap up your discussion?

TRY THIS

Revising Your Draft

- **When you return to a paper you started before, read from the beginning to the section you'll be working on now.** This helps you get back into the flow of thought.
- **Track your changes using word-processing software.**
- **Create multiple drafts.** Save each draft with a new file name and include the date in case you want to put something back in your draft.
- **Print out and read a hard copy.** This can help you get a sense of the whole paper.
- **Switch to "print preview" to see each whole page on the screen.** If one paragraph looks shorter than the others, it might need more development. If a paragraph seems too long, check if it should be divided into two.
- **Meet with a writing center tutor.** Tutors can help you take your work for a "test drive" and see if it meets the assignment.

FAQ

What should I do when I meet with a writing center tutor?

- **Plan ahead.** Give yourself enough time to prepare and ask questions, plus time after to revise your writing.
- **Bring along your assignment and any requirements.**
- **Think about the kinds of help you want—and tell your tutor.** Do you need help developing a thesis? Organizing ideas? Citing sources? Editing for grammatical issues?

- **Read your paper aloud, or ask the tutor to read the paper aloud to you.** You'll see and hear problems that won't be as evident when you read silently.
- **Remember that tutors do not just proofread.** They want to help you learn how to revise your own work.
- **Visit tutors for help with any project—from papers to résumés.**

2

Local Issues/Later-Order Concerns (LOCs)

When you edit and proofread, look closely at what are called local issues or later-order concerns (LOCs)—details of grammar, usage, punctuation, spelling, missing words, format requirements, and other mechanics.

TRY THIS

Proofreading for Local Issues/Later-Order Concerns (LOCs)

- **Edit on hard copy pages.**
- **Go backwards through your paper, sentence by sentence.** This can help you focus on grammar and spelling.
- **Slide a card down under each line as you reread.** This will help your eyes slow down.
- **Put the paper aside for a bit after you draft it.** It's easier to see problems with fresh eyes.
- **Track your changes.** Many word processors allow you to track changes between drafts.
- **Use spell checkers and grammar checkers with care.** They catch some but not all spelling and grammar problems and can only offer suggestions. (See Chapter 34a.)
- **Keep a list of the particular problems you tend to have when writing.** Use the Question and Correct sections in this book to find help with specific issues.

3

Arguments

Reading and writing persuasive arguments are parts of your everyday life. People actively persuade you to believe, act on, or accept their claims, just as you want others to accept or act on your claims. You can create arguments to justify your beliefs, solve problems, or evaluate products or works of art. Position papers, reviews of films and books, and literary analyses are also forms of argument.

3a   Claims and evidence

Arguments have two basic elements.

- A **claim** is the proposition or thesis to be proved.

- The **evidence** for an argument provides the reasons used to convince the audience. Such support or proof may include facts, data, examples, statistics, and the testimony of experts. Evidence may take the form of appeals.

  - *Logical appeals* are based on reason and facts.

  - *Emotional appeals* arouse the audience's emotions: sympathy, patriotism, pride, anger, and other feelings based on values, beliefs, and motives.

  - *Ethical appeals* act on the audience's impressions, opinions, and judgments about the person making the argument.

To write a convincing persuasive paper, try to find information to prove that your view should be accepted. Also, think about presenting yourself as a knowledgeable or experienced person who deserves to be listened to.

TRY THIS

Composing Persuasive Arguments

Show that your motives are reasonable and worthwhile.
Give your audience reasonable assurance that you are arguing for the general good or for a claim that shares the audience's motives.

Find common ground with your audience. Rather than thinking about how you differ from your readers, consider the values, interests, motives, or goals you share with them.

Use an appropriate tone. Employing a serious tone when writing about serious issues helps your readers recognize your professionalism and trust your judgment.

Avoid vague and ambiguous terms and exaggerated claims. Words such as *everyone, no one, always, never, best,* or *worst* usually invite someone in your audience to find an exception.

Acknowledge that you have thought about opposing arguments by including them. Readers who don't agree with you want to know that you aren't ignoring their views.

Rely upon knowledgeable, credible people as sources for your evidence. Introduce your sources by indicating who they are and why they should be trusted.

Cite your source material. Citing your sources will help show your credibility. (See Chapters 47–50.)

FAQ

What are some strategies to support my thesis?

If you were writing a paper encouraging readers to avoid texting while driving, these are some ways you could support your argument:

Logical Appeals: rely on facts and data

- Offer statistics showing the number of people injured or killed in texting-related accidents
- Include studies comparing effects of texting while driving with effects of drunk driving

Emotional Appeals: influence the audience's feelings

- Include stories about adults or children injured or killed in texting-related accidents
- Add photos of people affected by texting-related accidents

Ethical Appeals: demonstrate your credibility

- Discuss values you share with readers, such as safety
- Use credible sources, cited throughout the paper
- Consider opponents' viewpoints

3b Visual argument

Both written and visual arguments depend on connections between claims and evidence. In visual arguments, **claims** can be in the words that accompany an image, such as

▲ **Figure 3.1** This award-winning ad cleverly redefines typical arguments made about pet adoptions. What is the claim of this ad, and what evidence supports it? What kinds of appeals does it make?

a caption for a photograph or a title used for a graph or chart. More often, however, claims in visual arguments are implied rather than stated openly. **Evidence** is presented through the content and position of images as well as the words accompanying the images.

As you look at a visual argument or create one yourself, ask yourself these questions:

- **What is the purpose of the visual?** To inform? To persuade? To educate? To entertain?

- **Who is the target audience for the visual argument?** If you are creating a visual argument, to whom are you directing your image?

- **What is the claim of the visual argument?** Look carefully at the wording. The claim may be implied, however, rather than stated.

- **What kinds of evidence are offered in the visual argument?**

- **What kinds of appeals do the visuals make?** Are they logical, emotional, or both?

Writing about Literature

When we write about types of literature, such as stories, poems, and plays, we do so to enjoy the work, to think about it more closely, and to learn more about the world as seen through the eyes of the writer. To analyze a text, begin by reading the work closely and considering its meaning. How can the work be interpreted? Consider analyzing a work of literature in one of the following ways:

- **Analyze the theme.** What are some of the conflicts? Does the writer offer a lesson to be learned or a way of looking at life or the world?

- **Analyze characters.** Consider their behavior, how they are described, what they say, and how all this fits into the plot or theme of the work or its setting. Does this tell you anything more about the characters, the theme, the culture, or the time period in which the work is set? Do the characters change or stay the same?

- **Analyze the structure of the work.** Is it chronological? Does it skip around? Are you given clues by the writer as to what will happen?

- **Analyze the narrator.** Who is telling the story, someone outside the events or one of the characters? Does the narrator tell the reader the characters' thoughts? Does the narrator speak in the first person, using *I*? What is the narrator's tone or attitude?

- **Look at the type or genre of the work.** Is it a tragedy, comedy, sonnet, mystery, science fiction, or a work from another specific genre? How does it compare to others of its type? Does it blend several types of literature? Does it use elements common to this type of work?

- **Analyze the historical or cultural background.** How does the work reflect values and beliefs of the time and place in which it is set or in which it was written? What are some of the social or political forces at that time or that affected the author?

- **Analyze the work in terms of gender.** How does the work portray women or men? How does it define their roles in the family? In society? In the workplace?

- **Focus on the reactions of readers to the work.** Why do readers respond as they do to this work? What would influence their reactions?

- **Research the life of the author.** What about the author's life is reflected in this particular work?

- **Resist the obvious meaning of the work.** Read skeptically, look for internal inconsistencies, and focus on ambiguities in the work. How would you interpret the work?

TRY THIS

Avoiding Common Pitfalls in Literature Papers
- Write an interpretive analysis, not a plot summary.
- Offer a thesis that makes an interpretive claim about the work.

  Sample thesis: In E.M. Forster's *A Room with a View*, Lucy Honeychurch learns that her personal happiness not only requires her to break Edwardian society's rules but to escape them entirely.

- Include important information, such as key plot elements or details, needed to support your claims.

5

Portfolios

A portfolio is a collection of a writer's work. There are two key types of portfolios:

- **Process portfolio.** Includes rough drafts and final papers arranged chronologically to illustrate the growth of a writer's skills.
- **Presentation portfolio.** Showcases a writer's best work for course or program evaluation. Some job applicants compile presentation portfolios that include an introductory statement, a résumé, and samples of their best work.

TRY THIS

Revising Papers for Your Portfolio

- Does the overall message of your paper need to be expanded or narrowed?
- How can your thesis statement be stated more clearly and specifically?
- How can you make your introductory paragraph(s) more appealing?
- How can you improve the logical connections in your argument?
- Would additional research help support your claims? What kinds of evidence would back your thesis more effectively?
- Would reorganization make your argument more persuasive?
- Can you adjust your tone to appeal to your audience more effectively?
- Which word choices might communicate your message better?

Reflection

Both types of portfolios typically include *reflective statements* or a *reflective essay* explaining choices you made in drafting and revising as well as the significance of each work. For a *process portfolio*, reflect on your choices in selecting topics, researching information, and writing your papers. Consider how the selected papers demonstrate your growth as a writer and a scholar. For a *presentation portfolio*, discuss how the included works demonstrate your skills and abilities.

6

Document Design

6a Principles of document design

These principles will help you develop well-designed, readable pages.

- **Apply design elements consistently.** Use design elements, such as bullets, white space, spacing, font types, and so on, consistently throughout your document.

- **Include white space.** Well-placed white space makes your documents more readable and offers visual relief from blocks of text. White space in the margins helps frame the text and allows a reader to make notes.

- **Avoid clutter.** Remember, less is more.

- **Use contrasting design elements for emphasis.** Fonts in bold, italics, color, or varied size add emphasis by making words stand out from regular text. Indented text, graphics, and background shading highlight selected elements.

- **Insert headings and subheadings.** These help announce new topics or subsections. Make your headings and subheadings more noticeable by using a combination of bold, italics, and larger font sizes.

- **Create lists.** In research papers and professional documents, information is often presented more efficiently in lists. Use phrases or sentences containing key points and supporting details, and organize them with bullets, dashes, or numbers.

- **Use appropriate documentation style formats.** Style guides often contain specific formatting instructions for elements such as margins, titles, headers, and page numbers. For more information about formatting papers in Modern Language Association (MLA) format, see Chapter 47d; for American Psychological Association (APA) format, see Chapter 48d; for *Chicago Manual* format, see Chapter 49c; and for Council of Science Editors (CSE) format, see Chapter 50c.

6b Incorporating visuals

Visuals such as images, graphs, charts, and tables can help you communicate clearly, concisely, and effectively.

- **Images** Photographs, diagrams, maps, and illustrations add color, variety, and meaning to your documents. They help your readers see a subject in a new perspective, follow steps in a process, or pinpoint a location. Use multiple images placed next to each other to show contrast or changes over time (see Figure 6.1).

- **Graphs and charts** Use graphs and charts to illustrate data in visual form and explain relationships between items. These can be produced in a spreadsheet program such as Microsoft Excel (see Figures 6.2–6.7).

- **Tables** Create tables to show relationships between items. Use word-processing software to create your tables.

TRY THIS

Adding Visuals to a Text

- **Include a title.** Graphs, charts, and images are labeled as *figures*, and tables are labeled as *tables*. Add a title to explain the content, such as "Figure 1: Increases in Voter Registration" or "Table 5: Number of Registered Voters in Each Wisconsin County." Figures and tables each have separate numbering systems in your document.

- **Add labels.** In graphs and charts, provide a label on the x (horizontal) axis and y (vertical) axis to specify values indicated in each area of the visual. Column headings in tables also need clear labels.

- **Place visuals in their appropriate location in the text.** Check Chapter 47d for information on placement of visuals in MLA-formatted papers and Chapter 48d for APA-formatted papers.

- **Cite your sources.** See Chapters 47–50 for documentation formats.

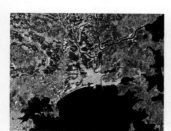 

▲ Figure 6.1 **Comparing Images** These satellite photographs, published by the U.S. Geological Survey, show the devastation of the Japanese city of Ishinomaki by the earthquake and tsunami that struck on March 11, 2011. Placed next to each other, these before-and-after photos demonstrate the force of the waves created by the tsunami.

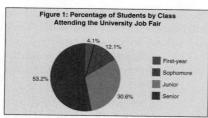

◀ **Figure 6.2 Pie Chart** Shows parts of a whole

Figure 6.3 Bar Graph ▶ Shows relationships among items

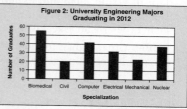

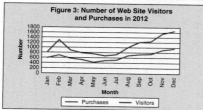

◀ **Figure 6.4 Line Graph** Shows change over a period of time

Figure 6.5 Map ▶ Identifies locations and visually represents data

Source: U.S. Geological Survey

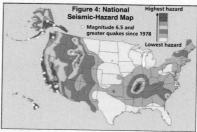

◀ **Figure 6.6 Flowchart** Illustrates a process or shows options in making decisions

Figure 6.7 Table ▶ Summarizes large amounts of data and shows relationships between items

Table 1: Dogs Available for Adoption

Name	Breed	Age	Spayed/ Neutered
Sammy	Spaniel	8–9 years	Yes
Missy	Pomeranian	1 year	Yes
Cabot	Pointer/Beagle Mix	4–5 years	Yes
Mimi	Chihuahua	6 months	No

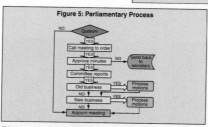

7

Multimodal Projects

A multimodal project combines more than one type, or mode, of communication. You can share your ideas with written text, as in a traditional academic paper, but with digital media tools, you can enhance communication with photographs, artwork, graphs, captions, video, audio, and more. Some examples include the following:

- Microsoft PowerPoint presentation
- Prezi
- Audio podcast
- Video or short film
- Website
- Blog
- Wiki
- Poster
- Advertisement
- Webzine

Some people also refer to these as *multimedia projects*. The word *multimodal* is used especially when focusing on the multiple methods of composing in different media.

7a Planning

Begin planning your project by thinking about purpose, audience, and topic. Consider which strategies would be most effective in motivating your audience to agree with your opinions, act upon your suggestions, or become interested in your topic. How can you include audio, visual, or other media to achieve your purpose?

TRY THIS

Planning Your Multimodal Project

Consider these elements as you plan your project:

- **What is your purpose?**
- **Who is your audience?**
- **What information should be included about your topic?**
  What do you need to say or show in order to achieve your purpose?

- **What will be the medium for your project?** Will you build a PowerPoint? Prezi? Video? Podcast? Website? Something else? What does your media format offer for sharing your views and fulfilling the purpose of your project? How will your audience view or experience your project?

7b   Format

There are many options for formatting projects constructed with digital media tools. Consider these general design principles as you work:

- **Create a consistent look for all sections of your project.** Don't switch background colors, fonts, or animation styles midway through your presentation. Set a tone and stick with it. This will make your project (and you) appear organized and focused.

- **Keep paragraphs or chunks of information focused.** Long passages of text are difficult for readers to follow when reading online. Insert a blank line between paragraphs.

- **Use easily readable fonts.** Widely available fonts such as Calibri, Cambria, Times New Roman, Arial, Georgia, Tahoma, and Verdana are good choices for online texts. Fonts that look like handwriting are difficult to read. Also, avoid using all capital letters; this is the equivalent of shouting at readers.

- **Choose contrasting background and font colors.** Use light background colors with dark font colors or vice versa. Avoid overly bright backgrounds; yellow backgrounds are particularly hard for readers to look at for long periods of time. Combinations of red on blue (and vice versa) are also problematic.

- **Use images that enhance your message.** Digital photographs and videos add to the impact of your project by explaining a fact or illustrating an example. Avoid clip art, which can look unprofessional.

- **Collect more than you need.** When working with multimodal projects, gather images, video clips, or audio clips (depending on your project). Give yourself options for editing. It is easier to remove images and clips you don't need than to go back and repeat your collection process to create new ones.

- **Back up your digital files in multiple places.**

- **Give credit to your sources.** Use the citation style requested by your instructor. In many programs, you can also insert links to the sources.

TRY THIS

Designing Presentations

Remember, *less is more* when designing presentations in programs such as Microsoft PowerPoint or Prezi.

Font Type. Use one of the fonts listed on p. 24.

Font Size. Vary your font sizes. Titles should be somewhat larger than headers, and headers should be larger than the main text. Words in fonts smaller than 20 point may be too difficult for your audience to read.

Graphics. Digital photographs that look professional serve to engage interest and reinforce your points. Cite your image sources in your presentation.

Animations. Animation can emphasize your key points and build interactions with your audience. However, too many animations can be distracting.

Layout. Balance your use of text and images to emphasize main points. Words, descriptive phrases, or short sentences—known as **talking points**—should be set off in bullets so your audience members can easily follow your arguments.

7c Organization

Regardless of how you design your project, you'll need to think about the way you organize information. With some multimodal projects, such as podcasts and presentations, your work will have a *linear organization*, a defined beginning, middle, and end. With *hypertexts*, such as websites and wikis, audience members will choose the way they experience your project, depending on where they click. As you design your project, consider the following elements.

- **Establish an introduction, beginning, or home.** This is where your audience will begin to experience your project. Think about what readers need to understand at the beginning. Introduce your topic and purpose. If appropriate, grab your reader's attention (see Chapter 1h) to build interest in proceeding with your project.

- **Provide general and specific information.** In projects with a linear structure, give general information before specifics.

- **Create a clear navigation system.** For projects such as websites and wikis, create a menu of links to show your reader how to interact with your project.

- **Build a memorable conclusion, if you have one.** For projects with a linear organization, end on a strong note by reemphasizing your ideas or projecting the future of your topic. (See Chapter 1i.) Hypertext projects, such as websites and wikis, don't have a defined ending.

FAQ

How should I organize my PowerPoint presentation?

1. *Title slide:* Provide the title of your presentation, your name, and your organization (if appropriate). An image can be added to increase your audience's interest in your topic.

2. *Introductory slide(s):* Grab the attention of your audience with questions, striking images, or an interesting quotation to lead into your main point.

3. *Thesis slide:* Present your main point to your audience. Map out your supporting claims or topics for discussion in short, bulleted statements.

4. *Body slides:* Prepare several slides to support claims listed on your thesis slide.

5. *Conclusion slide(s):* Complete your presentation by recapping your main points. Conclude with a strong written and visual statement that will make a lasting impression on your audience.

6. *Reference slide(s):* List all sources used in the presentation in the appropriate documentation style format.

Use your slides as supplements to your speech. Instead of including the text of your speech on your slides and reading it word-for-word, list key talking points on the slides and follow them as you talk, using notes if necessary. See Figure 7.1 for sample slides from a Microsoft PowerPoint presentation.

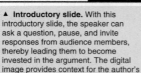

▲ Introductory slide. With this introductory slide, the speaker can ask a question, pause, and invite responses from audience members, thereby leading them to become invested in the argument. The digital image provides context for the author's argument.

▲ Body slide. This body slide covers the first point listed in the thesis slide. Note how the digital photograph complements the topic of the slide.

▲ **Figure 7.1** Sample Slides

Sentence Choices with Style

Contents of this section

Question and Correct

8

Clarity

8a Positive instead of negative

Use positive statements because negative statements are harder for people to understand.

Unclear Negative: Less attention is paid to commercials that lack human interest stories.

Revised: People pay more attention to commercials that tell human interest stories.

Negative statements can also make the writer seem evasive or unsure.

Evasive Negative: Senator Jamison does not disagree with the governor's entire proposal.

Revised: Senator Jamison agrees with the governor's proposed education funds but would like to see more tax cuts in his budget plan.

8b Double negative

Use only one negative at a time in your sentences. Using more than one negative creates a double negative, which is grammatically incorrect and may be difficult to understand.

Double Negative: He did **not** have **no** money.

Revised: He had no money. (*or*) He did not have any money.

Double Negative: I **don't** think he **didn't** have money left after he paid for his dinner.

(This sentence is particularly hard to understand because it uses both a double negative and negatives instead of positives.)

TRY THIS

Avoiding Double Negatives

Watch out for contractions that include negatives, like *doesn't*, *hasn't*, and *couldn't*. If you use these contractions, don't use any other negatives in your sentence. Also, watch out for negative words such as the following:

hardly	no one	nobody	nothing	scarcely
neither	no place	none	nowhere	

Sara hardly had ^any ~~no~~ popcorn left.

8c Known/familiar information to new/unfamiliar information

Begin your sentences or paragraphs with something that is generally known or familiar before you introduce new or unfamiliar material.

Familiar ⟶ Unfamiliar

Familiar to unfamiliar:

Every semester, after final exams are over, I'm faced with the problem of what to do with **lecture notes. They** might be useful
(OLD) (OLD)
someday, but **they** just keep cluttering **my computer's hard drive**.
(OLD) (NEW)
Someday, **the computer** will crash with all the information I might
(NEW)
never need.

(These sentences should be clear as the discussion moves from old to new information.)

The next example is not as clear.

Unfamiliar to familiar:

Second-rate entertainment is my description of most **movies** I've
(NEW) (OLD)
seen lately, but occasionally, there are some with **worthwhile themes**.
(NEW)
In the Southwest, the mysterious **disappearance** of an American
(NEW)
Indian culture is the **topic** of a recent movie I saw that I would
(OLD)
say has a **worthwhile theme**.
(OLD)

(These sentences are harder to follow because the familiar information comes after the new information.)

8d Verbs instead of nouns

Actions expressed as verbs are more easily understood and stated more briefly than actions named as nouns.

TRY THIS

Using Verbs Instead of Nouns

Try rereading your sentences to see which nouns could be changed to verbs.

Unnecessary Noun Form: The decision was to adjourn.

Revised: **They decided** to adjourn.

Some Noun Forms	Verbs to Use Instead
The negotiation of . . .	They negotiate . . .
The approval of . . .	They approve . . .
The preparation of . . .	They prepare . . .
The analysis of . . .	They analyze . . .
The usage of . . .	They use . . .

8e Intended subject as sentence subject

Be sure that the real subject (or the doer of the action in the verb) is the grammatical subject of the sentence. Sometimes the real subject of a sentence can get buried in prepositional phrases or other less noticeable places.

Subject buried in a prepositional phrase

For real music lovers, **it** is preferable to hear a live concert instead of an MP3.

(The grammatical subject here is **it**, *which is not the real subject of this sentence.)*

Who prefers to hear a live concert? Music lovers, so *music lovers* is the real subject of this sentence.

Revised: Music lovers prefer to hear a live concert instead of an MP3.

Real subject buried in the sentence

It seems like playing games online is something **Jonas** spends too much time doing.

(If the real subject, **Jonas**, *becomes the sentence subject, the entire sentence becomes clearer and more concise.)*

Revised: Jonas seems to spend too much time playing games online.

8f Predication

A logical sentence contains a subject and a predicate (the rest of the clause) that make sense together. When the subject and the predicate are not logically connected, that is referred to as faulty predication.

Faulty Predicate: The **reason** for her rapid promotion to vice-president **proved** she was talented.

(*In this sentence, the subject,* **reason,** *cannot logically prove* **she was talented.**)

Revised: Her **rapid promotion** to vice-president **proved** she was talented.

Faulty predication often occurs with forms of the verb *to be* because this verb sets up an equation in which the terms on either side of the verb should be equal.

Subject		Predicate
2×2	is	4
Dr. Streeter	is	our family doctor.

Faulty Predication: **Success is when** you have your own swimming pool.

(*The concept of success involves much more than having a swimming pool. Having a pool can be one example or a result of a type of success, but it is not the equivalent of success.*)

Revised: **One sign** of financial success **is having** your own swimming pool.

8g Missing words

Words that are unintentionally left out of sentences can cause confusion for readers.

Words needed for parallelism

Check for prepositions (like *in, to, for, of*) that follow verbs.

Marriages succeed when both partners have trust ^in and respect for each other.

(*We would have trust* **in** *someone, not trust* **for** *someone.*)

Words needed for comparisons

Check for words needed to complete a comparison. Name the two items being compared to each other.

This science class is more difficult. ^than the one I took last semester

> (*Without* **than the one I took last semester,** *readers will not know what the* **science class** *is being compared to.*)

The job fair was in a larger room than the ^office student government had.

> (*What is being compared here are the rooms. Without the missing word* **office,** *what is being compared are the* **larger room** *and the* **student government.**)

Words needed for grammatical correctness

Include words that are needed for correct grammatical constructions.

We have ^celebrated and will always celebrate Thanksgiving with our family.

> (*The word* **celebrated** *is needed to complete the past tense verb.*)

9

Variety

A series of short sentences or sentences with the same subject-verb order can be monotonous to read and sound choppy. Try these strategies to add variety.

- Combine two sentences (or independent clauses) into one longer sentence by using a comma and coordinating conjunction (see Chapter 25a), or a semicolon (see Chapter 27a).

  Comedians on *The Daily Show* mock politicians ^, but the .~~The~~ targets of the satire often miss their point.

- Combine the subjects of two independent clauses in one sentence when the verb applies to both clauses.

  Original: The **Wabash River** overflowed its banks. **Wildcat Creek** did the same.

  Revised: The **Wabash River and Wildcat Creek** ~~overflowed~~ overflowed their banks.

- Add a description, a definition, or other information about a noun after the noun.

  Professor Nguyen^, ~~is~~ a political science teacher^, .~~She~~ gives lectures in the community on current events.

- Turn a sentence into a *who, which,* or *what* clause.

  He was charged with breaking the city's newest law ~~. This law~~ ^, which^
  states that motorcyclists must wear helmets.

- Begin with dependent clauses that start with dependent
  markers such as the following words:

after	because	since	when
although	if	until	while

  After the trial ended, the lawyers filed for an appeal.

  When the stockholders met, they discussed the company's recent
  decline in profits.

- Add variety at the beginning of sentences by adding
  transitional words and phrases (see Chapter 15a).

  Original: The use of social media can involve invasion of your
  privacy. Social media laws are being passed to prevent invasion.
  Such laws are not always observed.

  Revised with transitions added and sentences combined:
  Although social media can involve invasion of your privacy,
  there are laws being passed to prevent invasion. **But** such laws
  are not always observed.

  Revised with phrases added and sentences combined:
  Currently, the use of social media can involve invasion of your
  privacy, though laws are being passed to prevent this. **However**,
  such laws are not always observed.

- Vary the length of sentences, writing some that are long
  and some that are short.

  Original: Traditionally, the game of squash has not been a
  popular sport in America. Recently ESPN carried
  some squash matches as one of their highlights.
  Televised squash matches are shown on terminals in
  Grand Central Station in New York City. This means
  thousands of commuters are seeing some matches.
  Squash is growing in popularity.

  Revised: **While** the game of squash has not traditionally
  been a popular sport in America, ESPN recently
  carried some squash matches as one of their highlights. Televised squash matches **now** are shown
  on terminals in Grand Central Station. This means
  thousands of New York City commuters are seeing
  some matches, and **as a result**, squash is growing
  in popularity.

10

Conciseness

By eliminating wordiness, you will communicate to your readers more clearly and are more likely to keep your readers' interest. This often means resisting the impulse to include everything you know about a subject or to add words that sound more formal or academic. To write concisely, omit

- what your readers do not need to know or already know
- whatever doesn't further the purpose of your paper.

FAQ

How do I know if I have wordy language?

- **Check for repetition of words or phrases.** If you find you're repeating the same words in a sentence or paragraph, try eliminating some or rephrasing your sentences.

  Smart phones are helpful tools ~~for~~ ~~Smart phones help with~~ tracking friends' phone numbers. ~~You can also use smartphones to send~~ *sending* email, and ~~search~~ *searching* online.

- **Check for phrases that say the same thing twice.**

  ~~first~~ beginning   6 p.m. ~~in the evening~~
  circular ~~in shape~~   ~~true~~ facts
  green ~~in color~~   prove ~~conclusively~~
  ~~positive~~ benefits   each ~~and every~~
  first ~~and foremost~~   the ~~end~~ result

- **Check for fillers.** Some phrases, such as the following, say little or nothing and can be omitted:

  there is (or) are   I am going to discuss
  in view of the fact that   I think that
  what I want to say is   it is my feeling that

  He said ~~that there is~~ a storm *is* approaching.

  He ~~made the statement that he~~ agreed ~~with the concept~~ that inflation could be controlled.

Strategies to revise sentences and paragraphs for conciseness

- **Combine sentences.** When the same nouns or pronouns appear in two sentences, combine the two sentences into one.

  The data was entered into the reports. ~~It was also~~ _{and} included in the graphs.

- **Eliminate** *who, which,* **and** *that.*

  The book ~~that is~~ lying on the piano belongs to her.

  The person ~~who is~~ responsible for this problem has not offered a solution.

  _{Artificial}
  ~~I am going to discuss artificial~~ intelligence~~, which~~ is an exciting field of research.

- **Turn phrases and clauses into adjectives and adverbs.**

  all applicants who are interested → all interested applicants

  spoke in a hesitant manner → spoke hesitantly

  the piano built out of mahogany → the mahogany piano

- **Turn prepositional phrases into adjectives or possessives**.

  the entrance to the station → the station entrance

  the windows of the building → the building's windows

  the photograph by Matthew → Matthew's photograph

- **Use active rather than passive voice. (See Chapter 11.)**

  _{research department} _{the figures.}
  The ~~figures were~~ checked ~~by the research department.~~

- **Remove unnecessary words and change to verbs whenever possible.**

  _{stores}
  The ~~function of the~~ box ~~is the storage of~~ wire connectors.

11

Active/Passive Verbs

An active verb expresses the action completed by the subject. A passive verb expresses action done to the subject. Passive voice uses forms of *to be* (*is, are, was, were*) and sometimes uses the word *by.*

Active: Paulo *wrote* the report.

(*The verb is* **wrote,** *and* **Paulo,** *the subject, did the writing.*)

Passive: The **report** *was written* by *Paulo*.

(*The verb is* **was written,** *and the* **report,** *the subject, was acted upon.*)

Using active verbs often results in clearer, more direct, and more concise sentences than those with passive verbs. Active verbs clarify who is doing the action and add a strong sense of immediacy and liveliness to your writing.

Active: After the eye of the hurricane passed, **ambulance drivers rushed** injured patients to the hospital. (*more immediate and direct*)

Passive: After the eye of the hurricane passed, **injured patients were rushed** to the hospital by **ambulance drivers**. (*wordy with weaker sense of action*)

FAQ

When is it appropriate to use passive voice?

- When the doer of the action is not important or is not known

  For the tournament game, more than five thousand **tickets were sold**.

  (*Who sold the tickets? That's not important; the number of tickets is what is being stressed here.*)

- When you want to focus on the action or the receiver of the action, not the doer

  Lara was chosen to receive the scholarship.

  (*The writer wanted to emphasize who got the scholarship, not who chose her.*)

- When you want to avoid blaming, giving credit, or taking responsibility

  It was announced that the **election was lost**.

  (*The candidate lost the election but wants to avoid stressing that.*)

- When you want a tone of objectivity, particularly in science writing

  Ten grams of sugar **were added** to the solution.

  (*The result, not who added the sugar, is important.*)

12

Voice, Formality, and Word Choice

12a Voice and formality

In writing, an appropriate voice is one that fits the level of formality in your paper and your subject.

Formal tone contains sophisticated phrasing not commonly used in conversation. Third-person pronouns *he* or *she* or *one* are often used instead of *I* or *you*. Formal tone may be expected in professional and legal documents and research writing. Jargon or language appropriate to the field and intended readers may also be used.

Formal: The tripartite narrative arc in classically constructed films requires initial exposition, rising action that delineates the central conflict, and then gradual movement towards a resolution.

Medium/semiformal tone uses standard sentence structures and vocabulary. Contractions are generally avoided. This tone is appropriate for most college writing assignments.

Medium/semiformal: The three-part narrative structure of movies follows the classical pattern of first exposing the audience to introductory information, then building action towards a conflict, and finally resolving the central problem of the film.

Informal tone uses language common in daily conversation and includes slang, colloquialisms, and regionalisms. Contractions and first- and second-person pronouns such as *I* and *you* are appropriate for this tone.

Informal: Movies usually start by telling us about the people and places in the story. Then some big problem comes up, but it's worked out by the end.

Slang

Slang terms are made up (such as *peeps, props, crunk, snarky,* or *woot*) or are given new definitions (such as *chops* for very talented or skilled). Over time, some slang may enter the general vocabulary and dictionaries of standard written English. However, slang is generally not considered appropriate for academic work. Abbreviations used in texting or tweeting, such as *LOL* or *IMHO*, and the shortened versions of words such as *thanx, thru*, or *lite*, are also not appropriate for academic writing.

Jargon

Jargon is the specialized language of various trades, professions, and groups. Specialists within the group use these terms to communicate with each other in a concise way when referring to complex concepts, objects, and techniques.

When you are writing about a specialized subject for a general audience and need to use a technical term, define the term in easily understandable language the first time you use it. You can then use the word later on and not lose the reader.

The term *jargon*, however, is also sometimes applied to *inflated expressions*, which sound pompous, and *euphemisms*, which are terms used to disguise unpleasant realities.

Specialized Language: subcutaneous hemorrhage, metabolic disorders, exhaust manifold, beta decay, data integrity, cloture

Inflated Expressions: learning facilitator (teacher), monetary remuneration (pay)

Euphemisms: revenue enhancement (taxes), pre-owned (used), nonmilitary collateral damage (dead civilians)

Unnecessary jargon reflects the writer's inability to write clearly. Note the wordiness and pompous tone of this example:

Original: Utilize this receptacle, which functions as a repository for matter to be removed.

Revised: Deposit litter here.

12b Tone shifts

Once you choose a formal or informal tone for a paper, keep that tone consistent in your word choices. Check that you didn't use a very formal phrase in an informal narrative or use slang when you're writing formally. This kind of shift can disrupt the tone of your writing.

Unnecessary shift: The welfare worker's responsibility is to assist in a family's struggle to obtain
food and clothing   children
˄stuff for the ̶k̶i̶d̶s̶.

(*The use of the informal words* **stuff** *and* **kids** *illustrates a shift in tone in this formal sentence.*)

12c Emphasis

When you want to stress a point or want your readers to realize the importance of what you're writing about, you can add emphasis to your writing in several ways:

- **Use parallelism.** When you have two or more items in a group or when you want to join two ideas, write them in parallel form (see Chapter 23a):

  "**Ask not what** your country can do for you; **ask what** you can do for your country." (President John F. Kennedy)

  "Too many people spend money they haven't earned, **to buy** things they don't want, **to impress** people they don't like." (Will Rodgers)

- **Use strong adverbs and adjectives.** Words that modify nouns and verbs can help you make your writing more vivid and memorable.

  Not vivid: The brightly colored sunset on the cliffs was pretty.

  Vivid: The flaming golden rays of the sunset glowed on the cliffs.

- **Use striking language.** You can use an interesting metaphor, concrete details, or an unusual way of stating something to add emphasis to your writing.

  Laughter illuminates faces and lights up our minds.

  Web browsers are portals because they open doors to the world.

- **Use visual design.** See Chapter 6 for ways to add visual impact and emphasis as you design your documents.

12d Denotation and connotation

The *denotation* of a word is the definition found in dictionaries. The *connotations* of a word are the associations, attitudes, and emotional overtones that some words have. While readers don't all share the same connotations, some connotations are widely known. Consider the word *snake:*

Denotation of the word *snake:* any of the many varieties of legless reptiles

Connotation of the word *snake:* something or someone who's evil, dangerous, treacherous

Weighing the denotative and connotative meanings of words can help you say what you really mean.

My boss is **firm** about the policy.

> (**Firm** *means strong and unwavering. It has a positive connotation.*)

My boss is **obstinate** about the policy.

> (**Obstinate** *means unwavering, but it also means stubborn and unwilling to consider other options. It has a negative connotation.*)

13

General and Specific Language

When we use general language, we are thinking broadly of a large category or class of items, such as, for example, "dangerous driving habits." But that applies to many different types of such habits and can be too vague or large a category when specifics are needed. To be more specific, we name an instance or example within the category we want to focus on, such as the danger of talking on a cell phone while driving, which identifies a more specific item or category within the general one. General statements can be made more specific, and general words can be made more specific.

General terms	Specific	More specific
animal	dog	cocker spaniel
clothing	pants	jeans

General statement: The number of problems in the service industry is growing.

More specific: Lack of adequate training among flight attendants has resulted in a rapidly increasing number of complaints by passengers.

Sometimes general terms are sufficient, depending on your purpose, but specific terms are often more precise and vivid, allowing readers to become more aware of your topic and its importance.

General term: unsafe food

More specific term: alfalfa sprouts contaminated with salmonella bacteria

14

Inclusive Language

14a Gender-inclusive language

Gender bias in English occurs when we use male pronouns and *man* as universals to indicate members of both sexes. To avoid offending readers by using language that seems to favor one sex over the other, use more inclusive terms and strategies such as the following.

● **Use alternatives to *man* or *men*.**

Instead of:	*Use:*
man	person, individual
man-made	machine-made, synthetic, artificial
stewardess	flight attendant
housewife	spouse
policeman or patrolman	police officer
congressman	congressional representative, member of Congress
businessman	business professional
saleswoman or salesman	salesperson, salesclerk, sales specialist

● **Use the plural.**

Not inclusive: A nurse is trained to understand her patients' emotions and physical symptoms.

Inclusive: Nurses are trained to understand their patients' emotions and physical symptoms.

● **Eliminate the pronoun or reword to avoid it.**

Not inclusive: If a taxpayer has questions about the form, he can call a government representative.

Inclusive: A taxpayer who has questions about the form can call a government representative.

● **Replace the pronoun with *one, he or she*, or an article (*a, an, the*).**

Not inclusive: The parent who reads to her infant helps increase the infant's sound discrimination.

Revised: The parent who reads to **an** infant helps increase
the infant's sound discrimination.

● **Address the reader directly in the second person.**

Not inclusive: Each applicant must mail **his** form by Thursday.

Revised: Mail **your** form by Thursday.

● **Address the person by his or her title when you
don't know the gender.**

Not inclusive: Dear **Sir**,

Revised: Dear **Customer Services Representative**,

FAQ

When referring to *everyone*, do I use *he or she* or *they*?

There are different views as to when to use the indefinite
pronouns *everybody*, *anybody*, *everyone*, and *anyone*.
Some people continue to use the singular pronoun (*everyone . . . he or she/his or her*) and consider the plural *they* to
be wrong.

Formal: When **everyone** has completed **his or her** test, **he or
she** may leave class.

However, the use of the plural pronoun (*everyone . . . they/
their*) has become acceptable in many informal contexts.

Informal: When **everyone** has completed **their** tests, **they** may
leave class.

In formal writing, it is still advisable to avoid using either
gender-specific or plural pronouns with these words.

14b   Respectful language

Writing inclusively also means avoiding assumptions about
our audience. When we write for a general educated audience, we can't assume that everyone will be of the same
race, religion, age, ethnicity, gender, or sexual orientation
as ourselves. To show respect for our audience members
and to be inclusive, we can acknowledge diversity by not
assuming our readers share our characteristics and beliefs.

Using inclusive language

Inclusive language also does not exclude or stereotype groups. It is disrespectful to make broad generalizations—even if they are seemingly positive—about an entire group of people. Here are some examples of assumptions to avoid:

I have an appointment with a female doctor.

> (*assumes it is unusual for a doctor to be a woman*)

My friend is gay, so he'll be the most fashionable one at the party.

> (*assumes all gay men are fashionable*)

Parents use their Biblical education to raise their children.

> (*assumes all parents are Christian*)

Senior citizens will require extra help using this computer program.

> (*assumes all senior citizens do not know how to use computers*)

Liu is Asian American, so she'll be able to help you with your math homework.

> (*assumes all Asian Americans are good at math*)

Choosing terms for ethnic or racial groups

For ethnic or racial groups, there are preferred choices, and some terms to avoid.

- Use *Native American* or *American Indian* instead of *Indian*

- Use *African American*, *Black*, or *black*

- Use *Hispanic* or *Latino* (or *Latina*, the feminine form)

- Use *Asian* instead of *Oriental*

When it's appropriate, use more specific terms, such as the name of a specific country or region of origin, as in *Cuban American*, *Chinese American*, and *Mexican American*. When referring to a specific American Indian tribal nation, use the group's name, such as *Navajo* or *Cherokee*. Current source materials, such as news or journal articles, are useful guides to the appropriate terms for groups you refer to in your writing. But it's important to remember that some people have strong preferences for one term or another.

15

Transitions

15a Transitional words and phrases

Transitions are words and phrases that build bridges between sentences, parts of sentences, and paragraphs. They help connect them together and show relationships.

The state government is determined not to raise property taxes this year. **Therefore**, some legislators were in favor of an increase in the cigarette tax, **but** the majority voted for a reduction in funding for educational programs. **As a result**, teachers, parents, and students protested in the state capitol yesterday.

FAQ

Which transitional word(s) should I use in my sentence?

Are you doing this?	Then use one of these words:
Adding:	and, besides, in addition, also, too, moreover, furthermore, next, first, second, third, likewise
Comparing:	similarly, likewise, in like manner, at the same time, in the same way
Contrasting:	but, yet, however, still, nevertheless, on the other hand, on the contrary, instead, rather, though, whereas, although
Emphasizing:	indeed, in fact, above all, and also, even more, in any event, in other words, that is, obviously
Ending:	after all, finally, in sum, for these reasons
Giving examples:	for example, for instance, to illustrate, that is, namely, specifically
Pointing to cause and effect, proof, or conclusions:	thus, therefore, consequently, because of this, hence, as a result, then, so, accordingly
Showing place or direction:	over, above, inside, next to, underneath, to the left, just behind, beyond, in the distance

Are you doing this?	Then use one of these words:
Showing time:	*meanwhile, soon, later, now, in the past, then, next, before, during, while, at last, since then, presently, at the same time, in the meantime*
Summarizing:	*to sum up, in conclusion, finally, as has been said, in general, to conclude, in other words*

15b Repetition of a key term or phrase

Restating an important word or phrase can help you draw connections between sentences and emphasize your main idea.

Among the recent food fads sweeping America and Europe is the interest in **molecular gastronomy**, which involves exploring the chemical composition of foods and the cooking process to create new and exciting dishes. While not all chefs agree that **molecular gastronomy** is the wave of the future, they cannot deny that it has had a significant impact on the culinary world.

15c Synonyms

Synonyms are words that have similar meanings. Using synonyms can help you build connections between sentences without repeating the same word too many times.

By experimenting with the physical and chemical composition of **food**, chefs concoct **edible delights** shaped as creams, gels, spheres, and foams. Applied properly, chemicals such as calcium chloride and liquid nitrogen transform standard **fare** into **delectable cuisine** in unexpected shapes and consistencies.

15d Pronouns

Pronouns (such as *he*, *she*, *it*, *they*) can help you refer to people, places, and things discussed in your writing. With pronouns, you can build the flow of your writing without overusing the same words.

During one such meal at Maze in London, I had a **bacon, lettuce, and tomato sandwich**, but **it** was a multilayered gel and mousse combination served in a martini glass. **It** was uniquely delicious, making this one of the most memorable dining experiences of my life.

III

Sentence Grammar

Contents

Question and Correct

LEARNING OBJECTIVE: Using adjectives and adverbs correctly

LEARNING OBJECTIVE: Placing modifying phrases appropriately in sentences

LEARNING OBJECTIVE: Being consistent in references to person, number, and verb tense

16

Fragments

A sentence fragment is an incomplete sentence

To recognize a fragment, consider the basic requirements of a sentence:

- A sentence is a group of words with at least one independent clause.

- An independent clause has at least one subject and a complete verb, plus an object or complement if needed. An independent clause can stand alone as a thought, even though other sentences may be needed to clarify the thought or idea.

  Independent clause: She saw a concert last night.

  (*We don't know who **she** is, but a pronoun can be a subject. And we don't know what concert **she** saw, but this type of additional information can appear in accompanying sentences.*)

  Not an independent clause: When it rains.

  (*Say that sentence out loud, and you will hear that it's not a complete sentence because we don't know what happens as a result of the **when** clause.*)

16a Unintentional fragments

1. A fragment can result when a subject or verb is missing from the sentence.

   Fragment: The week I spent on the beach just relaxing with a good book and soaking up the bright sun every day we were there.

   (**Week** *is probably the intended subject here, but it has no verb.*)

2. A fragment can be caused by misplaced periods. This happens when a dependent phrase or dependent clause gets detached from the sentence to which it belongs. Some writers do this when they worry about the sentence being too long. Such fragments can be

corrected by removing the period between the independent clause and the fragment.

Fragment: She decided to write her paper about the abuse of prescription drugs. **Then wondered if her choice was wise**. *(fragment)*

(The highlighted word group is a fragment with no subject for the verb **wondered**. *This phrase got disconnected from the independent clause that came before it and needs to be reattached.)*

Revision: She decided to write her paper about the abuse of prescription drugs, then wondered if her choice was wise.

Fragment: **Because he scored six three-point baskets** *(fragment)* **during the game**. Everyone applauded when he sat down on the bench.

(The highlighted word group is a dependent clause that was detached from the independent clause following it.)

Revision: Because he scored six three point baskets during the game, everyone applauded when he sat down on the bench.

FAQ

How can I find fragments in my writing?

1. When you read your paper backward, from the last sentence to the first, you'll be able to notice a fragment more easily when you hear it without the sentence to which it belongs.

2. To find dependent clauses separated from the main clause, look at the marker word, such as *after*, *although*, *because*, *before*, *during*, *if*, *since*, *unless*, *when*, or *while*. If the clause is standing alone, attach it to the independent clause that completes the meaning.

   If this happens———▶? *(Then what? By itself, this is incomplete.)*

16b Intentional fragments

Writers occasionally write an intentional fragment for its effect on the reader. However, intentional fragments should be used only when the writer could have written a whole sentence but preferred a fragment.

Fragment: Dilek walked quietly into the room, unnoticed by the rest of the group. **Not that she wanted it that way**. She simply didn't know how to make an effective entrance.

17

Comma Splices and Fused Sentences

A comma splice and a fused sentence (also called a run-on sentence) are punctuation problems in compound sentences. A compound sentence is one that contains two or more independent clauses.

TRY THIS

Using Commas and Semicolons in Compound Sentences

There are three patterns for commas and semicolons in compound sentences:

1. *Comma and conjunction:*

   Independent clause, and independent clause.

                     but
                     nor
                     so
                     for
                     or
                     yet

   Kuljit found some sources for his research paper, **but** he still needs more information.

2. *Semicolon:* Independent clause ; independent clause.

   Tiara majored in professional writing ; she is now a technical writer for a biomedical firm.

3. *Semicolon and comma:*

   Independent clause; however, independent clause.
                        therefore,
                        moreover,
                        consequently,
                        (etc.)

   Dina planned to give her presentation on Tuesday ; **however**, her professor asked her to speak on Thursday instead.

17a   Comma splices

The comma splice is a punctuation error that occurs in one of two ways:

- When independent clauses are joined only by a comma and no coordinating conjunction.

  Comma Splice: In Econ 150, students meet in small groups for

  and
  an extra hour each week, this helps them learn from each other.

- When a comma is used instead of a semicolon between two independent clauses.

  Comma Splice: The doctor prescribed a different medication;
  however, it's not helping.

17b   Fused or run-on sentences

The fused or run-on sentence is a punctuation error that occurs when there is no punctuation between independent clauses. This causes the two clauses to be "fused" or "run on" into each other.

, and (or ;)
Fused Sentence: I didn't know which job I wanted I couldn't decide.

FAQ

How can I fix comma splices, fused sentences, and run-ons?

- Between the two independent clauses, add a comma and then one of the seven joining words (*for, and, nor, but, or, yet, so*).
- Separate the independent clauses into two sentences.
- Change the comma to a semicolon.
- Make one clause dependent on the other clause.

18

Subjects and Verbs

18a Subject-verb agreement

Subject-verb agreement occurs when the subject and verb (or helping verb) endings agree in number and person. The subject of every sentence is either singular or plural (agreeing in number) and is in first (*I* or *we*), second (*you*), or third person (*he, she, it, they*). These determine the verb (or helping verb) ending. Verbs with singular subjects take singular endings, and verbs with plural subjects have plural endings.

Lavon   **takes**   lots of pictures with his phone.
(singular subject)   *(singular verb)*

Singular nouns, pronouns, and nouns that cannot be counted, such as *news, time*, and *happiness* (see 37b), take verbs with singular endings.

I chew.   Water drips.   Time flies.   You laugh.

Plural

Plural nouns and pronouns take verbs with plural endings.

Numbers show.   The shoes are blue.   They stretch.

FAQ

How can I find the subject and verb in a sentence?

1. It's easier to find the verb first because the verb is the word or words that change when you change the time of the sentence, from present to past or past to present.

   Nikki **bikes** to work.   Yesterday, Nikki **biked** to work.
   (verb is in present tense)   *(verb is in past tense)*

   Tomorrow, Nikki **will bike** to work.
           (verb is in future tense)

2. Eliminate phrases starting with the following words because they are normally not part of the subject:

   | including | along with | together with |
   | accompanied by | in addition to | as well as |

   Everyone, including my sister, **is** here.
   (subject)   *(verb)*

58

Buried subjects

It is sometimes difficult to find the subject word when it is buried among many other words. In such cases, disregard prepositional phrases; modifiers; *who, which,* and *that* clauses; and other surrounding words.

Almost **all** of my friends who live in Atlanta **are attending** the party.
   (subject)   *(verb)*

> (*In this sentence,* **Almost** *is a modifier of the subject* **all***;* **of my friends** *is a prepositional phrase; and* **who live in Atlanta** *is a who clause that describes* **friends***.*)

Compound subjects

Subjects joined by *and* take a plural verb (X *and* Y = more than one, plural).

The **dog** and the **squirrel are** running around the tree.

But sometimes the words joined by *and* act together as a unit and are thought of as one thing. If so, use a singular verb.

Peanut butter and jelly is a popular filling for sandwiches.

Or and *either/or* in subjects

When the subject words are joined by ***or, either . . . or, neither . . . nor***, or ***not only . . . but also***, the verb agrees with the subject word closer to it.

Either **Aleeza** or her **children are** going to bed early.

Not only the **clouds** but also the **snow was** gray that day.

Clauses and phrases as subjects

When a whole clause or phrase is the subject, use a singular verb.

What I want to know is why I can't retake the test.

Saving money is difficult to do.

However, if the verb is a form of *be* and the noun after it (the complement) is plural, the verb has to be plural.

What we saw were pictures of the experiment. (*What we saw =* *pictures*).

Indefinites as subjects

Indefinite words with singular meanings, such as *each, every*, and *any*, take a singular verb when they are the subject or precede the subject word.

Each has her own preference.

Each book is checked in by the librarian.

However, when indefinite words such as *none, some, most*, or *all* are the subject, the number of the verb depends on the meaning of the subject.

Some of the book **is** difficult to follow.

> (*The subject is a single portion of the book and needs a singular verb.*)

Some of us **are leaving** now.

> (*The subject is several people, so it's plural and needs a plural verb.*)

Collective nouns and amounts as subjects

Collective nouns refer to a group or a collection (such as *team, family, committee*, and *group*). When a collective noun is the subject and refers to the group acting as a whole or as a single unit, the verb is singular:

Our **family has** a new car.

In most cases, a collective noun refers to the group acting together as a unit, but occasionally the collective noun refers to members acting individually. In that case, the verb is plural.

The **committee are** unhappy with each other's decisions.

When the subject names an amount, the verb is singular.

More than 125 **miles is** too far.   Six **dollars is** the price.

Plural words as subjects

Some words with an *-s* ending, such as *civics, mathematics, measles*, and *news*, are thought of as a single unit and take a singular verb.

Physics is fascinating.   Modern **economics shows** contradictions.

Some words, such as those in the following list, are treated as plural and take a plural verb, even though they refer to one thing. (In many cases, there are two parts to these things.)

| jeans are . . . | sunglasses cost . . . | thanks were . . . |
| riches are . . . | pants fit . . . | scissors cut . . . |

Titles, company names, words, and quotations as subjects

For titles of written works, names of companies, words used as terms, and quotations, use singular verbs.

The Help **is** a good movie.

Thanks is not in his vocabulary.

Amazon is hiring.

"Cookies for sale!" she **said.**

Linking verbs

Linking verbs agree with the subject rather than the word that follows (the complement).

Her **problem is** frequent injuries.

Short **stories are** my favorite reading matter.

There is/are, Here is/are, and *It*

When a sentence begins with *there* or *here*, the verb depends on the complement that follows the verb.

There is an excellent old **movie** on TV tonight.

Here are my **friends**.

However, *it* as the subject always takes the singular verb, regardless of what follows.

It was bears in the park that knocked over the garbage cans.

Who, which, that, and *one of* as subjects

When *who, which*, and *that* are used as subjects, the verb agrees with the previous word it refers to (the antecedent).

They are the **students who study** hard. He is the **student who studies** the hardest.

In the phrase *one of those who* (or *which* or *that*), it is necessary to decide whether the *who, which,* or *that* refers only to the one or to the whole group. Only then can you decide whether the verb is singular or plural.

Chang is **one of those shoppers who buy** most things online.

(*In this case, Chang is part of a large group,* **shoppers** *who buy most things online, and acts like others in that* *group. Therefore,* **who** *takes a plural verb because it refers to* **shoppers***.*)

The American Dictionary is **one of the dictionaries** on that shelf **that includes** Latin words.

(*In this case,* **The American Dictionary***, while part of a group of dictionaries, is specifically one that includes Latin words. The other dictionaries may or may not. Therefore,* **that** *refers to one dictionary and takes a singular verb.*)

18b Verbs

Verbs that add *-ed* for the past tense and the past participle are regular verbs. The past participle is the form that has a helping verb such as "has" or "had." For a guide to using verb tenses, see 36a.

Regular Verb Forms			
	Present	Past	Future
Simple	I walk.	I walked.	I will walk.
Progressive	I am walking.	I was walking.	I will be walking.
Perfect	I have walked.	I had walked.	I will have walked.
Perfect progressive	I have been walking.	I had been walking.	I will have been walking.

Some brief samples of irregular verb forms are shown in the following tables. Consult a dictionary for more verbs.

Irregular Verb Forms				
	Present		Past	
Verb	Singular	Plural	Singular	Plural
be	I am	we are	I was	we were
	you are	you are	you were	you were
	he, she, it is	they are	he, she, it was	they were
have	I have	we have	I had	we had
	you have	you have	you had	you had
	he, she, it has	they have	he, she, it had	they had
do	I do	we do	I did	we did
	you do	you do	you did	you did
	he, she, it does	they do	he, she, it did	they did

Some Irregular Verbs		
Base (Present)	**Past**	**Past Participle**
be (am, is, are)	was, were	been
become	became	become
begin	began	begun
bring	brought	brought
come	came	come
do	did	done
eat	ate	eaten
find	found	found
forget	forgot	forgotten
get	got	gotten
give	gave	given
go	went	gone
grow	grew	grown
have	had	had
know	knew	known
lay	laid	laid
lie	lay	lain
make	made	made
mean	meant	meant
read	read	read
say	said	said
see	saw	seen
sit	sat	sat
speak	spoke	spoken
stand	stood	stood
take	took	taken
teach	taught	taught
think	thought	thought
write	wrote	written

18c *Lie/lay* and *sit/set*

Two sets of verbs, *lie/lay* and *sit/set*, can cause problems. Because they are related in meaning and sound, they are often confused with each other, but each one of each set has a different meaning.

Lie (recline)	She **lies** in bed all day. (*present*)
	She **lay** in bed all last week. (*past*)
Lay (put)	He **lays** his keys on the table. (*present*)
	He **laid** his keys on the table. (*past*)
Sit (be seated)	Please **sit** here by the window. (*present*)
	She **sat** by the window in class. (*past*)

Set (put)　　　　　Please **set** the flowers on the table. (*present*)
　　　　　　　　　　He **set** the flowers on the desk before
　　　　　　　　　　he left. (*past*)

18d　Verb voice

Verb voice tells whether the verb is in the active or passive voice. In the active voice, the subject performs the action on the verb. In the passive voice, the subject receives the action. The doer of the action in the passive voice may be omitted or may appear in a "by the" phrase.

Active: The **child sang** the song.

Passive: The **song was sung** by the **child**.

18e　Verb mood

The mood of a verb tells the following:

- It expresses a fact, opinion, or question (**indicative** mood).
- It expresses a command, request, or advice (**imperative** mood).
- It expresses a doubt, a wish, a recommendation, or something contrary to fact (**subjunctive** mood). In the subjunctive mood, present tense verbs stay in the simple base form and do not indicate the number and person of the subject. However, for the verb *be*, ***were*** is used for all persons and numbers.

Indicative:　　The new app **runs** well on this tablet computer.

Imperative:　　**Watch** the news to find out more about this issue.

Subjunctive:　The doctor recommends that Amit **stop** smoking.
　　　　　　　　I wish I **were** rich.

19

Pronouns

19a　Pronoun case

A pronoun is a word that substitutes for a noun. Pronouns change case according to their use in a sentence.

Subject case: **She** told a story.

Object case: Rosario told **them** a story.

Possessive case: The children liked **her** story.

Pronoun Cases					
Subject		Object		Possessive	
Singular	Plural	Singular	Plural	Singular	Plural
First person I	we	me	us	my, mine	our, ours
Second person you	you	you	you	your, yours	your, yours
Third person he	they	him	them	his, her	their, theirs
she	they	her	them	her, hers	their, theirs
it	they	it	them	it, its	their, theirs

TRY THIS

Correcting Common Problems with Pronouns

- Remember that *between, except,* and *with* are prepositions and take the object case.

  between you and ~~I~~ *me*   except Alexi and ~~she~~ *her*

  with ~~he~~ *him* and ~~I~~ *me*

- Don't use *them* as a pointing pronoun in place of *these* or *those*. Use *them* only as the object by itself.

  He liked ~~them~~ *those* socks. He liked them.

- Possessive case pronouns never take apostrophes.

  The insect spread ~~it's~~ *its* wings.

- Use possessive case before *-ing* verb forms.

  The crowd cheered ~~him~~ *his* making a three-point basket.

- Use reflexive pronouns (those ending in *-self* or *-selves*) to strengthen nouns they refer back to.

  Sarah puts too much suntan oil on herself.

- Don't use reflexive pronouns in other cases because you think they sound more correct. They aren't.

  They included ~~myself~~ *me* in the group.

Pronouns in compound constructions

To find the right case when your sentence has a noun and a pronoun, temporarily eliminate the noun as you read the sentence to yourself. You'll hear the case that is needed.

Jon and ~~him~~ *he* went to the store.

(*If* **Jon** *is eliminated, the sentence would be "*him *went to the store." It's easier to notice the wrong pronoun case this way.*)

Mrs. Weg gave the tickets to **Lutecia** and ~~I~~ *me*.

(*Try dropping the noun,* **Lutecia**. *You'll be able to hear that the sentence sounds wrong: "Mrs. Weg gave the tickets to* **I**.*" Because* **to** *is a preposition, the noun or pronoun that follows is the object of the preposition and should be in the object case.*)

Who/whom

In informal speech, some people may not distinguish between *who* and *whom*. But for formal writing, the cases are as follows:

Subject	Object	Possessive
who	whom	whose
whoever	whomever	

Subject: **Who** is going to the concert tonight? (**Who** is the subject of the sentence.)

Give this to **whoever** wants it. (**Who** is the subject of **wants**.)

Object: To **whom** should I give this ticket? (**Whom** is the object of the preposition **to**.)

Possessive: No one was sure **whose** voice that was. (**Whose** is the possessive marker for **voice**.)

FAQ

When do I use *who* and when do I use *whom*?

If you aren't sure whether to use *who* or *whom*, turn a question into a statement or rearrange the order of the phrase:

Question: (**Who, whom**) are you looking for?

Rearranged order: You are looking for **whom**.
(object of the preposition)

Sentence:	She is someone (**who, whom**) I know well.
Rearranged order:	I know **whom** well.
	(*direct object*)

Pronoun case after *than* or *as*

In comparisons using *than* and *as*, choose the correct pronoun case by recalling the words that are omitted.

He is taller than (**I, me**). (The omitted words here are *am tall*.) He is taller than **I** (am tall).

Our cat likes my sister more than (**I, me**). (The omitted words here are *he likes*.)

Our cat likes my sister more than (he likes) **me**.

Pronoun case *we* or *us* before nouns

When *we* or *us* is used before a noun, such as "we players" or "us friends," use the case appropriate for the noun. You can hear which to use by omitting the noun.

(*We, Us*) players paid for our own equipment.

> **Test:** *Would you say "Us paid for the equipment" or "We paid for the equipment"? (**We** is the correct pronoun here.)*

The barista gave (*we, us*) customers our coffee.

> **Test:** *Would you say "The barista gave **we** our coffee" or "The barista gave **us** our coffee?" (**Us** is the correct pronoun here.)*

Pronoun case with *to* + verb (infinitive)

When you use a pronoun after an infinitive (*to* + verb), use the object case.

Mira offered to drive Orin and (*I, me*) to the meeting.

> (*Would you say "Mira offered to drive **I** to the meeting"? The correct pronoun is **me**.*)

Pronoun antecedents

Because pronouns substitute for nouns, they should agree with the nouns they refer to in number and gender.

Singular: The *student* turned in *her* lab report.

Plural: The *students* turned in *their* lab reports.

19b   Pronoun reference

To avoid confusing your readers, be sure your pronouns agree with the words they refer to (their antecedents).

Unclear reference: Gina told Michelle that **she** took **her** car to the library.

(Did Gina take Michelle's car or her own car to the library?)

Revised: When Gina took **Michelle's** car to the library, she told Michelle she was borrowing it.

TRY THIS

Avoiding Vague Pronouns

Watch out for the vague uses of *they*, *this*, *it*, or *which* that don't refer to any specific group, word, or phrase (antecedent).

In Hollywood, ~~they~~ the screenwriters and producers don't know what the American public really wants in movies.

(Who *are* the **they** referred to here?)

When the town board asked about the cost of the next political campaign, the board was assured that ~~they~~ the politicians would pay for **their** own campaigns.

(*To whom do* **they** *and* **their** *refer? Most likely* **they** *refers to the politicians who will be campaigning, but* **politicians** *is only implied.*)

Martina worked in a national forest last summer, and ~~this~~ serving as a forest ranger may be her career choice.

(*What does* **this** *refer to? Because no word or phrase in the first part of the sentence refers to the pronoun, the revised version has one of several possible answers.*)

Many people who have cell phones let their ringtones go off loudly when sitting in movies or lectures, ~~which~~ and the loud ringing bothers me.

(*What does* **which** *refer to here? The fact that many people have cell phones, that they let their phones go off in movies or lectures, or maybe that the ringtones are so loud? The revised version has one of several possible answers.*)

Pronoun number

* **Pronouns for collective nouns:** For collective nouns, such as *group, committee,* and *family,* use either a singular or plural pronoun, depending on whether the group

acts as a unit or acts separately as many individuals within the unit.

The **committee** reached **its** decision before the end of the meeting.

(*Here the committee acted as a unit.*)

The **committee** relied on **their** own consciences to reach a decision.

(*Here each member of the committee relied separately on his or her own conscience.*)

- ***Consistent pronoun use:*** Don't let your writing shift from singular to plural or plural to singular unless it's necessary.

  The **company** made a profit last year, but ~~they~~ ^{it} lost money when ~~their~~ ^{its} sales declined this year.

Pronouns with compound subjects

Compound subjects with *and* take the plural pronoun.

The **table and chair** were delivered promptly, but **they** were not the style I had ordered.

For compound subjects with ***or*** or ***nor***, the pronoun agrees with the subject word closer to it.

The restaurant offered either regular **patrons** or each new **customer** a free cup of coffee with **his or her** dinner.

Pronouns with *who/which/that*

When ***who, which***, or ***that*** begins a dependent clause, use the word as follows:

- ***Who*** is used for people (and sometimes animals).

  He is a person **who** can help you.

- ***Which*** is used most often for nonessential clauses.

  The catalog, **which** I sent for last month, had some unusual merchandise.

  (*The **which** clause here is nonessential because the time when the catalog was ordered is not necessary to the meaning of the main clause.*)

- ***That*** is used most often for essential clauses.

  When I finished the book **that** she lent me, I was able to write my paper.

(*The* **that** *clause here is essential because the reader needs to know which book helped the writer compose his paper.*)

Indefinite words

Indefinite words such as ***any*** and ***each*** usually take the singular pronoun.

Each of the boys handed in **his** uniform.

Indefinite pronouns

Indefinite pronouns are pronouns that don't refer to any specific person or thing, such as ***anyone, no one, somebody***, or ***each***. Some of them may seem to have a plural meaning, but in formal writing, treat them as singular. When another pronoun refers to one of these words, you can use ***his or her***, switch to plural, use ***they***, or use ***a, an***, or ***the***. (See 14a on inclusive language.)

Everyone brought **his or her** coat. (or)

All the people brought **their** coats. (or)

Everyone brought **their** coats.

(*Some people view this example as incorrect. Others, such as the National Council of Teachers of English, accept this as a way to keep the language inclusive. See 14a.*)

(or) **Everyone** brought **a** coat.

20

Adjectives and Adverbs

20a Adjectives

Adjectives describe or add information about nouns and pronouns:

red	house		They	were **loud.**
(***adjective***)	(*noun*)		(pronoun)	(***adjective***)

Order of Adjectives

Physical Description

Determiner	Evaluation or Opinion	Size	Shape	Age	Color	Nationality	Religion	Material	Noun
a one her	lovely	big	round	old	green	English	Catholic	silk	purse

- the quiet Japanese rock garden
- a square blue cotton handkerchief
- my lazy old Siamese cat
- six excellent new movies
- many difficult physics problems
- every big green plant

To use adjectives and adverbs correctly:

- Use **-ed** adjectives (the **-ed** form of verbs, past participles) to describe nouns. Be sure to include the **-ed** ending.

  used clothing   **iced** tea   **experienced** driver

- Use adjectives following linking verbs such as *appear, seem, taste, feel*, and *look*.

  The sofa seemed **comfortable**. (sofa = comfortable)
  The water tastes **salty**. (water = salty)

20b Adverbs

Adverbs modify verbs, verb forms, adjectives, and other adverbs:

danced **gracefully**   **very**   tall
(*verb*)   (*adverb*)   (*adverb*) (*adjective*)

ran   **very**   quickly
(*verb*) (*adverb*) (*adverb*)

Many adverbs end in **–ly**

Adjective	Adverb
rapid	rapidly
nice	nicely
happy	happily

However, the **-ly** ending isn't a sure test for adverbs because some adjectives have an **-ly** ending (*early, ghostly*), and some adverbs do not end in **-ly** (*very, fast, far*). To be sure, check your dictionary to see whether the word is listed as an adjective or adverb.

Use adverbs to modify verbs.

quickly.   suddenly.   sweetly.
He ran ~~quick.~~   The glass broke ~~sudden.~~   She sang ~~sweet.~~
      ^   ^   ^

When you use adverbs such as *so, such,* and *too,* be sure to complete the phrase or clause.

Hailey was **so** tired. *that she left the office early.*

Malley's is **such** a popular restaurant. *that reservations are recommended.*

TRY THIS

Understanding Commonly Used Adjectives and Adverbs

Be sure to use the following adjectives and adverbs correctly:

Adjective	Adverb
sure	surely
real	really
good	well
bad	badly

She ~~sure~~ surely likes to dance.   The car runs ~~bad.~~ badly.   He sings ~~good~~ well.

FAQ

What is the difference between *good* and *well*?

Good is used as an adjective to modify a noun.

This is a **good** peach.
(adjective)

Well is most often used as an adverb.

Shake **well** before using.
(adverb)

Well is used an adjective when it refers to good health.

Despite her surgery, she looks **well**.
(adjective)

20c Comparisons

Adverbs and adjectives are often used to show comparison, and their forms indicate the degree of comparison. In comparisons, most adjectives and adverbs add *-er* and *-est* as endings or combine with the words *more* and *most* or *less* and *least*.

- **Positive form** is used when no comparison is made.
  a **large** box   an **acceptable** offer

- **Comparative form** is used when two things are being compared (with *-er, more,* or *less*).
  the **larger** of the two boxes   the **less acceptable** of the two offers

- **Superlative form** is used when three or more things are being compared (with *-est, most*, or *least*).
  the **largest** of the six boxes
  the **least acceptable** of all the offers

Adjectives and Adverbs in Comparison		
Positive	**Comparative**	**Superlative**
(for one: uses the base form)	*(for two: uses* **-er, more,** *or* **less***)*	*(for three or more: uses* **-est, most,** *or* **least***)*
tall	taller	tallest
pretty	prettier	prettiest
cheerful	more cheerful	most cheerful
selfish	less selfish	least selfish
Curtis is **tall**.	Curtis is **taller** than Rachel.	Curtis is the **tallest** player on the team.

Irregular Forms of Comparison		
Positive	**Comparative**	**Superlative**
(for one)	*(for two)*	*(for three or more)*
good	better	best
well	better	best
little	less	least
some	more	most
much	more	most
many	more	most
bad, badly	worse	worst

TRY THIS

Making Comparisons Correctly

Avoid double comparisons in which both the *-er* and *more* (or *-est* and *most*) are used.

the ~~most~~ farthest   ~~more~~ quicker

21

Modifiers

21a Dangling modifiers

A dangling modifier is a word or word group that refers to (or modifies) a word or phrase that has not been clearly stated in the sentence. When an introductory phrase does not name the doer of the action, the phrase then refers to (or modifies) the subject of the independent clause that follows.

Having finished the assignment, **Jillian** turned on the TV.

> (**Jillian**, *the subject of the independent clause, is the doer of the action in the introductory phrase. She finished the assignment.*)

However, when the intended subject (or doer of the action) of the introductory phrase is not stated as the subject of the independent clause, the result is a dangling modifier.

Having finished the assignment, the **TV** was turned on.

> (*This sentence says that* **the TV** *finished the homework. Since it is unlikely that TV sets can complete assignments, the introductory phrase has no logical word to refer to. Sentences with dangling modifiers say one thing while the writer means another.*)

Characteristics of dangling modifiers

- They most frequently occur at the beginning of sentences but can also appear at the end.

- They often have an *-ing* verb or a *to + verb* phrase near the start of the whole phrase.

TRY THIS

Revising Dangling Modifiers

1. Name the appropriate or logical doer of the action as the subject of the independent clause.

    Dangling Modifier: **Having arrived** late for practice, a **written excuse** was needed.

74

Revised: **Having arrived** late for practice, the **team member** needed a written excuse.

Dangling Modifier: After **getting** a degree in education, more **experience** in the classroom is needed to be a good teacher.

Revised: After **getting** a degree in education, **Lu** needed more classroom experience to become a good teacher.

Dangling Modifier: **To work** as a lifeguard, **practice** in CPR is required.

Revised: **To work** as a lifeguard, **you** are required to have practice in CPR.

2. Name the doer of the action in the dangling phrase.

Dangling modifier: Without **knowing** the guest's name, **it** was difficult for Marina to introduce him to her husband.

Revised: Because **Marina did** not **know** the guest's name, it was difficult to introduce him to her husband.

21b Misplaced modifiers

A misplaced modifier is a word or word group placed so far away from what it refers to (or modifies) that readers may be confused. Modifiers should be placed as closely as possible to the words they modify in order to keep the meaning clear.

Misplaced modifiers: The assembly line workers were told that they had been fired **by the personnel director.**

(*Were the workers told by the personnel director that they had been fired, or were they told by someone else that the personnel director had fired them?*)

Revised: The assembly line workers were told **by the personnel director** that they had been fired.

Single-word modifiers should be placed immediately before the words they modify. Note the difference in meaning in these two sentences:

I earned **nearly** $30.

(*The amount was almost $30 but not quite.*)

I **nearly** earned $30.

> (*I almost had the opportunity to earn $30, but it didn't work out.*)

FAQ

What should I look for to avoid misplaced modifiers?

When you proofread, check these words to be sure they are as close as possible to the words they refer to.

almost	hardly	merely	only
even	just	nearly	simply

21c Split infinitives

Split infinitives occur when modifiers are inserted between **to** and the **verb**. Some people object to split infinitives, but others consider them grammatically correct. In some cases, inserting a modifier between **to** and the **verb** is the more natural phrasing.

To **quickly** go

> (*Some people accept this, and others prefer to revise to* **to go quickly.**)

To **easily** reach

> (*Most writers prefer this as more natural than "He wanted* **easily** *to reach the top shelf."*)

22

Shifts

Consistency in writing involves using the same (1) pronoun person and number, (2) verb tense, and (3) tone (see 12b).

22a Shifts in person or number

Avoid shifts between first, second, and third person pronouns and between singular and plural. The following table shows the three persons in English pronouns:

Pronoun Person	Singular	Plural
First person (the person or persons speaking)	I, me	we, us
Second person (the person or persons spoken to)	you	you
Third person (the person or persons spoken about)	he, she, it, him, her, it	they, them

Unnecessary shift in person

Once you have chosen to use first, second, or third person, shift only with a good reason.

In a person's life, the most important thing ~~you do~~ *he or she does* is to decide
   (*third*)   (*second*)
on a type of job.

   (*This is an unnecessary shift from third to second person.*)

Unnecessary shift in number

To avoid pronoun inconsistency, don't shift unnecessarily in number from singular to plural (or from plural to singular).

~~A woman faces~~ *Women face* challenges to career advancement. When **they**
   (*singular*)   (*plural*)
take maternity leave, **they** should be sure that opportunities for
                (*plural*)
promotion are still available when they return to work.

   (*The writer uses the singular noun* **woman** *in the first sentence but then shifts to the plural pronoun* **they** *in the second sentence.*)

22b Shifts in verb tense

Because verb tenses indicate time, keep writing in the same time (past, present, or future) unless the logic of what you are writing about requires a switch.

Necessary shift: Many people today **remember** very little about the First Gulf War except the filmed scenes of fighting they **watched** on television news at the time.

   (*The verb* **remember** *reports a general truth in the present, and the verb* **watched** *reports past events.*)

Unnecessary shift: While we **were watching** the last game of the World Series, the picture suddenly **breaks up.**

(*The verb phrase* **were watching** *reports a past event, and there is no reason to shift to the present tense verb* **breaks up**.)

Revised: While we were watching the last game of the World Series, the picture suddenly broke up.

23

Parallelism

23a **Parallel structure**

Parallel structure involves using the same grammatical form or structure for equal ideas in a list or comparison. The balance of equal elements in a sentence helps your reader see the relationship between ideas and adds emphasis. Often, the equal elements repeat words or sounds.

Parallel: The instructor explained how to start the engine
(1)
and how to shift gears.
(2)

(*Phrases 1 and 2 are parallel in that both start with* **how to**.)

Parallel: Getting the model airplane off the ground was even
(1)
harder than building it from a kit.
(2)

(*Phrases 1 and 2 are parallel phrases that begin with* **-ing** *verb forms.*)

Parallelism is needed in the following constructions:

- *Items in a series or list*

Parallel: Our ideal job candidate will know how to

- manage team projects
- troubleshoot computer problems
- communicate effectively with clients.

(*parallelism with verbs*)

- *Both . . . and, either . . . or, whether . . . or, neither . . . nor, not . . . but, not only . . . but also* (correlative conjunctions)

  Parallel: Both his professional appearance and his knowledge of the company suggested he wanted to make a good impression during his job interview.

  (*parallelism with noun phrases*)

- *And, but, or, nor, yet, for, so* (coordinating conjunctions)

  Parallel: Job opportunities are increasing in the health fields **but** decreasing in many areas of engineering.

  (*parallelism using* **-ing** *verbs*)

- **Comparisons using** *than* **or** *as*

  Parallel: The mayor noted that it was easier to agree to the new budget **than** to veto it.

  (*parallelism in a comparison with* **to + verb**)

23b Faulty parallelism

Nonparallelism (or faulty parallelism) is grammatically incorrect and can also lead to a lack of clarity.

When the investigator took over, he started his inquiry by calling the *requesting* (1) witnesses back and requested that they repeat their stories. (2)

The article looked at future uses of computers and ~~what~~ their role (1)   (2) ~~will be~~ in the next decade.

TRY THIS

Proofreading for Parallel Structure

1. As you proofread, **listen** to the sounds when you are linking or comparing similar elements. Do they provide balance by sounding alike? Parallelism often adds emphasis by the repetition of similar sounds.
2. As you proofread, **visualize** similar elements in a list. Check to see that the elements begin with the same sentence structure.

Not Parallel: Braden wondered **whether to search** for a full-time job or **if he should apply** to graduate school.

Parallel: Braden wondered whether **to search** for a full-time job or **to apply** to graduate school.

Parallel: Braden wondered **if he should** search for a full-time job or **if he should apply** to graduate school.

IV

Punctuation

Contents of this section

Question and Correct

	SECTION	PAGE

LEARNING OBJECTIVE: Understanding common sentence patterns

LEARNING OBJECTIVE: Understanding how to use commas correctly

24

Sentence Punctuation Patterns (for Commas and Semicolons)

Commas and Semicolons in Sentences

- For simple sentences, use pattern 1.
- For compound sentences, use patterns 2, 3, and 4.
- For complex sentences, use patterns 5, 6, 7, and 8.

1. **Independent clause .**

   This novel has a memorable conclusion.

2. **Independent   coordinating   independent clause ,   conjunction   clause .**

and	*or*
but	*so*
for	*yet*
nor	

   Claire wanted a snack **,** **so** she ordered a pizza.

3. **Independent clause ; independent clause .**

   Jin is looking for a summer job **;** he wants to work in a hospital or a medical clinic.

4. **Independent   independent   independent clause ;   clause marker ,   clause .**
   however,
   nevertheless,
   therefore,
   consequently,
   (etc.)

   Fewer people are buying newspapers **;** **however** **,** more people are reading news online.

5. **Dependent**   **dependent**   **independent**
   clause marker   **clause ,**   **clause .**
   Because
   Since
   If
   When
   While
   After
   (etc.)

   When Oliver graduated from college **,** he started a new job as a reporter.

6. **Independent**   **dependent**   **dependent**
   clause   **clause marker**   **clause .**
                   because
                   since
                   if
                   when
                   while
                   after
                   (etc.)

   Emergency vehicles arrived quickly **after** the police officer called for help.

7. **Subject ,**   **nonessential ,**   **verb/predicate .**
             dependent
             clause

   (Use commas before and after the dependent clause if it is nonessential.)

   Sayid **,** **who is a talented mechanic ,** repaired the helicopter.

8. **Subject**   **essential**   **verb/predicate .**
             dependent
             clause

   (Do not use commas before and after essential clauses.)

   The fossils **that the scientist discovered last month** have been donated to a museum.

25

Commas

25a Commas between independent clauses

To use commas when you join independent clauses, you need to know the following:

Independent clause: a clause that can stand alone as a sentence

Compound sentence: a sentence with two or more independent clauses

Use the comma with one of the seven joining (coordinating) conjunctions. Some writers remember this list as "**FAN BOYS**," spelled out with the first letter of each word.

> For And Nor But Or Yet So
>
> (*Clause*), **and** (*clause*).
>
> The political debate covered many issues, **but** the candidates did not impress me.

Alternative: If one of the independent clauses has a comma, use a semicolon with the joining word instead.

> Alesha, not Mateya, is the team captain; **but** Mateya assists the coach during practice.

Exception: A comma may be omitted if the two independent clauses are short and there is no danger of misreading.

> We were tired **so** we stopped the game.

25b Commas after introductory elements

A comma is needed after introductory words, phrases, and clauses that come before the main clause in your sentence.

Introductory words

Well,   In fact,   First,

> **Well,** perhaps he meant no harm. **In fact,** he wanted to help.

Introductory phrases and clauses

Long phrases (usually four words or more) and clauses:

> **Without his new smartphone,** Rashaad could not remember his friends' phone numbers.

25c Commas with essential and nonessential elements

When you include words, phrases, or clauses that are not essential to the meaning of the sentence and could be included in another sentence, place commas before and after the nonessential element. If the word, phrase, or clause is essential to the meaning of the sentence, don't use commas.

> Dr. Tanar, **who is a cardiac surgeon,** retired after fifty years of practice.

TRY THIS

Identifying Essential and Nonessential Words and Clauses

You can decide if an element is essential by reading the sentence without it. If the meaning changes, that element is essential.

Essential: Apples **that are green** are usually very tart.

If you remove the clause *that are green*, the statement changes to indicate that all apples are usually very tart.

Nonessential: Madison, **who is my cousin**, will move to Denver when she graduates college.

Whether or not Madison is my cousin, she will still move to Denver. *Who is my cousin* is not essential.

25d Commas in series and lists

Use commas when three or more items are listed in a series. The items can be words, phrases, or clauses. In a list of three items, some writers prefer to omit the comma before the "and."

> He first spoke to Julio, then called his roommate, and finally phoned me.

Americans' favorite spectator sports are football, baseball, and basketball.

(The comma after baseball *is optional.)*

FAQ

Do I need a comma between a list of two items or phrases?

You need at least three items or phrases in a list in order to use commas. Some writers mistakenly put a comma between two items (often verbs) in a sentence.

Misused comma: No one has ever been able to locate the source of the river, and follow it to its starting place.

Revised: No one has ever been able to locate the source of the river and follow it to its starting place.

25e Commas with adjectives

Use commas to separate two or more adjectives that describe the same noun equally.

cold, dark water   happy, healthy baby

But when adjectives are not equal, do not use commas to separate them.

six big dogs   bright green sweater

25f Commas with dates, addresses, geographical names, and numbers

- **With dates listing month and day before the year**

In a heading or list: May 27, 2013 (*or*) 27 May 2013

In a sentence: The order was shipped on March 18, 2012, but not received until April 14, 2012.

- **With addresses:** In a letter heading or on an envelope:

  Jim Johnson, Jr.
  216 Oakwood Drive
  Mineola, NM 43723-1342

In a sentence:

> You can write to Senator Michael Jameson, Jr., 1436 West-wood Drive, Birlingham, ID 83900, for more information.

- ### With geographical names

Put a comma after each element in a place name.

> The convention next year will be in Chicago, Illinois, and in Washington, D.C., the year after that.

- ### With numbers

> 4,300,150   27,000   4,401 (*or*) 4401

25g Commas with interrupting words or phrases

Use commas to set off words and phrases that interrupt the sentence.

> The committee was, however, unable to agree.

> The weather prediction, much to our surprise, was accurate.

25h Commas with quotations

Use a comma before quotations that begin or end with words such as *he said*.

> Everyone was relieved when the chairperson said, "I will table this motion until the next meeting."

> "I forgot," Serkan explained, "to complete the materials section of my lab report."

25i Unnecessary commas

- Don't separate a subject from its verb.

> **Unnecessary comma:**   An eighteen-year-old in most states, is now considered an adult.

- Don't put a comma between two verbs that share the same subject.

> **Unnecessary comma:**   We turned off our phones, and began to study.

- Don't put a comma in front of every *and* or *but*.

> **Unnecessary comma:**   We decided that we should not lend her the money, and that we should explain our decision.

*(The **and** in this sentence joins two **that** clauses.)*

- Don't put a comma in front of a direct object. Remember that clauses beginning with *that* can be direct objects.

    Unnecessary comma: He explained to me, that he is afraid to fly because of terrorists.

- Don't put commas before a dependent clause when it comes after the main clause except for extreme or strong contrast.

    Unnecessary comma: She texted me, because she was going to miss class.

    Extreme contrast: The movie actor was still quite upset, although he did win an Academy Award.

- Don't put a comma after *such as* or *especially*.

    Unnecessary comma: There are several kinds of dark bread from which to choose, such as, whole wheat, rye, oatmeal, pumpernickel, and bran.

26

Apostrophes

26a Apostrophes with possessives

The apostrophe shows ownership, but this is not always obvious.

TRY THIS

Testing Words for Possession

Turn the words around into an **of the** phrase.

day's pay

the pay of the day

Mike's shoes

the shoes of Mike

- For singular nouns, use *'s*.

    the book**'s** author   a flower**'s** smell

- For a singular noun ending in -s, the s after the apostrophe is optional, especially if it would make pronunciation difficult.

    James**'s** car   (*or*)   James**'** car

    Euripides**'** story *(Saying* Euripides's story *is difficult.)*

- For plural nouns ending in -s, add only an apostrophe.

    both teams**'** colors   six days**'** vacation

- For plural nouns not ending in -s (such as *children* or *mice*), use *'s*.

    the children**'s** game   six men**'s** coats

- For indefinite pronouns (pronouns ending in -*body* and -*one*, such as *no one* and *everybody*), use *'s*.

    no one**'s** fault   someone**'s** hat

- For compound words, add *'s* to the last word.

    brother-in-law**'s** job   everyone else**'s** preference

- For joint ownership by two or more nouns, add *'s* after the last noun in the group. When individually owned, add *'s* after each noun.

    Lisa and Vinay**'s** house   *(Lisa and Vinay own the house jointly.)*

    Lisa**'s** and Vinay**'s** houses   *(Lisa and Vinay each own different houses.)*

FAQ

Where does the apostrophe go to show possession?

For singular nouns that don't end in **'s:**

Word	Possessive Marker	Result
cup	**'s**	cup**'s** handle

When you aren't sure whether the word is plural or not, remember this sequence:

- Write the word.
- Then write the plural, if needed.
- Then add the possessive apostrophe.

Thus everything to the left of the apostrophe is the word and its plural, if needed.

Word	Plural Marker	Possessive Marker	Result
cup	s	'	cups' handles

26b Apostrophes with contractions

Use the apostrophe to mark the omitted letter or letters in contractions.

it's = it is   don't = do not   that's = that is   '79 = 1979
he's going = he is going

26c Apostrophes with plurals

Use apostrophes to form plurals of letters, abbreviations with periods, numbers, and words used to refer to the word itself, not the thing or meaning it represents. The apostrophe is optional if the plural is clear.

Plural of a word used as the word itself:

Madison uses too many *wow*'s in her e-mails.

Necessary apostrophes:

a's   B.A.'s   *A*'s

Optional apostrophes:

9s (*or*) 9's   UFOs (*or*) UFO's   ands (*or*) and's

&s (*or*) &'s   Ph.D.'s (*or*) Ph.D.s

26d Unnecessary apostrophes

Don't use the apostrophe with possessive pronouns (such as *hers* and *its*) or with the regular plural forms of nouns.

Not correct:	it's sound	yours'	I bought five apples'.
Correct:	its sound	yours	I bought five apples.

27

Semicolons

The semicolon is a stronger mark of punctuation than a comma, and it is used with two kinds of closely related equal elements:

- between independent clauses
- between items in a series when any of the items contains a comma.

27a Semicolons in compound sentences

Use the semicolon when joining independent clauses not joined by the seven connectors that require commas: *and, but, for, nor, or, so, yet*.

Here are two patterns for using semicolons:

- **Independent clause + semicolon + independent clause**

  He often watched TV reruns; she preferred to read instead.

- **Independent clause + semicolon + joining word or phrase + comma + independent clause**

  He often watched TV reruns; **however**, she preferred to read instead.

Transitional words or phrases are all the joining words other than *and, but, for, or*, or *nor* that can be used to connect two independent clauses.

also	finally	instead
besides	for example	nevertheless
consequently	however	still
even so	in addition	therefore

A semicolon can be used instead of a comma with two independent clauses joined by *and, but, for, nor, or, so*, or *yet* when one of the clauses contains a comma.

- **Independent clause with commas + semicolon + independent clause**.

  Senator Dowson, who was accused of bribery, has resigned; he

  (independent clause #1 with commas)

  has refused to discuss his resignation with reporters.

  (independent clause #2)

27b Semicolons in a series

For clarity, use semicolons to separate a series of items in which one or more of the items contain commas. Semicolons are also preferred if items in the series are especially long.

- Items with their own commas:

  Among her favorite movies were old Cary Grant pictures, such as *Arsenic and Old Lace*; any of Woody Allen's films; and children's classics, including *The Sound of Music* and *The Wizard of Oz*.

- Long items in a series:

  When planning the trip, she considered the length of travel time between cities where stops would be made; the number of people likely to get on at each stop; and the times when the bus would arrive at major cities where connections would be made with other buses.

27c Semicolons with quotation marks

Place semicolons after quotation marks.

  Her answer to my question was "I'll have to think about that"; she clearly had no answers.

27d Unnecessary semicolons

Don't use a semicolon between a clause and a phrase or between an independent clause and a dependent clause.

Unnecessary semicolon: They wanted to see historical buildings; especially the courthouse. *(should be a comma)*

Unnecessary semicolon: He tried to improve his tennis serve; because that was the weakest part of his game. *(should be no punctuation)*

Don't use a semicolon in place of a dash, comma, or colon.

Incorrect semicolon: The office needed more equipment; a laptop, an iPad, and a paper shredder. *(should be a colon, not a semicolon)*

28

Quotation Marks

28a Quotation marks with direct and indirect quotations

Quotation marks with prose quotations

Direct quotations: the exact words said by someone you heard or read and are recopying. Enclose exact quotations in quotation marks.

Indirect quotations: not someone's exact words but a rephrasing or summary of those words. Don't use quotation marks for indirect quotations.

If a quotation is longer than four lines, set it off as a block quotation by indenting one inch or ten spaces from the left margin. Use the same spacing between lines as in the rest of your paper, and don't use quotation marks.

- Direct quotation of a whole sentence: Use a capital letter to start the first word of the quotation.

  Mr. and Mrs. Yoder, farm owners, said, "We refuse to use that pesticide because it might pollute the nearby wells."

- Direct quotation of part of a sentence: Don't use a capital letter to start the first word of the quotation.

  Mr. and Mrs. Yoder stated that they "refuse to use that pesticide" because of possible water pollution.

- Indirect quotation:

  According to their statement, the Yoders will not use the pesticide because of potential water pollution.

- Quotation within a quotation: Use single quotation marks (' at the beginning and ' at the end) for a quotation inside another quotation.

  The agriculture reporter explained, "When I talked to the Yoders last week, they said, 'We refuse to use that pesticide.'"

If you leave some words out of a quotation, use an ellipsis (three spaced periods, see 29h) to indicate omitted words. If you need to insert something within a quotation, use brackets [ ] to enclose the addition. (See 29g.)

Quotation marks in poetry

When you quote a single line of poetry, write it like other short quotations. Separate two lines of poetry with a slash (/) at the end of the first line. Leave a space before and after the slash. If the quotation is three lines or longer, set it off, indented one inch or ten spaces, like a longer quotation, and do not use quotation marks.

Quotation marks in dialogue

Write each person's speech, however short, as a separate paragraph. Use commas to set off *he said* or *she said*. Closely related bits of narrative can be included in the paragraph. If someone's speech goes on for several paragraphs, use quotation marks at the beginning of each paragraph but not at the end of any paragraph except the last one.

28b Quotation marks for minor titles and parts of wholes

Use quotation marks for the titles of parts of larger works (titles of book chapters, magazine articles, and episodes of television and radio series) and for short or minor works (songs, short stories, essays, short poems, and other literary works that are shorter than book length).

> "The Star-Spangled Banner"
> "Bowling for Votes" (an episode of *Parks and Recreation*)

Use italics for larger, more complete works (*Hamlet*). Don't use quotation marks or italics for the titles of most religious texts (The Bible) or legal documents. (See 31a.)

28c Quotation marks for words

Use quotation marks or italics for words used as words rather than for their meaning.

> The word "accept" is often confused with "except." OR
> The word *accept* is often confused with *except*.

28d Quotation marks with other punctuation

- Put commas and periods inside quotation marks. When a reference follows a short quotation, put the period after the reference.

  "Adonais," a poem by Percy Bysshe Shelley, memorializes John Keats.
  . . . after the stunning success" (252).

- Put a colon or semicolon after the quotation marks.

  . . . until tomorrow";

- Put a dash, a question mark, or an exclamation point inside the quotation marks when these punctuation marks are part of the quotation and outside the quotation marks when the marks apply to the whole sentence.

  He asked, "Do you need this book?"
  Does Dr. Lim tell all her students, "You must work harder"?

28e Unnecessary quotation marks

Don't put quotation marks around the titles of your essays, common nicknames, bits of humor, technical terms, and well-known expressions.

29

Other Punctuation

29a Hyphens

Hyphens have a variety of uses:

- **For compound words:**
  Some compound words are one word:
  weekend   granddaughter   hometown

  Some compounds are two words:
  high school   executive director   turn off

  Some compounds are joined by hyphens:
  father-in-law   president-elect   clear-cut

Fractions and numbers from twenty-one to ninety-nine that are spelled out have hyphens.

one-half   thirty-six   nine-tenths

For new words or compounds you are forming, check your dictionary. But not all hyphenated words appear there, especially new ones, and usage varies between dictionaries for some compounds.

e-mail (*or*) email   witch-hunt (*or*) witch hunt
wave-length (*or*) wavelength (*or*) wave length

For hyphenated words in a series, use hyphens as follows:

five- and six-page essays

(Leave an extra space after the hyphens in all hyphenated words except the last one.)

- **For two-word units:**
  Use a hyphen when two or more words before a noun work together as a single unit to describe the noun. When these words come after the noun, they are not hyphenated.

  He needed up-to-date statistics. (*or*) He needed statistics that were up to date.
  They repaired the six-inch pipe. (*or*) They repaired the pipe that was six inches long.

  Do not use a hyphen with adverbs ending in *-ly*.

  That was a widely known fact.

- **For prefixes, suffixes, and letters joined to a word:**
  Use hyphens between words and prefixes *self-, all-,* and *ex-*.

  self-contained   all-encompassing   ex-president

  For other prefixes, such as *anti-, pro-,* and *co-*, use the dictionary as a guide.

  co-op   antibacterial   pro-choice

  Use a hyphen to join a prefix to a capitalized word or with figures and numbers.

  anti-American   non-Catholic   pre-1998

  Use a hyphen when you add the suffix *-elect*.

  president-elect

  Use a hyphen to avoid doubling vowels and tripling consonants and to avoid ambiguity.

  anti-intellectual bell-like re-cover re-creation

- **To divide words between syllables when the last part of the word appears on the next line.**

  Every spring the nation's capital is flooded with tour-
  ists snapping pictures of the cherry blossoms.

- **When dividing words at the end of a line:**
  - Don't divide one-syllable words.
  - Don't leave one or two letters at the end of a line.
  - Don't put fewer than three letters on the next line.
  - Don't divide the last word in a paragraph or on a page.
  - Divide compound words between the parts of the compound. If a word contains a hyphen, break only at the hyphen.
  - Don't insert hyphens in website addresses.

29b Colons

Use colons as follows:

- **To announce items at the end of the sentence**
  The company sold only electronics they could service: computers, printers, and television sets.

- **To separate independent clauses** Use a colon instead of a semicolon to separate two independent clauses when the second clause restates or amplifies the first.
  The town council voted not to pave the gravel roads: it did not have the funds for road improvement.

- **To announce long quotations**
  Use a colon to announce a long quotation (more than one sentence) or a quotation not introduced by words such as *said* or *stated*.
  The candidate offered only one reason to vote for her: "I will not raise parking meter rates."

- **In salutations and between elements**
  Dear Dr. Philippa: 6:12 a.m.   Genesis 1:8

- **With quotation marks**
  When colons are needed, put them after closing quotation marks.
  "Don't argue with your boss": that's her motto for office harmony.

- **Unnecessary colons**
  Do not use a colon after a verb or phrases like *such as* or *consisted of*.

Unnecessary colon:	The two best players were: Timon Lasmon and Maynor Field.
Revised:	The two best players were Timon Lasmon and Maynor Field.

| Unnecessary colon: | The camping equipment consisted of: tents, lanterns, matches, and dehydrated food. |
| Revised: | The camping equipment consisted of tents, lanterns, matches, and dehydrated food. |

29c End punctuation

Periods

- Use periods at the ends of sentences that are statements, mild commands, indirect questions, or polite questions to which answers aren't expected.

    Electric cars are growing in popularity. (*statement*)

    Turn off your cell phones during class. (*mild command*)

    Would you please let me know when you're done. (*polite question*)

- Use a period with abbreviations, but don't use a second period if the abbreviation is at the end of the sentence.

    R.S.V.P.   U.S.A.   Mr.   8 a.m.

- A period is not needed after agencies, common abbreviations, names of well-known companies, and U.S. Postal Service state abbreviations.

    NATO   NBA   CIA   YMCA   IBM   DNA   TX

- Put periods that follow quotations inside the quotation marks. But if there is a reference to a source, put the period after the reference.

    She said, "I'm going to Alaska next week."
    Neman notes that "the claim is unfounded" (6).

Question marks

- Use a question mark after a direct question but not after an indirect one.

    Did anyone find my flash drive? (*direct question*)

    Jules wonders if he should buy a new iPhone. (*indirect question*)

- Place a question mark inside quotation marks if the quotation is a question. Place the question mark outside quotation marks if the whole sentence is a question.

    Drora asked, "Is she on time?"
    Did Eli really say, "I'm in love"?

- Question marks may be used between parts of a series.

    Would you like to see a movie? go shopping? eat at a restaurant?

- Use a question mark to indicate doubt about the correctness of a date, number, or other piece of information. But do not use it to indicate sarcasm.

    The ship landed in Greenland about 1521 (?) but did not keep a record of where it was.

    Not polite: Matti's sense of humor (?) evaded me.

    Revised: Matti's sense of humor evaded me.

Exclamation points

- Use the exclamation point after a strong command or a statement said with great emphasis or with strong feeling. But don't overuse the exclamation point.

    Correct: I'm absolutely delighted!
    Unnecessary: Wow! What a great party! I enjoyed every minute of it! The food was delicious, and the music was fantastic!

- Enclose the exclamation point within the quotation marks only if it belongs to the quotation.

    As he came in, he exclaimed, "I've won the lottery!"

29d Dashes

The dash is informal but can be used to add emphasis or clarity, to mark an interruption or shift in tone, or to introduce a list. If you use a word processor without the dash, use two hyphens to indicate the dash with no space before or after the hyphens.

    The cat looked at me so sweetly—with a dead rat in its mouth.

29e Slashes

Use the slash to mark the end of a line of poetry and to indicate acceptable alternatives. For poetry, leave a space before and after the slash. For alternatives, leave no space. The slash is also used in website addresses.

    He repeated Milton's lines: "The mind is its own place, and in itself / Can make a Heaven of Hell, a Hell of Heaven."

    pass/fail   and/or   http://www.whitehouse.gov

29f Parentheses

Use parentheses to enclose supplementary or less important material added as further explanation or example or to enclose figures or letters in a numbered list.

> The newest officers of the club (those elected in May) were installed at the ceremony.

> They had three items on the agenda: (1) the budget, (2) parking permits, and (3) election procedures.

29g Brackets

Use brackets to add your comments or additional explanation within a quotation and to replace parentheses within parentheses. The Latin word *sic* in brackets means you copied the original quotation exactly as it appeared, but you think there's an error.

> We agreed with Fellner's claim that "this great team [the Chicago Bears] will go to the Super Bowl next year."

> The lawyer explained, "We discussed the matter in a fiendly [*sic*] manner."

29h Omitted words (ellipsis)

Use an ellipsis (a series of three periods, with one space before and after each period) to indicate that you are omitting words or part of a sentence from the source you are quoting. If you omit a whole sentence or paragraph, add a fourth period with no space after the last word preceding the ellipsis.

> "modern methods . . . with no damage."

> "the National Forest System . . ." (Smith 9).

> "federal lands . . . . They were designated for preservation."

If you omit words immediately after a punctuation mark (such as a comma) in the original, include that mark in your sentence.

> "because of this use of the forest, . . ."

V

Mechanics

Contents

Question and Correct

	SECTION	PAGE

LEARNING OBJECTIVE: Correctly capitalizing words

LEARNING OBJECTIVE: Using italics correctly

LEARNING OBJECTIVE: Writing numbers correctly

30

Capitalization

30a **Proper nouns and common nouns**

Capitalize proper nouns, which are words that name one particular thing, most often a person or place rather than a general type or group of things. Listed here are categories of words that should be capitalized. If you are not sure about a particular word, check your dictionary.

Proper noun	Common noun
James Joyce	man
Thanksgiving	holiday
University of Maine	state university
Macintosh	computer
May	month

- Persons
  - Vincent Baglia   Rifka Kaplan   Masuto Tatami
- Places, including geographical regions
  - Milwaukee   Alberta   Northeast
- Peoples and their languages
  - French   Swahili   Portuguese
- Religions and their followers
  - Buddhist   Judaism   Christianity
- Members of national, political, racial, social, civic, and athletic groups
  - Democrat   African American   Green Bay Packers
  - Danes   Friends of the Library   Olympics Committee
- Institutions and organizations
  - Girl Scouts   Library of Congress   Lions Club
- Historical documents
  - Declaration of Independence   Magna Carta
- Periods and events, but not centuries
  - Middle Ages   World War II   twentieth century
- Days, months, and holidays, but not seasons
  - Tuesday   Thanksgiving   winter
- Trademarks
  - Coca-Cola   Toyota   Google

- Holy books and words denoting the Supreme Being (pronouns referring to God may be capitalized or lowercased)

  Talmud   Bible   Lord

- Words and abbreviations derived from specific names, but not the names of things that have lost that specific association and now refer to general types

  Stalinism   Freudian   NBC
  french fries   pasteurize   italics

- Place words, such as *street, park*, and *city*, that are part of specific names

  New York City   Wall Street   Zion National Park

- Titles that precede people's names, but not titles that follow names

  Governor Chris Christie   Aunt Sue   President Barack Obama
  Chris Christie, governor Sue, my aunt Barack Obama, president

- Words that indicate family relationships when used as a substitute for a specific name

  Here is a gift for   Li Chen sent a gift to his
    Mother.   mother.

- Titles of books, magazines, essays, movies, plays, and other works, but not articles (*a, an, the*), short prepositions (*to, by, on, in*), or short joining words (*and, but, or*) unless they are the first or last word. With hyphenated words, capitalize the first and all other important words.

  The Taming of the Shrew   *The Indo-European Languages*
  The Ground Beneath Her Feet   *A Brother-in-Law's Lament*

- The pronoun *I* and the interjection *O*, but not the word *oh*

  "Sail on, sail on, O ship of state," I said as the canoe sank.

- Words placed after a prefix that are normally capitalized

  un-American   anti-Semitic   pro-Israel

30b Capitals in sentences, quotations, and lists

- Capitalize the first word of every sentence.

- Capitalize the first word of a comment in parentheses if the comment is a complete sentence. Use lowercase if the comment is not a full sentence.

  The American Olympic ski team (which receives some government support) spent six months training for the elimination trials, whereas the German team trained for over two years. (Like most European nations, Germany provides financial support for its team.)

- Do not capitalize the first word in a series of questions in which the questions are not full sentences.

  What did the interviewer want from the rock star? details of her personal life? news about her next project?

- Capitalize the first word of directly quoted speech, but not a continuation of an interrupted direct quotation or a quoted phrase or clause that is integrated into the sentence.

  She answered, "Everyone will know the truth."

  "Everyone," she answered, "will know the truth."

  When Bataglio declined the nomination, he explained that he "would try again another year."

- Capitalize the first word in a list after a colon if each item in the list is a complete sentence or if each item is displayed on a line of its own.

  The popularity of walking as an alternative to jogging has led to various improvements: (1) better designs for walking shoes, (2) an expanding market for walking sticks, and (3) a rapid growth in the number of manufacturers selling walking shoes.

  (*or*)

  The popularity of walking as an alternative to jogging has led to various improvements:

  1. Better designs for walking shoes
  2. An expanding market for walking sticks
  3. A rapid growth in the number of manufacturers selling walking shoes

31

Italics

Italics have generally replaced underlining for titles of long works in word-processed documents. When you are writing by hand, use underlining (a printer's mark to indicate words to be set in italics) for the kinds of titles and names indicated in this section.

31a Titles

- Use italics for titles and names of long or complete works, including the following:

Books	*The Hunger Games*
Magazines	*Entertainment Weekly*
Newspapers	*The Washington Post*
Works of art (visual and performance)	*Swan Lake*

Pamphlets	*Saving Energy in Your Home*
Television/radio series (not titles of individual episodes, such as "Choke")	*Glee*
Films and videos	*The Artist*
Long plays	*Macbeth*
Long musical works	*Canon in D*
Long poems	*In Memoriam*
Software	*Adobe InDesign*
Recordings	*Born This Way*
Websites (not individual webpages)	*The Onion*
Ships, airplanes, and trains	*Orient Express*

- Do not use italics or quotation marks for references to the Bible and other religious works, legal documents, the Internet, and titles of websites used as verbs.

Genesis	Bible	Upanishads
Torah	U.S. Constitution	Declaration of Independence
Internet	Google	Facebook

31b Other uses of italics

- Foreign words and phrases and scientific names of plants and animals
  de rigueur   *Felis domesticus*

- Trademarked names used as words
  Some words, such as *Kleenex*, are brand names for products.

- Letters used as examples or terms
  In English, the letters *ph* and *f* often have the same sound.

- Words being emphasized
  It *never* snows here at this time of year.

  (Use italics for emphasis sparingly.)

Do not use italics for the following

- Words of foreign origin that are now part of English
  | alumni | cliché | manga |
  | blitz | chutzpah | karaoke |

- Titles of your own papers

32

Numbers

Style manuals for different fields and companies vary. The suggestions for writing numbers given here are generally useful as a guide for academic writing.

- Spell out numbers that can be expressed in one or two words, and use figures for other numbers.

Words	Figures
eight pounds	284 days
six dollars	$49.99
thirty-seven years	8,962 bushels
forty-three people	3.43 liters

- Use a combination of figures and words for numbers that are close together when such a combination will make your writing clearer.

    The club celebrated the birthdays of six 90-year-olds born in the city.

Use Figures for the Following

- Days and years

September 18, 2013	(*or*)	18 September 2013
A.D. 1066		
in 1931–1932	(*or*)	in 1931–32
the 1990's	(*or*)	the 1990s

- Time of day

8:00 A.M. (*or*) a.m.	(*or*)	eight o'clock in the morning
4:30 P.M. (*or*) p.m.	(*or*)	half past four in the afternoon

- Addresses

15 Tenth Street		
350 West 114 Street	(*or*)	350 West 114th Street
Prescott, AZ 86301		

- Identification numbers

Room 88	Channel 603
Interstate 95	Elizabeth II

- Page and division of books and plays

page 30	Book I
Act 3, sc. 2	Ch. 3

- Decimals and percentages

6.1 average	13½ percent
0.057 metric ton	

- Numbers in series and statistics
  two apples, six oranges, and three bananas
  115 feet by 90 feet
  Be consistent, whichever form you choose.

- Large round numbers
  | $14 billion | (*or*) | fourteen billion dollars |
  | 11.5 million | (*or*) | 11,500,000 |

- Repeated numbers (in legal or commercial writing)
  Notice must be given at least ninety (90) days in advance.

Do not use figures for the following

- Numbers that can be expressed in one or two words
  in his forties   the twenty-first century

- Dates when the year is omitted
  June sixth

- Numbers beginning sentences
  Ninety-five percent of our students are from South Carolina.

33

Abbreviations

In writing government, business, social science, science, and engineering documents, abbreviations are used frequently. However, for writing in the humanities, only a limited number of abbreviations are generally used.

33a Abbreviating titles

- *Mr., Mrs.*, and *Ms.* are abbreviated when used as titles before a name.
  Mr. Toyagama   Ms. Patuk   Mrs. Begay

- *Dr.* and *St.* ("Saint") are abbreviated only when they immediately precede a name; they are written out when they appear after the name.
  Dr. Marlen Chafo   Marlen Chafo, doctor of internal medicine

- *Prof., Sen., Gen., Capt.*, and similar abbreviated titles can be used when they appear in front of a full name or before initials and a last name but not when they appear before the last name only.
  Gen. R. G. Brindo   General Brindo

- *Sr., Jr., J.D., Ph.D., M.F.A., C.P.A.,* and other abbreviated academic titles and professional degrees can be used after the name.

    Leslie O'Brien, Ph.D.　　Kim Takamota, C.P.A.

- *Bros., Co.,* and similar abbreviations are used only if they are part of the exact name.

    Bass & Co.　　Warner Bros.

33b Abbreviating places

In general, spell out names of states, countries, continents, streets, rivers, and so on. But there are a few exceptions:

- Use the abbreviation *D.C.* in Washington, D.C.
- Use *U.S.* only as an adjective, not as a noun.

    U.S. training bases　　training bases in the United States

- If you include a full address in a sentence, use the postal abbreviation for the state.

    For further information, write to us at 100 Peachtree Street, Atlanta, GA 30300, for a copy of our free catalog.

    The company's headquarters, on Peachtree Street in Atlanta, Georgia, will soon be moved.

33c Abbreviating numbers

- Write out numbers that can be expressed in one or two words.

    eighteen　　fifty-six　　345

- The dollar sign is generally acceptable when the written-out phrase would be three words or more.

    $29 million　　thirty dollars

- For temperatures, use figures, the degree symbol, and F (for Fahrenheit) or C (for Celsius).

    10°F　　25°C

33d Abbreviating measurements

Spell out units of measurement, such as *acre, meter, foot*, and *percent*, but use abbreviations for measurements in tables, graphs, and figures.

33e Abbreviating dates

Spell out months and days of the week.

    January　　Tuesday

The abbreviations B.C., B.C.E. (before the common era), and C.E. (common era) are placed after the year, while A.D.

is placed before. With dates and times, the following are acceptable:

57 B.C	57 B.C.E	329 C.E.	A.D. 329
A.M., P.M. (*or*) a.m., p.m.		EST (*or*) E.S.T.	

33f Abbreviating names of familiar organizations or other entities

Use abbreviations for names of organizations, agencies, countries, and things usually referred to by their initials.

IBM	NAACP	NASA	NOW
PTA	UNICEF	the former USSR	DVD

If you are using the initials for a term that may not be familiar to your readers, spell it out the first time and give the initials in parentheses. From then on, you can use the initials.

The study of children's long-term memory (LTM) has been difficult because of the lack of a universally accepted definition of childhood LTM.

33g Abbreviating Latin expressions and documentation terms

Some Latin expressions always appear as abbreviations.

Abbreviation	Meaning
cf.	compare
e.g.	for example
i.e.	that is
et al.	and others
etc.	and so forth
vs. (*or*) v.	versus

The following abbreviations are appropriate for bibliographies and footnotes, as well as in informal writing, but for formal writing, use the full phrase instead. The format for abbreviations may vary among style manuals, so use the abbreviations appropriate for the style you are following.

Abbreviation	Meaning
ed., eds.	editor (*or*) edited by, editors
n.d.	no date of publication given
n.p.	no place of publication given
n. pag.	no page number given
p., pp.	page, pages
vol., vols.	volume, volumes

34

Spelling

English spelling is difficult because it contains many words from other languages that have different spelling conventions. In addition, English has several ways to spell some sounds. But correct spelling is important, partly to be sure your words are understood correctly and partly because you don't want to signal your reader that are you are careless or not very knowledgeable.

TRY THIS

Improving Your Spelling

Following these strategies can help you improve your spelling.

- **Learn some common spelling rules.** Read the useful spelling rules in 34b.

- **Look up words in the dictionary.** If you are unsure of a spelling, try looking it up in a print or online dictionary. Many word-processing programs, such as Microsoft Word, also have built-in dictionaries.

- **Create your own memory aids.** Keep a journal or list of words that cause you problems, and study it.

- **Make up associations that will help you remember tricky words.** For example, you could try remembering that *dessert* is the sweet treat you'd like seconds of. So it has an extra s. And *desert*, with one s, is the one that refers to barren sandy places.

34a Proofreading

Proofreading means reading your work more slowly and carefully than your normal reading speed to catch misspellings and typographical errors. This is best done after you have finished writing and are preparing to turn your paper over to your readers.

TRY THIS

Proofreading for Spelling Errors

Try these strategies to catch your spelling errors:

- **Slow down.** Proofreading requires slowing down your reading rate so that you can see all the letters in each word.

- **Zoom in.** If you proofread on your computer, set the display at 125 percent or more so that you can clearly see each word.

- **Focus on each word.** One way to slow yourself down is to point a pencil or pen at each word as you say it aloud or quietly to yourself.

- **Read backward.** Move backward through each line from right to left. In this way, you won't be listening for meaning or checking for grammatical correctness.

FAQ

Won't a spell-checker catch all of my spelling errors?

Spell-checkers are useful tools, particularly when used as a final proofreading step in combination with other strategies. However, they can't catch all spelling errors:

- **Sound-alike words (homonyms).** Spell-checkers cannot always distinguish between words that sound alike, such as *there* and *their*, *its* and *it's*, or *brake* and *break*.

- **Substitution of one word for another.** For example, if you meant to write *own* and typed *one* instead, the spell-checker is not likely to catch the error.

- **Many proper nouns.** Some well-known proper nouns, such as *Washington*, may be in the spell-checker dictionary, but many others will not be.

- **Misspellings that the spell-checker can't match to an appropriate word.** If you misspell words, the spell-checker may highlight the error, but it might not be able to suggest the correct spelling. If this happens, use a dictionary to find the word.

- **Missing words.** If you forget to type a word, the spell-checker will not flag it for you.

34b Some spelling guidelines

ie/ei

Write *i* before *e* / except after *c* / or when sounded like "*ay*" / as in *neighbor* and *weigh*. This rhyme reminds you to write *ie* except under two conditions:

- When the two letters follow a *c*.
- When the two letters sound like *ay* (as in *day*).

Some *ie* Words		Some *ei* Words	
believe	field	ceiling	eight
chief	yield	receive	deceive

- The following common words are exceptions to this rule:

conscience	foreign	neither	species
counterfeit	height	science	sufficient
either	leisure	seize	weird

Doubling Consonants

- **One-Syllable Words** If the word ends with a single short vowel and a consonant, double that last consonant when you are adding a suffix beginning with a vowel.

shop	shopped	shopping	shopper
wet	wetted	wetting	wettest

- **Two-Syllable Words** For words with two or more syllables that end with a vowel and then a consonant, double the consonant when (1) you are adding a suffix beginning with a vowel, and (2) the last syllable of the base word is accented.

occur	occurred	occurring	occurrence
regret	regretted	regretting	regrettable

Final Silent -*e*

Drop the final silent -*e* when you add a suffix beginning with a vowel. But keep the final -*e* when the suffix begins with a consonant.

line	lining	care	careful
smile	smiling	like	likely

Words such as *true / truly* and *argue / argument* are exceptions to this rule.

Plurals

- Most plurals are formed by adding *-s*. But add *-es* when words end in *s, sh, ch, x,* or *z* because another syllable is needed to make the ending easy to pronounce.

one ankle	two ankles
one box	two boxes
one wish	two wishes
one batch	two batches

- With phrases and hyphenated words, pluralize the last word unless another word is more important.

one systems analyst	two systems analysts
one sister-in-law	two sisters-in-law
one attorney general	other attorneys general

- For words ending in a consonant plus *-y*, change the *-y* to *-i* and add *-es*. For proper nouns, keep the *-y*.

one company	four companies
a monkey	two monkeys
Mr. Henry	the Henrys

- For some words, the plural is formed by changing the base word. Other words have the same form for singular and plural. And other words, taken from other languages, form the plurals in the same way as the original language.

one child	several children
one woman	two women
one deer	nine deer
one medium	some media

FAQ

Are apostrophes needed when making single words into plurals?

Apostrophes are used to show possession (like *Sara's book*) or in contractions (such as *didn't* or *would've*), not for making words plural. For most plurals, just add *s*. See Chapter 26 for more information about the correct use of apostrophes.

two bikes	NOT: two bikes'
four oranges	NOT: four orange's

34c Sound-alike words (homonyms)

Word	Meaning	Example
accept:	to agree/receive	I have to accept the facts.
except:	other than	I called everyone except him.
affect:	to influence	Pollen affects my allergies.
effect:	a result	Sneezing is the effect.
anyone:	any person at all	This problem would make anyone angry.
any one:	specific person or thing in a group	Any one of those children could have taken the ball.
apart:	not together	Jim and Sue divorced and are now apart.
a part:	joined to a group	She is a part of the chorus.
than:	used to compare	He is smarter than I.
then:	indicates time	Then I read a book.
their:	shows possession	The boys flew their kites.
there:	indicates location	They found it over there.
they're:	they are	They're happy now.
to	preposition	We are going to the movies.
two	number	He has two dogs.
too	very or also	This cake is too sweet.
your:	shows possession	Your suit looks great.
you're:	you are	You're ready for your interview.

VI

Multilingual Speakers

Contents

Question and Correct

	SECTION	PAGE

LEARNING OBJECTIVE: To understand the differences between American English and World Englishes

35

American Style in Writing/ ESL Resources

If your first language is not English, you may have writing style preferences that are different from American style and questions about English grammar and usage. Your style preferences and customs will depend on what language(s) you are most familiar with, but in general, consider the following differences between the languages you know and academic style in American English.

	Language Styles of Other Cultures	American Academic Language and Style
Conciseness	In some cultures, writers try for a style with a variety of words and phrases. Ideas can be repeated in various ways.	Effective academic and public writing style in American English is concise and avoids unnecessary words.
Introduction of topic	In some languages, the topic is not immediately announced or stated at all. Instead, suggestions lead readers to develop the main ideas themselves.	In American English, there is a strong preference for announcing the topic in the opening paragraph or near the beginning of the paper.
Organization	Digressions, or moving off the main topic into related matters, are encouraged in some cultures because they add to the richness of ideas.	In American English, there is a preference for staying on the topic and not moving away, or digressing, from it.

(continued)

	Language Styles of Other Cultures	American Academic Language and Style
Pattern of reasoning	Writers in some cultures prefer inductive reasoning, moving from specifics to the more general conclusion.	American academic writing is usually deductive, beginning with general ideas and moving to more specific reasons or details.
Citation of sources	In some cultures, there is less attention to citing sources, ideas, or the exact words used by others. Ideas of great scholars, for example, can be used without citation because it is assumed that readers know the sources.	In American academic writing, writers are expected to cite all sources of information that are not generally known by most people. A writer who fails to credit the words or ideas of others is in danger of being viewed as a plagiarist.

For writers from some other cultures, the American academic preference to organize a paper from general to specific (deductive) may require a different way of thinking. This is because writing in some cultures moves toward the general thesis or main point of an argument by the end of the document. This is described as writing inductively.

35b American English and World Englishes

American academic English is the English explained in this book, but it is only one form of spoken and written English. Other varieties of English used around the globe are referred to as World Englishes. No variety of English is better or more correct than another; each is appropriate for the circumstances and purposes for which it is being used. They are just different forms of a language widely used around the world and may vary in pronunciation, vocabulary, spelling, punctuation, and grammatical rules.

You will want to write in grammatically correct and stylistically appropriate American English when you are studying in American schools and communicating with Americans. But when you are communicating with other World English speakers and writers, the World English you use elsewhere is acceptable for social and sometimes business purposes.

35c Resources for learning English as another language

Some websites where you can find useful resources for learning English as another language include the following:

dictionary.cambridge.org
The site offers definitions in American, British, business, and learner's dictionaries, plus listings of dictionaries useful for people learning English as another language.

owl.english.purdue.edu/owl/resource/678/01/
Purdue University's Online Writing Lab page includes links to handouts on ESL issues as well as other resources.

www.openculture.com/category/freelanguagelessons
Open Culture offers links to a variety of educational language resources, including audio podcasts and online videos.

www.eslcafe.com
Dave Sperling's ESL Café provides discussion forums, help with pronunciation and slang, idioms, grammar lessons, quizzes, and other aids.

www.1-language.com
1-Language.com offers free English courses; an audio listening center; and English courses for those who speak Chinese, German, or French; and other resources.

www.englishforum.com/00
Aardvark's English Forum includes dictionaries, interactive exercises, resources for teachers, world weather and news, and links to other useful sites.

36

Verbs

Unlike sentences in some other languages, verbs are required in English sentences because they indicate time and person (also see 18b-e for information about verb forms, voice, and mood). The basic building blocks of English sentences are the subject and verb (see also Chapters 18 and 40), and when appropriate, the direct object. The order for sentences that are not questions is subject → verb → object.

Sentences that are questions have helping verbs before the subject, and sentences that are commands do not state the subject because it is understood as *you*.

Standard order: Amit bought a new car.

Question: Did Amit buy a new car?

Command: Change the TV channel.

(The subject **you** *is understood.)*

36a Verb tenses

Progressive tenses: Use a form of *be* plus the *-ing* form of the verb, such as *going* or *running:*
She **is going** to the concert tonight.

Perfect tenses: Use a form of *have* plus the past participle, such as *walked* or *gone*.
They **have finished** the project.

Present tense

Simple Present:

- present actions or conditions
  She **feels** happy.

- a general action or literary truth
  The sun **sets** later during the summer.

- habitual actions
  I **take** my dog to the park every morning.

- future time
  The concert **begins** at 7:00 p.m. this evening.

Present Progressive: activity in progress, not finished, or continuing
He **is studying** Swedish.

Present Perfect: actions that began in the past and lead up to and include the present
She **has lived** in Alaska for two years.

Present Perfect Progressive: action that began in the past, continues to the present, and may continue into the future
They **have been building** that parking garage for six months.

Past tense

- **Simple Past:** completed actions or conditions
  They **ate** breakfast in the cafeteria.

- **Past Progressive:** past action that took place over a period of time or was interrupted by another action

   He **was swimming** when the storm began.

- **Past Perfect:** action or event completed before another event in the past

   No one **had heard** about the crisis when the newscast began.

- **Past Perfect Progressive:** ongoing condition in the past that has ended.

   I **had been** majoring in engineering, but now I'm studying economics.

Future tense

- **Simple Future:** actions or events in the future.

   The store **will open** at 9:00 a.m.

- **Future Progressive:** future action that will continue for some time

   I **will be working** on that project next week.

- **Future Perfect:** action that will be completed by or before a specified time in the future

   Next summer, they **will have been** here for twenty years.

- **Future Perfect Progressive:** ongoing action or condition until a specific time in the future

   By tomorrow, I **will have been waiting** for the delivery for one month.

36b Helping verbs with main verbs

Helping or auxiliary verbs combine with other verbs.

Forms of Helping Verbs

be	am	is	are	were +*ing* form of verb
have	have	has	had	
do	do	does	did	

36c Modal verbs

Modal verbs are helping verbs that indicate possibility, uncertainty, necessity, or advisability. Use the base form of the verb after the modal.

can	may	must	should	would
could	might	shall	will	ought to

Your car battery **can die** if you leave your headlights on all night.

May I take this?

36d Two-word (phrasal) verbs

Some verbs are followed by a second (and sometimes a third) word that combine to indicate the meaning. Many dictionaries will indicate the meanings of these phrasal verbs.

look over ("examine")	She **looked over** the contract.
look up ("search for")	I need to **look up** that phone number.

The second word of some of these verbs can be separated from the main verb by a noun or pronoun. For other verbs, the second word cannot be separated from the main verb.

Manuel told the team to *count* him *in*. *(separable)*

The team could *count on* **him** to help. *(cannot be separated)*

36e Verbs with *-ing* and *to* + verb form

Some verbs combine only with the *-ing* form of the verb (the gerund), some combine only with the *to* + verb form (the infinitive), and some can be followed by either form.

Verbs Followed Only by *-ing* Forms (Gerunds)

admit	enjoy	recall
appreciate	finish	recommend
deny	keep	risk
dislike	practice	suggest

He *admits spending* that money.

She *risked losing* her scholarship.

Verbs Followed Only by *to* + Verb Forms (Infinitives)

agree	have	plan
ask	mean	promise
claim	need	wait
decide	offer	wish

We *agree to send* an answer soon.

They *planned to go* on vacation.

Verbs That Can Be Followed by Either Form

begin	like	remember
continue	love	start
hate	prefer	try

They *begin to sing*. *(or)* They *begin singing*.

I *tried to fix* the car. *(or)* I *tried fixing* the car.

Nouns (Count and Noncount)

Proper and common nouns

Proper nouns name specific places, things, and people. They begin with capital letters; all other names are **common nouns** and are not capitalized.

Count and noncount nouns

Common nouns are of two types: count and noncount nouns. **Count nouns** name things that can be counted because those things can be divided into separate and distinct units. Count nouns have plurals and usually refer to things that can be seen, heard, touched, tasted, or smelled.

Count Nouns

book	one book, two books
chair	a chair, several chairs
child	the child, six children

Noncount nouns name things that cannot be counted because they are abstractions or things that cannot be cut into parts. Noncount nouns do not have plurals and may have a collective meaning. Noncount nouns are used with singular verbs and pronouns. They are never used with *a* or *an*, but they can be used with *some*.

Noncount Nouns

air	humor	oil
furniture	literature	weather

The names of many foods and materials are noncount nouns.

bread	corn	electricity
coffee	spaghetti	steel

To indicate the amount for a noncount noun, use a count noun first. If you use *some*, use a singular verb.

a pound of coffee	a loaf of bread
an ear of corn	a gallon of oil

128

Articles (*A, An,* and *The*)

A/An

A and *an* identify a noun in a general or indefinite way and refer to any member of a group. *A* and *an,* which mean "one among many," are generally used with singular count nouns (see 37b).

She likes to read a book before going to sleep.

> (*This sentence does not specify which book but refers to any book.*)

He ordered an egg for breakfast.

The

The identifies a particular or specific noun in a group or a noun already identified in a previous phrase or sentence. *The* may be used with singular or plural nouns.

She read the book that I gave her.

> (*This sentence identifies a specific book.*)

A new model of computer was introduced yesterday. The model will cost much less than the older model.

> (**A** *introduces the noun the first time it is mentioned, and then* **the** *is used afterward whenever the noun is mentioned.*)

Some uses of *the*

- Use *the* when an essential phrase or clause follows the noun.
  The man who is standing at the door is my cousin.

- Use *the* when the noun refers to a class as a whole.
  The ferret is a popular pet.

- Use *the* with names that combine proper and common nouns.
  the British Commonwealth   the Gobi Desert   the University of Illinois

- Use *the* when names are plurals.
  the Netherlands   the Balkans

- Use *the* with names that refer to rivers, oceans, seas, points on the globe, deserts, forests, gulfs, and peninsulas.

  the Nile **the** Pacific Ocean **the** Persian Gulf

- Use *the* with superlatives.

  the best reporter **the** most expensive car

No articles

Articles are not used with names of streets, cities, states, countries, continents, lakes, parks, mountains, languages, sports, holidays, universities and colleges without *of* in the name, and academic subjects.

He traveled to Botswana. She applied to Brandeis University.

She is studying Mandarin. My major is political science.

39

Prepositions

Prepositions in English show relationships between words. The following guide will help you choose among *on, at, in, of, for*, and *with* to indicate time, place, and logical relationships.

Prepositions of time

on Use with days (**on** Monday).

at Use with hours of the day (**at** 9:00 p.m.) and with *noon, night, midnight*, and *dawn* (**at** midnight).

in Use with other parts of the day: *morning, afternoon, evening* (**in** the morning); use with months, years, seasons (**in** the winter).

They are getting married **on** Sunday **at** four o'clock **in** the afternoon.

Prepositions of place

on Indicates a surface on which something rests
She put curtains **on** the windows.

at	Indicates a point in relation to another object I'll meet you **at** Second Avenue and Main Street.
in	Indicates an object is inside the boundaries of an area or volume She is **in** the bank.

Prepositions to show logical relationships

of	Shows relationship between a part (or parts) and the whole One **of** her teachers gave a quiz.
of	Shows material or content They gave me a basket **of** food.
for	Shows purpose We bought seeds **for** our garden.
with	Shows the means used He dug the hole **with** a shovel.
with	Shows cause or origin Matt was sick **with** the flu.
with	Shows possession The car **with** the Indiana license plate is mine.

40

Omitted and Repeated Words

40a Omitted words

Subjects and verbs can be omitted in some languages but are necessary and must appear in English sentences. The only exception in English is the command, which has an understood subject: "Move those chairs here." (The understood subject here is "you.")

Subjects

Include a subject in the main clause and all other clauses. *There* and *it* may sometimes serve as subject words. The subject is left out only when expressing a command (*Put that box here, please.*).

there
Certainly, are many confusing rules in English spelling.

It
is about ten miles from here to the shopping mall.

Verbs

Verbs such as *am, is,* and *are* and other helping verbs are needed in English and cannot be omitted.

is
Nurit studying to be a computer programmer.

has
She been studying ancient Mayan ruins in Mexico for many summers.

40b Repeated words

In some languages, the subject can be repeated as a pronoun before the verb. In English, the subject is included only once.

The plane that was ready for takeoff ~~it~~ stopped on the runway.

(**Plane** *is the subject of the verb* **stopped***, and* **it** *is an unnecessary repetition of the subject.*)

When relative pronouns such as *who, which,* and *that* or relative adverbs such as *where* or *when* are the object of the verb, no additional word is needed.

The woman tried on the hat that I left ~~it~~ on the seat.

(**That** *is the object of the verb* **left***, and* **it** *is an unnecessary repetition.*)

The city where I live ~~there~~ has two soccer fields.

(**Where** *is the object of the verb* **live***, and* **there** *is an unnecessary repetition.*)

41

Idioms

An **idiom** is an expression that means something beyond the literal meaning of the words. An idiom such as *kick the bucket* (meaning "die") cannot be understood by examining the meanings of the individual words. Many idioms are used only in informal English. Dictionaries of American English, such as the *Cambridge International Dictionary of Idioms* (http://dictionary.cambridge.org) define many commonly used phrases.

bottom line	the last figure on a financial balance sheet; the result or final outcome or ultimate truth
hand over fist	very rapidly, with rapid progress
hold water	be proved, be correct
on one's toes	eager, alert
on the table	open for discussion
pig out	eat a lot and eat quickly
throw in the towel	give up and stop trying, quit in defeat
see the light	understand something clearly at last, realize one's mistake

The meanings of two-word (phrasal) verbs (see 36d) also change according to the prepositions that follow the verbs. Note the difference in the meanings of the two-word (phrasal) verbs *look after*, *look over*, and *look for:*

look after   take care of
Could you **look after** my dog while I am away on vacation?

look over   examine something (briefly)
I'll **look over** the report you gave me.

look for   to seek or search
I'll **look for** some bargains when I am shopping.

VII

Research

Contents

Question and Correct

	SECTION	PAGE

LEARNING OBJECTIVE: Selecting and revising an arguable topic for a research project

LEARNING OBJECTIVE: Developing a research question and answering it with a thesis statement

LEARNING OBJECTIVE: Gaining familiarity with primary and secondary sources and library resources, including print materials and databases

LEARNING OBJECTIVE: Understanding how
to search the Internet for credible sources

LEARNING OBJECTIVE: Learning about
firsthand research, including observations,
surveys, and interviews

LEARNING OBJECTIVE: Evaluating the
credibility of primary and secondary sources

LEARNING OBJECTIVE: Understanding the
academic importance and ethical value of
attributing sources

42

Finding a Topic

42a Selecting a topic

Selecting a topic is one of the most important decisions you will make in the research process. You'll want to find a topic that is interesting, fits the guidelines of your assignment, and can be researched effectively with the resources and time available to you.

TRY THIS

To Select a Topic

- **Read newspapers, magazines, and online news sites.** Issues discussed in the news can often serve as effective paper topics. (See 43c for links to news sites.)

- **Use Internet search engines and library databases.** Type in search terms for a topic interesting to you. (See 43b and 43c for a list of Internet search engines and library databases.)

- **Check reference guides.** Browse through any book or online catalog of subject headings, such as the *Library of Congress Subject Headings* and the *Readers' Guide to Periodical Literature.*

42b Focusing your topic

Once you have identified a general subject, you'll need to focus your topic so that it is specific and manageable.

General subject: Bullying
Narrowed topic: Cyberbullying among high school students

General subject: Themes in Christopher Nolan films
Narrowed topic: The role of chaos in Christopher Nolan's *The Dark Knight*

TRY THIS

Thinking About the Guidelines for Your Assignment

- How much time will you have to complete the research?
- Is there a number or type of sources required for this assignment?
- How long will your project need to be?
- Does your assignment specify a purpose for your writing? To inform? To persuade? To educate? To call to action?
- Who is the intended audience for your writing project? Your peers? A group of readers who resist your idea? A person or group who has the power to make the changes or solutions you suggest?

As you define your topic, think about whether it is too broad, too narrow, or too obvious. You may need to revise your approach to make the topic more manageable and a better fit for your assignment guidelines.

- **Narrowing Topics That Are Too Broad** As you begin, consider whether your topic idea is manageable for the time and resources you have. Often, your initial idea is too general and might need to be narrowed down.

  Broad topic: America's overreliance on oil

  This is a big issue that has many political, economic, and scientific dimensions. Narrowing this down to a more specific aspect of the problem will make it more manageable.

  More manageable topic: Federal miles-per-gallon requirements for vehicles sold in the United States

  As you start your research, you may find that the topic still covers too much and may need to be narrowed even more.

- **Broadening Topics That Are Too Narrow** Sometimes a topic is too narrow, especially when very little or only specialized information exists on the topic.

  Too narrow topic: I have to take twelve credits of a foreign language to complete my college's general education requirement, and I don't want to.

This question affects only you. How might you make your topic relevant for a wider audience?

More manageable topic: Is knowing a foreign language useful for a career in nursing?

After collecting more research, you will be in a better position to offer your point of view on this issue, as well as show its relevance to others in addition to yourself.

- **Rethinking Topics That Are Too Obvious** There are also topics that are no longer interesting or controversial because we know the answers, such as "smoking is harmful to our health." However, you can think about a purpose and audience to revise the topic. Perhaps you want to investigate the question of whether insurance companies should charge smokers higher rates for health insurance or the problems associated with teens and flavored cigars.

42c Developing a research question

As you start your research process, try listing all of the questions you need to answer so that you understand your topic more fully. Thinking first about the journalist's questions—*who, what, when, where, why,* and *how*—can help you gather basic information. Once you understand the basics about your topic, you'll develop more specific questions that can lead you to your thesis.

After completing your research and reviewing your sources, you should have enough information to create a research question about your topic. A research question is the main question you will answer in your paper. The answer to your research question is the thesis, or main point, of your paper.

TRY THIS

To Develop an Effective Research Question
- **Why** is this issue important?
- **Who** is affected by this issue?
- **What** is at stake for each group affected by this issue?
- **Who** has the power to do something about this issue?
- **Where?** Is this a local or national issue? An issue about a specific place?
- **When and how** did this issue arise?

These sample research questions focus the writer's investigation into specific aspects of each topic.

Research Question:	How can parents and schools help reduce the number of cyberbullying incidents among high school students?
Research Question:	What comment does director Christopher Nolan make about the role of chaos in society through his characterization of The Joker in *The Dark Knight*?

42d Formulating your thesis statement

After completing your research and reviewing the information you've collected, you can begin to formulate a tentative thesis statement. Your thesis statement will answer your research question, communicate the main idea of your paper, and help you create a working outline. The thesis states your position or the point you are arguing and researching and shows what you, as a knowledgeable writer, have learned about your topic. Your thesis may need to be revised further as you revise your paper.

These two thesis statements communicate the writer's conclusions about each topic.

Thesis Statement:	Schools need the legal authority to get involved in cyberbullying cases to protect teens and educate them about the dangers of online harassment.
Thesis Statement:	In *The Dark Knight*, director Christopher Nolan shows through his characterization of The Joker that introducing chaos among citizens of a civilized society is far more dangerous than any actions taken by a single madman.

A good thesis statement will provide the main idea of the essay as well as suggest your purpose for writing (such as *to explain*, *to persuade*, or *to interpret*). And it will guide your writing as you compose the paper. See 1d for more about thesis statements.

43

Searching for Information

43a Choosing primary and secondary sources

Primary sources are original or firsthand materials.
Primary sources include the following:

- Words written or spoken by the original author, such as essays, novels and nonfiction books, articles, web pages, podcasts, autobiographies (but not, for example, articles, reviews, web pages, podcasts or biographies *about* that person), speeches, e-mails, discussion group postings, tweets, or posts on social networking sites or blogs

- Surveys, studies, or interviews you conduct

- Any creative works by the original author (poems, plays, web pages, art forms such as photos and sculptures)

- Accounts of events by people who were present

Primary sources may be more accurate because they have not been distorted by others. Primary sources are not always unbiased, however, because some people present pictures of themselves and their accomplishments that may not be objective.

Secondary sources are secondhand accounts, information, or reports about primary sources written or delivered by people who weren't direct participants in the events or issues being examined. Typical secondary sources include the following:

- News articles about events

- Reviews

- Biographies

- Documentaries

- Encyclopedia entries

- Other material interpreted or studied by others

Although reading secondary sources may save time, they are *interpretations* and may be biased, inaccurate, or incomplete. However, they can also support or challenge other secondary sources as well as your thinking based on primary sources.

43b Searching libraries and library databases

Libraries have the types of scholarly resources your instructor will probably want you to use for your research.

General Reference Sources The library's reference section contains a variety of scholarly sources, including:

* Encyclopedias, including those for specific areas of study
* Dictionaries
* Biographies
* Almanacs, such as the *World Almanac* and *Book of Facts*
* Atlases
* Government publications

When you read an entry in a subject encyclopedia or other scholarly sources, you know you're reading information from authors who are selected because of their expertise.

Library Indexes and Catalogs Your library will have book indexes such as *Books in Print*, periodical indexes such as the *Readers' Guide to Periodical Literature*, and other online indexes. Most library catalogs are online, so you can search the library's holdings by author, title, keyword, and subject heading. When you request a *keyword search*, the search engine will look for the word in any part of the entry in the catalog (title, subtitle, abstract, etc.), whereas the *subject heading* has to match, word for word, the Library of Congress headings (listed in the *Library of Congress Subject Headings*). When doing a keyword search, try synonyms for your topic or broader or alternate terms that might include it. For example, when searching for information about "**hybrid cars**," you might also try "**fuel-efficient vehicles**," "**zero-emissions vehicle**," or "**alternative energy sources**" as keywords.

Library Databases and Subscription Services Many libraries subscribe to periodical databases and other services that can access electronic versions of articles from journals, magazines, and newspapers. You'll often find them through links on the library's webpage. These databases are free for anyone registered with the college. Some databases can also be found on public library sites.

Resources in library databases are a good place to start because they are considered scholarly or newsworthy, don't contain advertisements, have current information about issues and events, and have already been fact-checked and edited. Some companies, such as ProQuest, offer a wide range of specialized databases. Some of the most widely used library databases include the following:

- *Academic Search Premier* (EBSCOhost)—includes a wide range of newspaper, magazine, and journal articles.
- *Expanded Academic ASAP* (InfoTrac)—provides an extensive number of newspaper, magazine, and journal articles.
- *JSTOR*—has full-text articles from many academic journals.
- *LexisNexis*—offers news articles, including transcripts of speeches, news shows, and other events.
- *ProQuest Central*—provides full-text articles from academic journals, newspapers, and magazines as well as dissertations and theses.
- *Project Muse*—provides full-text articles from academic journals.
- *ScienceDirect*—specializes in science, technical, and medical articles.

Check your library's website or ask your reference librarians to find what other database resources your library offers and how to access them. You will probably need your student ID or a password to log in.

TRY THIS

To Conduct a Search on Library or Subscription Databases

- **Start by deciding on a search term or a keyword term.** Would a subject search or keyword search be more helpful for finding information on your topic?
- **Search by subject.** When you search a broad subject, like "**globalization**" or "**cancer**," some databases will connect you to a list of subdivided topics that allow you to narrow your search.
- **Search by keyword.** If you have a more narrow or specific topic, such as the laws needed to protect the nesting grounds of loggerhead turtles on the South Carolina coast,

you might search by using a list of relevant keywords ("**log-gerhead turtles**," "**nesting**," "**South Carolina**," and "**law**") to find relevant hits in the title or full text of articles.

- **Use terms that refine your search.** Place quotation marks around search phrases to find sources containing that exact phrase. Use "OR" for choices between search terms and "NOT" to exclude certain items from your search.
- **Read the help section.** Start your database search by reading the directions for using the database's search engine. The help section of your database helps you find the ways that program works to narrow your search.
- **Use a flash drive or other storage device.** Many articles will be available in PDF files that you can download and save directly to your flash drive or computer.

Many "full-text" databases provide entire texts of articles that originally appeared in journals, magazines, or newspapers. In many cases, you'll be able to see a webpage showing the digitized text of the article. In other cases, you may be able to view a PDF file of the document. This allows you to see the article as it originally appeared in a journal, magazine, or newspaper with the same layout, colors, and photographs.

Sometimes databases may provide just the bibliographic citations needed to locate relevant articles or an abstract, which is a brief summary of the article. To locate the full text of these materials, you should check your library's catalog to see whether the library has these resources in print form or on microfiche. You can also ask your reference librarians to see whether these materials are available through its interlibrary loan service.

TRY THIS

Using Library Databases for Research in Various Disciplines

Art: *Art Full Text, JSTOR, Project Muse, Oxford Art Online*

Business: *ABI/INFORM, Business Source Complete, Business and Company Resource Center, Dun and Bradstreet's Million Dollar Database, General Business File ASAP, Standard and Poor's Net Advantage*

Communications and Journalism: *Communication and Mass Media Complete, Communication Abstracts, LexisNexis*

Computer Science/Technology: *Computers and Applied Sciences Complete, INSPEC, ProQuest Computing*

Education: *ERIC, Education Research Complete*

Engineering: *Compendex, INSPEC*

History: *America: History and Life, Historical Abstracts, JSTOR*

Law: *LegalTrac, LexisNexis, Criminal Justice Periodicals*

Literature: *MLA International Bibliography, Literature Resource Center, JSTOR, Project Muse*

Mathematics: *Math SciNet, Science Direct*

Medicine: *Medline, Health Source, Cochrane Library, CINAHL, Nursing Resource Center*

Political Science: *Political Science Complete, Public Affairs Index, Worldwide Political Science Abstracts, JSTOR*

Psychology: *PsycARTICLES, PsycINFO, Psychology and Behavioral Sciences Collection*

Sciences: *Science Direct, Science Citation Index, Cambridge Scientific Abstracts, Environment Complete, BIOSIS Previews*

Sociology: *Sociological Abstracts, Social Sciences Abstracts*

43c Searching the Internet

The Internet can be an extremely useful research tool. However, its resources may be best used in combination with other materials in your library. For current events topics, searching your library's databases can often be a better first step than starting with the Internet (see 43b).

Also, despite the ocean of information you can access online, your library is more likely to provide access to older books, collections of reference works, the content of some journals, and old archives of newspapers. Before you consider using Wikipedia, check with your instructor as to whether it's a credible source.

Search Engines Often researching starts with using search engines. Search engines locate websites based on keywords you enter into the engine's search function. Search engines scan huge numbers of (but not all) websites, and they can help you find materials from a vast variety of resources. Most search engines allow you to specify whether you want to search the web, images, news, videos, blogs, and so on. In addition, try "Advanced Search" functions to locate results in books, government documents, and sites in other languages. When you search online, be sure to continue looking at results beyond the first page.

Google is a very powerful search engine and a good starting point for most searches. But a common mistake is to depend only on Google. Each search engine will turn up its own list of links based on its unique search formula. Many search engines will also personalize their results to your search patterns, location, and preferences, which can sometimes limit you from getting information you need. Also, many search engines include sponsored links (links that advertisers pay for) listed prominently on the first page of results. Google, Yahoo!, and others identify their paid links, but some search engines don't.

Some popular search engines include the following:

Google www.google.com	Bing www.bing.com
Yahoo! www.yahoo.com	Ask www.ask.com

TRY THIS

To Use Internet Search Engines Effectively

Keep these suggestions in mind to make your search more efficient.

- Use specific phrases instead of single words to define your search.

- Think of a variety of keywords that apply to your topic. If a keyword doesn't turn up useful results, switch to a different one.

- Enclose the whole term (as a unit) in quotation marks to ensure that the entire term is the object of the search.

- Talk to a tutor in your writing center about possible search strategies for your topic.

- When you find a useful site, look for links that connect you to related sites.

- Be sure your terms are spelled correctly.

- Use search engine directories or categories when they exist.

FAQ

How can I make my web search produce more specific results?

Each search engine has its own tips (and Help section) for refining your search. These are some examples:

site: Use this term directly in front of a website's URL if you want the engine to search for keywords on a particular site. For example, you can limit searches about earthquakes to CNN's website by typing **site:cnn.com earthquake**.

" " Put terms in quotation marks to find pages using a specific phrase.

– or NOT Use the minus sign directly (with no spaces) in front of words you want excluded from your search. You can also type "NOT," insert a space, and list the words to exclude from the search.

OR Use OR if you want to see sites using one term or the other, but not both.

+ Use the plus sign directly in front of terms you absolutely require in your search.

Using Directories Some search engines have materials arranged by general subjects in a directory. For example, in Yahoo!'s directory (http://dir.yahoo.com), you'll find broad categories such as "Health," "Science," and "Recreation & Sports." Within each subject, you can find related sites. For example, under "Health," you'll find subheadings including "Diseases and Conditions," "Nutrition," and "Pharmacy." These can be very helpful to browse through when you're looking for a topic for a paper or keywords to use in your searching.

Writers' resources

Bartlett's Familiar Quotations	www.bartleby.com/100
Biographical Dictionary	www.s9.com
Cambridge Dictionaries Online	dictionary.cambridge.org
Dictionary.com/ Writing Resources	dictionary.reference.com/ writing
Google Scholar	scholar.google.com
IWCA Resources for Writers	writingcenters.org/resources
Library of Congress	www.loc.gov

Merriam-Webster Online Dictionary	www.m-w.com
OWLs (Online Writing Labs)	writingcenters.org/owcdb
Purdue Online Writing Lab	owl.english.purdue.edu
Roget's International Thesaurus	www.bartleby.com/110
Strunk's *Elements of Style*	www.bartleby.com/141
Thesaurus.com	thesaurus.reference.com

Online Books (E-Books)

Bartleby.com	www.bartleby.com
Complete Works of William Shakespeare	thetech.mit.edu/shakespeare
Google Books	books.google.com
Online Books Page	onlinebooks.library. upenn.edu
Project Gutenberg	www.gutenberg.org
Scholars' Lab Digital Resources	www.lib.virginia.edu/ scholarslab/resources

Magazines, Journals, and News Media Most newspapers, television networks, and print publications have online databases of information. However, some magazines, journals, and news media websites allow only subscribers to access their archives. You may be able to access full-text articles from these sites by entering them through your university's library databases.

ABC News	abcnews.go.com
Arts and Letters Daily	www.aldaily.com
ArtsJournal.com	www.artsjournal.com
BBC News	news.bbc.co.uk
CBS News	www.cbsnews.com
CEO Express	www.ceoexpress.com
Chicago Tribune	www.chicagotribune.com
CNN News	www.cnn.com
Fox News	www.foxnews.com
Google News	news.google.com
The *Guardian* (London)	www.guardian.co.uk
Los Angeles Times	www.latimes.com
NBC News	www.nbcnews.com
New York Times	nytimes.com
NPR (National Public Radio) News	www.npr.org
Reuters	www.reuters.com

Roper Center for Public Opinion	www.ropercenter.uconn.edu
Salon	www.salon.com
SciTechDaily	www.scitechdaily.com
Slate	www.slate.com
United Press International	www.upi.com
USA Today	www.usatoday.com
Washington Post	www.washingtonpost.com
Washington Times	www.washtimes.com

Government Information

Bureau of Labor Statistics	www.bls.gov
Census Bureau	www.census.gov
Centers for Disease Control and Prevention	www.cdc.gov
Central Intelligence Agency	www.cia.gov
Childstats.gov	www.childstats.gov
Data.gov *(access to federal datasets)*	www.data.gov
Department of Health and Human Services	www.hhs.gov
Department of Homeland Security	www.dhs.gov
Department of Housing and Urban Development	www.hud.gov
Department of Justice, Bureau of Justice Statistics	bjs.ojp.usdoj.gov
Department of Transportation, Bureau of Transportation Statistics	www.bts.gov
Environmental Protection Agency	www.epa.gov
Federal Bureau of Investigation	www.fbi.gov
Government Printing Office	www.gpo.gov
National Aeronautics and Space Administration	www.nasa.gov
National Archives	www.archives.gov
National Center for Education Statistics	nces.ed.gov

National Institutes of Health	www.nih.gov
National Oceanic and Atmospheric Administration	www.noaa.gov
NATO	www.nato.int
Regulations.gov	www.regulations.gov
Smithsonian Institution	www.si.edu
Supreme Court of the United States	www.supremecourt.gov
THOMAS: Legislative Information	thomas.loc.gov
United Nations	www.un.org/english
United States House of Representatives	www.house.gov
United States Senate	www.senate.gov
White House	www.whitehouse.gov
World Health Organization	www.who.int/en

Online Media, Images, Art, and Photographs The following links offer a good place to start searching for images to use in educational projects. Before you use any images you find online, check the website's permissions and copyright information.

CDC Public Health Image Library	phil.cdc.gov
Library of Congress American Memory Map Collections	memory.loc.gov
NASA Image Gallery	www.nasa.gov/multimedia/ imagegallery
NOAA Photo Library	www.photolib.noaa.gov
U.S. Geological Survey Multimedia Gallery	gallery.usgs.gov
Wikimedia Commons	commons.wikimedia.org

Blogs, Podcasts, and Social Media Blogs are websites with dated entries listed in reverse chronological order with the most recent post first. Podcasts are streaming audio and video programs. Some blogs and podcasts are personal and informally presented, but others are a form of editorial writing or journalism. They may have themes, such as health care or education. Reading about blog and podcast owner(s) and writer(s) can help you determine their credibility, including how widely viewed and influential they are. In addition, links posted by friends and organizations on social media sites like Twitter and Facebook can lead to useful blog entries, podcasts, and articles.

Other Online Sources In addition, you'll find sites maintained by public interest groups (such as environmental groups or consumer safety organizations) and nonprofit organizations (such as museums and universities) with information about their areas of interest; directories that help you locate companies and people; and company sites with information about their services and products (and discussion groups on the company site about its products and services). There are also biased sites that post propaganda to influence others to adopt their views. To sort out such sites from more trustworthy sites, evaluate your sources carefully (see Chapter 44).

43d Conducting firsthand research

Firsthand research involves investigating sources on your own. This can be done through taking notes on your own observations, conducting surveys, and interviewing people. These forms of information-gathering can add credibility and authority to your writing.

Observations

Conducting observations can help you gather information about your topic. You can learn a lot by watching a particular place and taking notes about what you see.

TRY THIS

To Conduct an Effective Observation

- **Ask permission, if necessary.** When observing in a public place, asking permission usually is not necessary. However, when observing in a place with restricted access, such as an emergency room or an elementary school, ask the person in charge for permission.

- **Carry along something to write with and record your observations.** Bring along some method of recording your observations, such as a pen or pencil, a notebook, a video camera, or an audio recorder.

- **Bring consent forms, if necessary.** Ask each person you record to sign a consent form before you begin. A consent form should include a statement giving you permission to record each person as well as a place for their signatures.

- **Answer basic questions.** Ask the journalistic questions first: *who, what, when, where, why,* and *how.* This will guide you to ask more specific questions as your observe.

- **Write detailed notes.** Jot down your impressions of the place you are visiting. Note the time order of events, what people are doing, how people are interacting, and what is said.

Surveys

Conducting surveys can be another effective method of gathering information. A survey can provide you with quantitative information, or numerical data, about the attitudes or beliefs of a group of people about a specific topic. There are two basic types of survey questions: closed questions and open questions.

Closed questions Closed questions have a limited number of answers. Closed questions are easier to count than open questions, making it easier to show the results in graphs or charts. Closed questions include the following types:

- **True/false or yes/no:** These are best for gathering respondents' opinions on specific issues.

- **Multiple choice:** These are useful for asking respondents about their actions or practices regarding a topic. You can ask people to select one or all responses that apply.

- **Likert scales:** These give readers a range of responses to choose from. Responses are selected from a numerical scale (e.g., 1 = most likely to 5 = least likely) or include descriptive phrases (e.g., strongly agree, agree, neutral, disagree, strongly disagree).

- **Rankings:** These types of questions ask readers to rate their preferences from strongest to weakest.

Open questions Open questions ask for short-answer or narrative responses. This makes them harder than closed questions to count and represent in charts and graphs. But they can be helpful when you want individualized viewpoints on an issue. You can use quotations from responses to these open questions to support points in your paper.

Analyzing and Presenting Your Results Once you have your survey results, review them and think about their implications. Your readers expect that you are a credible researcher who has reviewed the data and presented the results fairly and accurately.

You can include pie charts or bar graphs to help your readers understand your results. Use pie charts to show the parts of a whole and bar graphs to show comparisons between items. See 6b for strategies for including visuals in your paper.

Interviews

Interviews are also a good method for gathering firsthand information. Talking with someone who is an authority or expert or has a specific connection to your topic may provide important information.

TRY THIS

To Conduct an Effective Interview

- **Do some preliminary searching.** Before conducting your interview, spend some time learning about the person. Then you'll have background on his or her expertise or position of authority.

- **Be prepared with written questions.** Include some open-ended questions that begin with *who, what, when, where, why,* and *how.* Having your notes to refer to can help you keep the conversation on track and gather the information you need for your paper.

- **Set up a time and place for your interview.** It's polite to contact your subject ahead of time to ask for and set up an interview.

- **Explain the purpose of your interview.** Make sure your interview subjects know that their words may be used in your paper. Also tell them if your work will be published in a newspaper or on the Internet.

- **Bring a pen, pencil, notebook, and/or recorder.** Because you'll want to take notes during the interview, consider using a video or audio recorder during your conversation.

- **Have your subject fill out a consent form, if needed.** If you record your interview, ask your subject to sign a consent form before you begin recording. A consent form should include a statement giving you permission to record this person as well as a blank line on which to sign his or her name.

- **Show you are an interested listener.** Demonstrate that you are actively listening by maintaining eye contact, sitting up in your seat, and nodding or responding to what the person says.

- **Use interview material responsibly.** When you include quoted or paraphrased material from your interview in your paper, you'll want to be sure you present the person's viewpoints fairly, accurately, and respectfully.

44

Evaluating Sources

We live in an age of such vast amounts of information that we can't know everything about a subject. All information that comes streaming at us from newspapers, magazines, the media, books, journals, brochures, podcasts, blogs, websites, and so on is also of very uneven quality.

Evaluating sources, then, is a skill we rely on constantly, and applying that skill to research projects is equally important.

44a Getting started

To begin, ask yourself what type of information you are looking for and where you're likely to find appropriate sources for it.

- **What kind of information are you looking for?** Do you want facts? opinions? news reports? research studies? analyses? historical accounts? personal reflections? data? public records? scholarly essays reflecting on the topic? reviews?

- **Where would you find such information?** Which sources are most likely to be useful: the Internet? online library databases and subscription services? libraries with scholarly journals, books, and government publications? public libraries with popular magazines? newspapers? community records? people on your campus or in your town?

For example, if you're searching for information on some current event, a reliable newspaper such as the *New York Times* will be a useful source, and it is available on the web and in a university or public library. If you need statistics on the U.S. population, government census documents on the web and in libraries are useful places to search. If you want to do research into local history, however, the archives and websites of local government offices and the local newspaper are better places to start.

Consider whether there are organizations that gather and publish the types of information you're seeking. For example, if you want information about local teen drinking and driving, a useful source would be a local office of Mothers Against Drunk Driving (MADD). If you want national or regional information, the MADD website is also likely to be helpful.

Be sure to ask yourself whether the sponsoring organization's goal for the site is to be objective, gain support for its viewpoint, or sell you something. For example, an energy consortium funded by a large oil company is not likely to be an unbiased source of information about the hazards of offshore oil drilling.

44b Evaluating authors' credibility

As you start looking at your sources, do some investigating to learn about the author of your source. Your goal is to get some sense of who the author is, what the author's organization or institution represents, and why it's worth reading what the author wrote. That may be important as you write the paper and build your case.

Ask yourself the following questions to decide whether a source's viewpoint or knowledge of the topic is important to read or include in your research project.

Author

- How reputable is the person listed as the author?

- What has the author written in the past about this topic? If this is the author's first publication in this area, perhaps the author isn't yet an expert.

- Why is this person considered an expert or a reliable authority? Who considers this person an expert? Would that source have any bias?

- If the author is an organization, what can you find out about it? How reputable is it?

- Did you see the person or organization listed in other sources that you've already determined to be trustworthy?

FAQ

How can I learn more about the credibility of an author?

- Check a search engine and the Library of Congress catalog to see what else this person has written. Also look up the author's organization or institution.

- Review library databases that may lead you to other articles by this person or sources in which the author has been cited.
- Look through the *Book Review Index* or *Book Review Digest* to read reviews of the author's other books, if available.
- Check a biography index or database to learn more about the author.

Institutional or organizational affiliation

- With what organization, institution, or company is the author associated? If the name is not easily identified, perhaps the group is less than reliable.

- What are this group's goals? Is there a bias or reason for the group to slant the truth in any way?

- Does the group monitor or review what is published under its name?

- Does the organization have a profit motive? Is this group trying to sell you something or convince you to accept its views?

- Do its members conduct objective, disinterested research? Are they trying to be sensational or attention-getting to enhance their own popularity or ratings?

Publisher, producer, or sponsor

- Who published or produced the material?

- Is that publisher or sponsor reputable? For example, a university press or a government agency is likely to be a reputable source that reviews what it publishes.

- Is the group recognized as an authority?

- Is the publisher or group an appropriate one for this topic?

- Might the publisher be likely to have a particular bias? (For example, a brochure printed by a right-to-life group is not going to contain much objective material on abortion.)

- Is there any review process or fact-checking? (If a pharmaceutical company publishes data on a new drug it is developing, is there evidence of outside review of the data?)

44c Evaluating content

When you are deciding about using a source, you can evaluate the content by considering the following important criteria:

Accuracy. What reasons do you have to think the facts are accurate? Do they agree with other information you've read? Are there sources for the data given?

Comprehensiveness. Is the topic covered in adequate depth, or is it too superficial or limited to only one aspect that overemphasizes only one part of the topic?

Timeliness. When was the source published? Is the information current enough to be useful? How necessary is timeliness for your topic? (For websites, look at the "last revised" date at the end of the page. If no date is available, are all the links still live?) Is the source a revision of an earlier edition? If so, it is likely to be more current, and a revision indicates the source is sufficiently valuable to revise. (For a print source, check a library catalog or *Books in Print* to see whether you have the latest edition.)

References. Is the source of the material generally considered trustworthy? Does the source have a review process or do fact-checking? Is there a Works Cited or Reference List? Does the source provide links or references to other credible sources?

Fairness. If the author has a particular viewpoint, are differing views presented with some sense of fairness, or are opposing views presented as irrational or silly?

Objectivity. Is the language objective or emotional? Does the author acknowledge differing viewpoints? Are the various perspectives presented fairly? If you are reading an article in a magazine or in an online publication, do other articles in that source promote a particular viewpoint?

Relevance. How closely related is the material to your topic? Is it really relevant or merely related? Is it too general or too specific? Is it too technical?

Audience. Can you tell who the intended audience is? Is that audience appropriate for your purposes? Is the material too specialized or too popular or brief to be useful?

TRY THIS

Evaluating the Content and Quality of Sources

- Read the preface, introduction, or summary. What does the author want to accomplish?

- Browse through the links to other pages on the site or the table of contents and the index. Is the topic covered in enough depth to be helpful?

- Is there a list of references to show that the author has consulted other sources? Can the sources lead you to useful material?

- Are you the intended audience? Consider the tone, style, level of information, and assumptions the author makes about the reader. Are they appropriate to your needs? If there is advertising in the publication or on the website, it may help you determine the intended audience.

- Is the content of the source fact, opinion, or propaganda? If factual, are the sources of these facts clearly indicated? Is the language emotional or objective?

- Are there broad, sweeping generalizations that overstate or simplify the matter?

- Do you think enough evidence is offered? Is the coverage comprehensive?

- Does the author use a mix of primary and secondary sources (see 43a)?

- To determine accuracy, consider whether the source is outdated. Do some cross-checking. Do you find some of the same information elsewhere?

- Are there arguments that are one-sided with no acknowledgment of other viewpoints?

44d Evaluating online sources

Many of the ways to evaluate Internet sources are similar to those for evaluating sources found elsewhere, but there are also some special matters to consider when deciding whether to use online sources. The Internet is a worldwide medium where anyone can post anything from anywhere. No monitors, evaluators, or fact-checking organizations regulate or review much of what is posted on the web. In addition, the sponsor or organization name on the site can be misleading. Although excellent sources of information exist online, many sites or pages on sites can lead unsuspecting readers into accepting as fact whatever biased, false, stolen, or fake information turns up in a search.

TRY THIS

Understanding Domain Names

A website's *domain* consists of two or three letters that appear after the last dot in its URL. The domain can sometimes give you clues about the website's source or publisher.

.gov	government sites (These are usually dependable.)
.edu	educational institutions (These are dependable, though personal student websites may not be.)
.org	organizations (These include nonprofit or public service organizations that may have their own biases.)
.com, .biz, .net	commercial sites (Business websites are likely to have a profit motive. Individuals, however, may also post their personal websites and blogs on corporate servers.)
.uk, .de, .ca, .jp	foreign sites (.uk = England; .de = Germany, .ca = Canada, .jp = Japan; there are two-letter abbreviations for all countries of the world.)

It is quite easy for businesses and individuals, however, to purchase most types of domain names (except .gov) for their corporate or personal websites. Also, new domain names are occasionally created. To check the names of people or groups who have registered their website domains, conduct a "whois" search at the following website:

www.networksolutions.com/whois

In addition to questions in 44b and 44c about evaluating an author's credibility and a source's content, you should do some additional searching when evaluating a website.

- **Find the site's home page.** You can get to a site's home page by deleting all of the URL after the domain name (all of the information after the first slash) and hitting "Enter."

- **Double-check information from .edu sites.** If the domain name is .edu, determine if you are reading information written by college or university professionals or by students completing a class project.

- **Check the currency of the site.** Is there a date of origin and any sign the site has been maintained and revised in the recent past? If there are links to other sites, are they live links or links that no longer work?

- **Determine whether the site is trying to sell you something.** Do you see a "shopping cart" or "checkout" link? This could be a sign that the site may be providing you information with the hope you will buy its products or services.

- **Check for ads.** Is there advertising (or pop-up windows) on the site? Does that interfere with the site's credibility? (Sites with .gov as the domain will not have advertising.)

- **Look for an "About Us" link on the site.** Be wary of sites that want to hide their sponsors or publishers.

- **Consider how you accessed the site.** Did you link to it from another reliable site? If you found the site through a search engine result, that means only that the site contains your search keywords; it says nothing about the site's trustworthiness or credibility.

45

Attributing Sources and Avoiding Plagiarism

45a **Attributing sources**

When we use primary and secondary sources in our writing, we show that we are aware of others who have knowledge about our topics. And we do that by indicating our sources in the text and citing them using a specific documentation format, such as MLA, APA, *Chicago Manual*, or CSE format. (See Chapters 47–50 for more information on these styles.) There are several reasons why we should attribute sources:

- **Attributing sources is ethical.** Recognizing our sources is part of the American academic writing process. We should "give credit where credit is due" and acknowledge that we made use of other sources to develop our own ideas and arguments.

- **Showing our use of sources is part of the learning process.** When we attribute our sources, we assure readers (and instructors) that we are learning about our topic, developing critical thinking skills, and engaging with the ideas of others.

- **Documenting sources demonstrates our credibility as writers.** When we attribute our sources, we invite others to view our sources and see how we have developed our opinions and conclusions. This kind of transparency allows readers to see our thinking and development process, which in turn gives greater legitimacy to our ideas.

- **Citing sources shows respect for intellectual property.** Attributing our sources acknowledges other people's creativity and hard work. In a similar way, it would be unfair to us as writers if we had an interesting or important idea that was used by someone else in his or her work without acknowledging the real source.

- **Citing sources helps others.** Just as we read the work of others and find references to works we want to read or see, we too can be useful sources for others looking for information or ideas we found.

45b Avoiding plagiarism

Attributing sources properly also helps to avoid plagiarism. Plagiarism results when a writer fails to document a source and presents the words or ideas of someone else as the writer's own work. Plagiarism can occur in the following ways:

- Using someone's exact words without putting quotation marks around the words and without citing the source.

- Changing another person's words into your own words by paraphrasing or summarizing without citing the source.

- Stating ideas or research specifically attributed to another person or persons without citing the source.

- Claiming authorship of a paper written by someone else.

Why is avoiding plagiarism important?

- **Plagiarism is unethical.** When a writer uses someone else's words, information, or ideas and doesn't acknowledge using that work, that is considered an act of stealing, even if it happens because of carelessness or rushing too fast to write the paper.

- **Plagiarism means losing a learning opportunity.** Professors assign research projects to help students learn how to use sources as well as gain knowledge about their topics. If we plagiarize instead of researching and citing our sources, we lose the opportunity to learn about our topics and the chance to practice critical thinking and research skills needed in college and the workplace. Moreover, readers who want to find sources mentioned in the paper so that they can learn more also lose when those citations are missing.

- **Plagiarism diminishes credibility.** Drawing upon other people's ideas and words is appropriate when writing research papers. Our arguments are more compelling when we cite the opinions of experts. To be considered credible writers, however, we need to let readers know where we located those ideas and words. Blending our own ideas and language in conversation with information from other sources is an important goal of the research process.

- **Plagiarism may result in serious penalties.** Plagiarism is considered a violation of academic honesty and may result in a variety of penalties, including expulsion. After college, plagiarism can negatively affect careers and reputations. Plagiarists can be sued for copyright violations or for use of intellectual property without permission.

45c Distinguishing information requiring documentation vs. common knowledge

While most ideas borrowed from other sources will require documentation, there are a few exceptions.

Information that requires documentation

When we use the ideas, findings, data, conclusions, arguments, and words of others, we need to acknowledge that we are borrowing their work. We do that by documenting what we use. If you are arguing for a particular viewpoint and find someone who expresses that viewpoint, you may want to include it. Whenever you summarize, paraphrase, or quote someone else, provide documentation for those sources, including the author and the location of the source.

Common knowledge: information that does not require documentation

Common knowledge is that body of general ideas and facts most readers already know because it is widely repeated. It does not have to be documented. Specific details or statistics about topics might not be considered common knowledge, however. In such cases, proper documentation should be provided to show where the ideas or study results came from.

Common knowledge consists of the following:

* **Common historical facts.** For example, it is common knowledge that the Declaration of Independence was adopted in 1776 and that George Washington was the first U.S. president.

* **Common physical or scientific facts.** Most people know basic scientific facts such as the earth is the third planet from the sun and water is composed of hydrogen and oxygen molecules.

* **Facts widely available in a variety of standard reference books.** Many reference books, for example, would note that Brazil is the largest country in South America, Great Britain has a parliamentary system of government, and the language most commonly spoken in Australia is English.

* **Information that is widely shared and found in numerous sources without reference to any source.** For example, it has been widely reported in the news and in health sources that obesity is a major health problem in the United States. A statement about that does not need to be documented. However, if you are writing about the occurrence of obesity and find statistics for various segments of the population, cite your sources.

* **Studies or surveys that you have personally conducted.** If you're reporting the results or data from your own study or survey, you should explain when and how the study or survey took place, but you don't need to cite it unless it has been previously published in another source. If you quote someone you interviewed, you do need to document how you conducted the interview (personal interview, e-mail message, phone), the person's name, and the date of the interview or exchange.

Common knowledge may also include more specific ideas or concepts, depending on the expertise of your audience. For example, if your audience is composed of educators, it's common knowledge among this group that U.S. schoolchildren aren't well acquainted with geography. However, if you cite test results documenting the extent of this problem or reference the ideas of a specific person about the causes of the problem, that is not common knowledge and needs documentation. If you are unsure of whether the information you are using is considered common knowledge, consult your instructor.

FAQ

Are there cultural differences about the documentation of sources?

In some cultures, documenting something, particularly from a well-known work of literature, can be interpreted as an insult because it implies that the reader is not familiar with that work. In American academic writing, however, it is very important to document sources. This may be a skill that is new or needs sharpening, but it is a vitally important skill.

45d Checking work for plagiarism

Give yourself time to check your work to make sure you have attributed sources responsibly and have not inadvertently plagiarized any source materials. Follow these steps to check your work:

- Ask yourself whether your readers can properly identify which ideas and words are yours and which are from the sources you cite.

- Re-read what you wrote to see if you cited all ideas that aren't your own and aren't considered common knowledge.

- Check to ensure that all quotations are punctuated with quotation marks and contain in-text citations.

- Review paraphrased and summarized material to ensure language and sentence structures aren't too close to the original text.

- Check to see that all paraphrased and summarized material is attributed with in-text citations (see Chapter 46).

- Consider whether your paper predominantly reflects your words, phrases, and integration of ideas.

- Check to make sure your paper isn't a string of quotations from your sources.

- Check the sources in your Works Cited or References page to be sure they are cited in the body of the paper and vice versa.

Avoiding plagiarism: an example

Original source

Fans of raw milk (meaning milk that hasn't been pasteurized or homogenized) credit it with having more beneficial bacteria and enzymes than its processed counterpart, but science hasn't proven any of these claims. And raw milk can become contaminated in a number of ways: by coming into contact with cow feces or bacteria living on the skin of cows, from an infection of the cow's udder, or from dirty equipment, among others. The special heating process we know as pasteurization is the only effective way of killing most, if not all, harmful bacteria—which can include listeria, salmonella, and *E. coli*.

Lowenstein, Kate. "Not Safe to Eat." *Health* Oct. 2011: 86+. Print.

Plagiarized passage

Some people believe that raw milk is better for you than pasteurized milk, but science has not proven these claims. Milk can become contaminated by bacteria on cows. The special heating process called pasteurization is the only real way of killing dangerous bacteria—which can include listeria, salmonella, and *E. coli*.

(This example illustrates plagiarism. A parenthetical citation is needed for all the material that is paraphrased from the original passage. The last sentence is too close to the original text. It needs either to be paraphrased more completely or have quotation marks around the direct quote. This also needs a parenthetical citation.)

Acceptable passage—No plagiarism

According to *Health* writer Kate Lowenstein, there is no scientific evidence that raw milk is healthier than pasteurized milk. On the contrary, unpasteurized milk poses a danger to human health because microorganisms on milking tools and bovine skin, udders, and feces can infect the milk supply and cause a variety of foodborne illnesses (86). Lowenstein states, "The special heating process we know as pasteurization is the only effective way of killing most, if not all, harmful bacteria—which can include listeria, salmonella, and *E. coli*" (86).

(In the first two sentences, the main ideas of the original are communicated in the writer's own language and sentence structure. The last sentence is quoted accurately. References to the author and parenthetical citations indicate where the original ideas came from.)

45e Taking notes

As you develop your research projects, try to develop a system of keeping your notes organized. Think about how you are going to store, categorize, and process the materials you gather.

TRY THIS

Keeping Your Research Materials and Notes Organized

- Save researched articles from library databases or websites on a flash drive, on your computer's hard drive, or in your e-mail account.

- Bookmark websites you may want to revisit later.

- Highlight passages in your notes that are quoted, paraphrased, or summarized from your original sources to avoid accidental problems with plagiarism.

- Divide your major topics into subtopics, and then save your research materials and notes in separate file folders labeled by subtopic.

- Have some highlighters or colored pens handy so you can assign a color for each subtopic, and then color-code your printouts related to that subtopic.

- Be prepared to find that you need to add, change, or modify your subtopics as you learn more about the topic.

45f Writing an annotated bibliography

You may be asked to create an annotated bibliography as a step towards preparing your research project. Annotated bibliographies give you the opportunity to review, summarize, and organize your research materials on a particular topic. Each entry in an annotated bibliography contains three parts:

- **A bibliographic citation formatted in the documentation style required for your course.** See Chapters 47–50 for information on Works Cited and References citations.

- **An abstract (brief summary) of the source.** Fairly and objectively inform your readers of the main ideas in the work being discussed. Think about the situation or argument the author is addressing. What is the author's purpose? What are the key points stressed in the work? What conclusions does the author draw about the subject?

- **A short reflection about the significance of the source and its relevance for your research project.** Explain how the work will help you with your research project. How does the source expand your understanding of a topic? How and where might you use information from the work in your project?

Here is a sample entry from an MLA-formatted annotated bibliography developed for a paper about contemporary political protests.

Wasik, Bill. "Crowd Control." *Wired* Jan.
    2012: 76+. Print.

> **Bibliographic citation**

In 2003, Wasik helped to pioneer the concept of flash mobs, events where people connected via social networking technology spontaneously gather together to perform humorous and entertaining group activities. The author explores how the flash mob concept has mutated. The label has now been applied to outbreaks of group criminal behavior, such as the 2011 youth riots around London, as well as political movements, such as the Occupy Wall Street protests. In each instance, social networking platforms have been used to organize crowd behavior and shape a group identity. Authorities are becoming savvier about the role of social networking tools in organizing crowd behavior and now monitor these networks to diffuse crowds before they can become unruly or violent. This article provides an in-depth analysis of the psychology of crowd behavior.

> **Abstract**

For my research paper, this article will help me to discuss the role of social networking in political protests.

> **Reflection**

46

Integrating Sources

46a Summarizing

A summary is a brief restatement, using your own words, of the main ideas in a source. Unlike paraphrases (see 46b), summaries are shorter than the original source because they convey only the main points of the source.

FAQ

What are the characteristics of a summary?

- Summaries use fewer words than the source being summarized.
- Summaries include only the main points, omitting details, facts, examples, illustrations, direct quotations, and other specifics.
- Summaries are written in your own words, not copied from your source, and use your own sentence structures.
- Summaries are objective and do not include your own interpretation or reflect your slant on the material.
- Summaries represent the viewpoint(s) of the author(s) fairly and accurately.
- Summaries must be cited in the documentation format (MLA, APA, *Chicago Manual*, CSE, etc.) you are using for your paper.

Summary: an example

Original Source: book excerpt

Most of us are already aware of the direct effect we have on our friends and family; our actions can make them happy or sad, healthy or sick, even rich or poor. But we rarely consider that everything we think, feel, do, or say can spread far beyond the people we know. Conversely, our friends and family serve as conduits for us to be influenced by hundreds or even thousands of other people. In a kind of social chain reaction, we can be deeply affected by events we do not witness that happen to people we do not know. It is as if we can feel the pulse of the social world around us and respond to its persistent rhythm. As part of a social network, we transcend ourselves, for good or ill, and become a part of something much larger. We are connected.

Christakis, Nicholas A., and James H. Fowler. *Connected: The Surprising Power of Social Networks and How They Shape Our Lives— How Your Friends' Friends' Friends Affect Everything You Feel, Think, and Do.* New York: Back Bay-Little, 2011. Print.

Unacceptable Summary: too close to original language and sentence structure and missing a parenthetical citation

We are all part of a social chain reaction, where everything we think, feel, or do can affect our friends and family. We can also affect and are affected by hundreds or even thousands of people we do not know. As part of a social network, we are connected.

> (*The language and sentence structure of this example are too close to the original text and could be considered plagiarized. This example is also missing a parenthetical citation.*)

Acceptable Summary

Researchers Nicholas A. Christakis and James H. Fowler argue that our individual emotions and behaviors inadvertently make an impression on other people. We are intertwined into the communities in which we live. Therefore, our emotions and behaviors have an impact on those closest to us, who in turn have an impact on those immediately around them. This process also works in the reverse, unconsciously shaping our own moods and decisions (30).

> *(The key idea of the original passage is communicated here in the writer's own language and sentence structure. A reference to the authors and a parenthetical citation indicate where the original idea came from.)*

TRY THIS

Writing a Summary

1. Read the original source carefully and thoughtfully.
2. After the first reading, ask yourself what the author's major point is.
3. Go back and reread the source, making a few notes in the margin.
4. Look away from your source, and then, like a newscaster, panelist, or speaker reporting to a group, finish the sentence: "This person is saying that . . . "
5. Write down what you've just said.
6. Go back and reread both the source and your notes in the margins to check that you've correctly remembered and included the main points.
7. Revise your summary as needed.

46b Paraphrasing

A paraphrase restates information from a source, using your own words.

FAQ

What are the characteristics of a paraphrase?

- A paraphrase has approximately the same number of words as the source. (A summary, by contrast, is much shorter.)
- Paraphrases use your own words, not those of the source, and are written in your own sentence structures.
- Paraphrases are objective and do not include your own interpretation or slant on the material.

- Paraphrases represent the viewpoint(s) of the author(s) fairly and accurately.
- A paraphrase is approximately the same length as the passage from the original source and contains more detail than a summary would.
- Paraphrases must be cited in the documentation format (MLA, APA, *Chicago Manual*, CSE, etc.) you are using for your paper.

Paraphrase: an example

Original Source: magazine article excerpt

To ignite a pandemic, even the most lethal virus would need to meet three conditions: it would have to be one that humans hadn't confronted before, so that they lacked antibodies; it would have to kill them; and it would have to spread easily—through a cough, for instance, or a handshake. Bird flu meets the first two criteria but not the third.

Specter, Michael. "The Deadliest Virus." *New Yorker* 12 Mar. 2012: 32–37. Print.

Unacceptable Paraphrase: wording and sentence structure too close to the original source

To start a pandemic, a disease needs to meet three conditions. First, it would need to be new to humans so that they lacked antibodies to fight it off. Second, the disease would have to kill them. Third, it would need to spread easily through coughs or handshakes. Bird flu doesn't spread easily, but it meets the first two criteria (Specter 32).

(The language and sentence structure of this example are too close to the original text and could be considered plagiarized.)

Acceptable Paraphrase

H5N1, a new strain of avian influenza, proved fatal for many of those infected with it; their immune systems were unable to resist this mutation of the disease. However, because H5N1 did not effectively proliferate through airborne or surface contact, it did not reach the level of a worldwide epidemic (Specter 32).

(The main ideas of the original are communicated here in the writer's own language and sentence structures. A parenthetical citation indicates where the ideas originally came from.)

TRY THIS

Writing a Paraphrase

1. Read the original passage as many times as is needed to understand its full meaning.
2. As you read, take notes, using your own words, if that helps.
3. Put the original source aside and write a draft of your paraphrase, using your notes if needed.
4. Check your version against the original source by rereading the original to be sure you've included all the ideas from the source.
5. If you find a phrase worth quoting in your own writing, use quotation marks in the paraphrase to identify the words you're borrowing, and note the page number.

46c Quoting

A quotation records the exact words of a written or spoken source. Place quotation marks directly before and after the quoted words.

FAQ

What are the characteristics of quotations?

- Quotations are written exactly as they appear in the source.
- Quotations must be surrounded by quotation marks.
- Quotations are introduced by text that indicates the author of the quotation.
- Quotations must be cited in the documentation format (MLA, APA, *Chicago Manual*, CSE, etc.) you are using for your paper.

Short quotations

Introduced with a comma. Use a comma to connect the signal phrase to the quotation. (See 46d for signal phrases.)

Psychologists Jean M. Twenge and W. Keith Campbell argue, "American culture encourages self-admiration with the belief that it will improve our lives" (13).

Introduced with a colon. Use a colon at the end of a full sentence.

Twenge and Campbell assert that narcissists do not have logical reasons to support their inflated self-perceptions: "Measured objectively, narcissists are just like everyone else. Nevertheless, narcissists see themselves as fundamentally superior—they are special, entitled, and unique" (19).

Introduced mid-sentence: Blend the quotation into your sentence so that your sentence remains grammatically correct.

Twenge and Campbell argue that Americans "have taken the desire for self-admiration too far—so far that our culture has blurred the distinction between self-esteem and narcissism in an extreme, self-destructive way" (17).

Long quotations (block quotations)

If the quotation is more than four typed lines, set it off by indenting one inch or ten spaces from the left margin in MLA style (one-half inch or five spaces in APA style). Double-space the quotation, and don't use quotation marks.

Twenge and Campbell suggest that one of the causes behind the increase in narcissistic personality disorder among young adults may be overindulgent parenting:

> Some early psychodynamic theorists believed that narcissism resulted from cold, neglectful parents, but empirical data has not supported that conclusion very strongly except in some forms of vulnerable or covert narcissism. More modern behavioral theories argue that narcissism instead arises from inflated feedback—if you're told over and over that you are great, you'll probably think you are great. (80)

The MLA citation for this source would appear as follows:

Twenge, Jean M., and W. Keith Campbell. *The Narcissism Epidemic: Living in the Age of Entitlement.* New York: Free-Simon, 2009. Print.

Quotes are needed when . . .

* the writer's words are especially vivid, memorable, or expressive.

* an expert's explanation is so clear and concise that a paraphrase would be confusing or wordy.

* you want to emphasize the expertise or authority of your source.

* the words the source uses are important to the discussion.

Example: source worth quoting

In a Senate hearing about the recent financial catastrophe, Senator Carl Levin argued that reform is necessary: "To rebuild our defenses, it is critical to understand that the recent financial crisis was not a natural disaster. It was a man-made economic assault. People did it. Extreme greed was the driving force. And it will happen again unless we change the rules."

Levin, Carl. "Opening Statement of Senator Carl Levin, U.S. Senate Permanent Subcommittee on Investigations Hearing on Wall Street and the Financial Crisis." *Carl Levin: United States Senator*. United States Senate, 13 Apr. 2010. Web. 1 Mar. 2012.

(This statement is worth quoting because restating it in different words would probably take more words and have less punch.)

Example: source worth paraphrasing

Senator Carl Levin criticized the bank's questionable loan practices: "Once a Main Street bank focused on financing mortgages for its customers, Washington Mutual was taken in by the short-term profits that even poor-quality mortgages generated on Wall Street" (qtd. in Javers).

Javers, Eamon. "Levin Probe Faults Washington Mutual for Risky Loans." *Politico*. Capital News Co., 14 Apr. 2010. Web. 1 Mar. 2012.

(This statement by Senator Levin is a good candidate for paraphrasing rather than quoting. The statement is not particularly concise or uniquely phrased, plus some additional background information would be needed for readers to understand its full meaning.)

TRY THIS

To Use Quotations Effectively

- Use quotations as evidence, support, or further explanation of what you have written. Quotations are not substitutes for stating your point in your own words.

- Use quotations sparingly. Too many quotations strung together with very little of your own writing makes a paper look like a scrapbook of pasted-together sources, not a thoughtful integration of what you know about a subject.

- Use quotations that illustrate the author's own viewpoint or style, or quote excerpts that would not be as effective if rewritten in different words. Effective quotations are succinct or particularly well phrased.

- Introduce quotations with words that signal the relationship of the quotation to the rest of your discussion (see 46d).

46d Using signal words and phrases

When you summarize, paraphrase, or quote from outside sources in your writing, identify each source and explain its connection to what you are writing about. You can do this by using signal words that tell the reader what to expect or how to interpret the material. These words can help you integrate material smoothly into your writing.

TRY THIS

To Introduce Quoted, Paraphrased, or Summarized Words

Try using the following signal words:

acknowledges	condemns	points out
adds	considers	predicts
admits	contends	proposes
agrees	describes	reports
argues	disagrees	responds
asserts	explains	says
believes	finds	shows
claims	holds	speculates
comments	insists	suggests
concedes	notes	warns
concludes	observes	writes

FAQ

How can I integrate my sources smoothly into my paper?

- **Explain how the source material is connected to the rest of the paragraph.** Show your readers the connection between the reference and the point you are making. Introduce the material by showing a logical link, or add a follow-up comment that integrates a quotation into your paragraph.

- **Use the name of the source and, if appropriate, that person's credentials as an authority.** Name your source's job title or professional affiliation as you introduce quoted, paraphrased, or summarized material (According to Kathleen Sebelius, **Secretary of the United States Department of Health and Human Services**, ". . . . ")

- **Use a verb to indicate the source's stance or attitude toward what is quoted, paraphrased, or summarized.**
  - Does the source think the statement is very important (Professor Mehta **stressed**, ". . . .")?
  - Does the source take a position on an issue (The senator **argued**, ". . . .")?
  - Does the source remain neutral about what is stated (The researcher **reported**, ". . . .")?

- **Use the appropriate verb tense.** When writing about literature and most other humanities subjects, use the present tense. Science writers generally use present tense verbs, except when writing about research that has been completed (When studying the effects of constant illumination on corn seedlings, Jenner **found** that ". . . .").

- **Include each source on your Works Cited or References page.** See Chapters 47, 48, 49, and 50 for examples of citation formats.

In the following two MLA-formatted examples, notice the difference in the way the writer's ideas and source material are integrated into the text.

Unacceptable Paragraph: sources not introduced and not integrated well

   Food production uses up one-tenth of America's energy costs each year (Webber 76). There are ways that food production can become more efficient. Vertical greenhouses or urban farms can help to reduce costs. They have "the potential for even greater biomass production per square foot of land than local farms" (Webber 77). A company called Plantagon is building a vertical greenhouse in the city of Linköping in Sweden. "Essentially, as urban sprawl and lack of land will demand solutions for how to grow industrial volumes in the middle of the city, solutions on this problem have to focus on high yield per ground area used, lack of water, energy, and air to house carbon dioxide" (Hassle qtd. in Ma). The cone-shaped glass skyscraper will be seventeen stories high and will be energy-efficient. Plants will travel on tracks throughout the building for "maximum sun exposure" (Ma). Focusing on getting food from local farms is not always cost-efficient in the long run, but urban farms might make a difference (Webber 77).

(The quotations here are abruptly dropped into the paragraph without introductions and without clear indications from the writer as to how these statements connect together and relate to the main idea of the paragraph.)

Acceptable Paragraph: sources introduced and integrated effectively

Food production can become a more cost- and energy-efficient process. Currently, food production uses up one-tenth of America's energy costs each year (Webber 76). Some environmentalists believe that buying food from local farms reduces the energy costs associated with transporting food from other global regions. Michael W. Webber, associate director for the Center for International Energy and Environmental Policy, argues that while there are benefits to supporting local farms, local fields may actually require more energy for food production to grow non-native crops (77). However, new technologies, such as vertical greenhouses or urban farms, can help to reduce costs (77). For example, a company called Plantagon is currently building a vertical greenhouse in Linköping, Sweden. The seventeen-story, cone-shaped, glass skyscraper will rotate plants on tracks throughout the building for "maximum sun exposure" and energy-efficiency (Ma). Plantagon CEO Hans Hassle explains the benefits of vertical farms: "Essentially, as urban sprawl and lack of land will demand solutions for how to grow industrial volumes in the middle of the city, solutions on this problem have to focus on high yield per ground area used, lack of water, energy, and air to house carbon dioxide" (qtd. in Ma). Webber agrees that vertical farms have "the potential for even greater biomass production per square foot of land than local farms" (77).

Works Cited

Ma, Julie. "A 'Vertical Greenhouse' Could Make a Swedish City Self-Sufficient." *GOOD*. GOOD Worldwide, 12 Mar. 2012. Web. 14 Mar. 2012.

Webber, Michael E. "More Food, Less Energy." *Scientific American* Jan. 2012: 74–79. Print.

VIII

Documentation

Contents

Question and Correct

	SECTION	PAGE

LEARNING OBJECTIVE: Understanding how to acknowledge sources in MLA format

	SECTION	PAGE
✦ What are major features of MLA style?	47	181
✦ How do I refer to sources in the body of my paper in MLA style?	47a	182
✦ What is a parenthetical reference?	47a	182
✦ When do I use notes (or endnotes) in MLA, and what is the appropriate way to type them?	47b	188
✦ What are the parts of a citation in the Works Cited list?	47c	189
✦ How do I cite magazine and journal articles I located on library databases?	47c	202
✦ How do I cite Internet sources in my Works Cited list?	47c	208
✦ What do MLA-formatted pages of a research paper look like?	47d	220

47

MLA

Documenting in MLA Style

For research papers in most of the humanities, use the format recommended by the **Modern Language Association (MLA)**. The latest style manuals published by the MLA are the following, but check to see whether more current guidelines have succeeded them (www.mla.org/style):

> Modern Language Association. *MLA Handbook for Writers of Research Papers*. 7th ed. New York: MLA, 2009. Print.

> Modern Language Association. *MLA Style Manual and Guide to Scholarly Publishing*. 3rd ed. New York: MLA, 2008. Print.

Major features of MLA style

- For parenthetical references, place the author's last name and the page number of the source at the end of the sentence and before the period. Parenthetical references placed after long quotations (which are indented one inch from the left margin) are placed after the sentence and after the period.

- In the Works Cited list, use full first and last names and middle initials of authors.

- Capitalize all major words in book and periodical titles, and put the titles in italics. Enclose article and chapter titles in quotation marks. If the title of another work appears within an italicized title, do not italicize the title of the other work.

- In the Works Cited list at the end of the paper, give full publication information, alphabetized by author's last name.

FAQ

What are the different parts of MLA citation format?

1. **Parenthetical references.** In your paper, use in-text citations to acknowledge words, ideas, and facts you've taken from outside sources. (See 47a.)

MLA

2. **Endnotes.** If you are adding material that would disrupt your paper if it were included in the text, include such notes at the end of the paper. But an endnote section is not required. (See 47b.)

3. **Works Cited list.** At the end of your paper, include a list of the sources from which you have quoted, summarized, or paraphrased. (See 47c.)

47a Parenthetical references

In-text citations, also referred to as "parenthetical references" because they are enclosed in parentheses, help your reader find the citation of the source in the Works Cited list at the end of the paper. Try to be brief, but not at the expense of clarity, and use signal words and phrases to introduce the citation (see 46d).

Examples of MLA In-Text Citations

1. **Print or PDF Source with a Single Author** For sources in print or PDF format (an electronic source that looks exactly the same as the original print publication), if the author's name is not in your sentence, put the last

name in parentheses, leave a space with no punctuation, and then include the page number.

> One of the most commonly accepted theories is that "a dream is the fulfillment of a wish" (Freud 154).

If you include the author's name in the sentence, only the page number is needed in parentheses.

> According to famed psychoanalyst Sigmund Freud, "a dream is the fulfillment of a wish" (154).

2. **Web Source with a Single Author** Because webpages may vary in length when printed out on paper (due to printer and font settings), page numbers for web sources are not considered permanent references for citation purposes. So don't use page numbers to cite web sources unless they are in PDF format. (For citing PDF sources, see example #1).

> In fact, "certain bacteria can be induced to reproduce plasmids along with themselves, doubling their number about twice per hour" (Mullis).

If the author's name is included in the sentence, no parenthetical reference is needed for web sources. (For web sources with numbered paragraphs, see example #17.)

> According to Nobel-prize winning chemist Kary Mullis, "certain bacteria can be induced to reproduce plasmids along with themselves, doubling their number about twice per hour."

3. **Two or More Works by the Same Author** If you used two or more different sources by the same author in your paper, when you cite one of them, put a comma after the author's last name and include a shortened version of the title and the page reference. If the author's name is in the text, include only the title and page reference. If your source is not in print or PDF format, omit the page reference.

> One current theory emphasizes the principle that dreams express "profound aspects of personality" (Foulkes, *Sleep* 144).
>
> (*or*)
>
> Foulkes' investigation shows that young children's dreams are "rather simple and unemotional" ("Children's Dreams" 90).

4. **Two or Three Authors** If your source has two or three authors, either name them in your sentence or include

the names in parentheses. If your source is not in print or PDF format, omit the page reference.

> Jeffrey and Milanovitch argue that the recently reported statistics for teen pregnancies are inaccurate (112).
>
> (*or*)
>
> The recently reported statistics for teen pregnancies are said to be inaccurate (Jeffrey and Milanovitch 112).

5. **More Than Three Authors** If your source has more than three authors, either use the first author's last name followed by *et al.* (which means "and others") or list all the last names. If your source is not in print or PDF format, omit the page reference.

> The conclusion drawn from a survey on the growth of the Internet, conducted by Martin et al., is that global usage will double within two years (36).
>
> (*or*)
>
> Recent figures on the growth of the Internet indicate that global usage will double within two years (Martin, Ober, Mancuso, and Blum 36).

6. **Unknown Author for a Print Source or Website** If the author is unknown, use a shortened form of the title in your citation. This includes titles for pages that appear within a website.

> More detailed nutritional information in food labels is proving to be a great advantage to diabetics ("New Labeling Laws" 3).
>
> Native plants, instead of being planted in lawns, should be in gardens where there is very little rain ("Habitats").

7. **Work in an Anthology** Cite the name of the author of the work, not the editor of the anthology, in the sentence or in parentheses.

> When the author describes his first meeting with Narum, he uses images of light to show "the purity of the man's soul" (Aknov 262).

8. **Corporate Author or Government Document** Use the name of the corporation or government agency, shortened or in full. If the name is long, try to include it in your sentence to avoid a long parenthetical reference.

If your source is not in print or PDF format, omit the page reference.

> The United Nations Regional Flood Containment Commission has been studying weather patterns that contribute to flooding in Africa (4).

9. **Entire Work** If you cite an entire work, it is preferable to include the author's name in the text.

> Lafmun was the first to argue that small infants respond to music.

10. **Literary Work** If you refer to well-known prose works, such as novels or plays, that are available in several editions, it is helpful to provide more information than just a page reference in the edition you used. A chapter number, for example, might help readers find the reference in any copy they find. In such a reference, give the page number first, add a semicolon, and then give other identifying information.

> In *The Prince*, Machiavelli reminds us that although some people manage to jump from humble origins to great power, such people find their greatest challenge to be staying in power: "Those who rise from private citizens to be princes merely by fortune have little trouble in rising but very much trouble in maintaining their position" (23; ch. 7).

For poems, omit page numbers and use canto (if available) and line numbers separated by periods. For lines, use the word *line* or *lines* in the first reference, and then afterward give only the numbers. Use slash (/) marks to separate lines of verse, with a single space on either side of the slash.

> Eliot again reminds us of society's superficiality in "The Love Song of J. Alfred Prufrock": "There will be time, there will be time / To prepare a face to meet the faces that you meet" (lines 26-27).

For verse plays and poems, omit page numbers and use act, scene, canto, and line numbers separated by periods.

> Hamlet decides to test his uncle by staging a play: "The play's the thing / Wherein I'll catch the conscience of the King" (2.2.633-34).

11. **Biblical and Other Sacred Texts** Because sacred texts are available in several editions from various publishers, your reader needs more information than just a page

reference. For the first reference in your document, give the shortened title of the work (italicized), followed by a comma. Then add the abbreviated title of the chapter. Add the verse number, followed by a period, and the line numbers. For additional references, give only the abbreviated chapter title, verse, and line numbers.

> Ecclesiastes emphasizes the seriousness of the passage to adulthood: "Banish anxiety from your mind, and put away pain from your body; for youth and the dawn of life are vanity" (*New Oxford Annotated Bible*, Eccles. 11.10). In his first letter, Paul echoes this sobering view of adulthood (1 Cor. 13.11-12).

12. **Multivolume Work** When you cite a volume number as well as a page reference for a multivolume work, separate the two by a colon and a space. Do not use the word *volume* or *page*.

> In his *History of the Civil War*, Jimmersen traces the economic influences that contributed to the decisions of several states to stay in the Union (3: 798-823).

13. **Indirect Source** Using original sources is preferable, but when you have to rely on a secondhand source—words from one source quoted in a work by someone else—start the citation with the abbreviation *qtd. in*.

> Although Newman has established a high degree of accuracy for such tests, he reminds us that "no test like this is ever completely and totally accurate" (qtd. in Mazor 33).

14. **Two or More Sources** If you refer to more than one work in the same parenthetical citation, separate the references by a semicolon. If your source is not in print or PDF format, omit the page reference.

> Recent attempts to control the rapid destruction of the rainforests in Central America have met with little success (Costanza 22; Kinderman 94; Lazilo).

15. **Work Listed by Title** For sources listed by title in your list of works cited, use the title (if the title is short) or a shortened form of the title that begins with the word by which it is alphabetized in your Works Cited list. If your source is not in print or PDF format, omit the page reference.

> The techniques used in those early construction projects have been modernized in contemporary building designs ("Architectural" 27).

16. **Work from a Library Database** For works from library databases, start with the word by which the source is alphabetized in your Works Cited list. If you are able to view a PDF version of the original print file (meaning that it looks exactly the same as the original print publication), use the exact page numbers (also see example #1).

> Mountain biking has yet to be considered a full-fledged mainstream sport, due in part to the challenges faced by the advertising industry in marketing the mountain-biking lifestyle (Smith 66).

If you are viewing the work in web page format, do not use page numbers (also see example #2).

> Advertisers are now using custom-designed bottles, superheroes, and new flavors to market bottled water to children (Hein).

17. **Work from a Web Source with Numbered Paragraphs** If the web source contains numbered paragraphs, follow the words with which you begin your citation with a comma. Then add *par* or *pars* (followed by a period) to indicate paragraphs, and then add the paragraph number or numbers used. (For works in PDF format, see example #1.)

> A number of popular romantic comedies from the late 1990s suggest that women can only succeed at maintaining their femininity by paying less attention to their careers (Negra, par. 6).

18. **Long Quotation** If a quotation runs more than four typed lines, set it off by indenting one inch or ten spaces from the left margin. Double-space the quotation, and do not use quotation marks. At the end of the quote, put the parenthetical citation after the period. Do not put another period after the final parenthesis.

> Eli Pariser argues that when search engines filter results based on a user's personal characteristics, they can hamper people's ability to gather information needed to develop new ideas:
>
> > Personalization can get in the way of creativity and innovation in three ways. First, the filter bubble artificially limits the size of our "solution horizon"—the mental space in which we search for solutions to problems. Second, the information environment inside the filter bubble will tend to lack some of the key traits that spur creativity. Creativity is a context-dependent trait: We're more likely to come

> up with new ideas in some environments than in
> others; the contexts that filtering creates aren't the
> ones best suited to creative thinking. Finally, the
> filter bubble encourages a more passive approach
> to acquiring information, which is at odds with the
> kind of exploration that leads to discovery. (94)

The bibliographic information for this long quotation
would appear on the Works Cited page:

> Pariser, Eli. *The Filter Bubble: What the Internet Is Hiding
> from You.* New York: Penguin, 2011. Print.

19. **Lecture, Speech, or Other Oral Presentation** For lec-
    tures, speeches, and similar oral sources, include the
    name or word you used to alphabetize it.

    > The speaker indicated there would be no change in current
    > student loan policies (Lefevre).

20. **E-Mail** Use the last name of the person who sent the
    e-mail.

    > The Department of Natural Resources is reviewing the sta-
    > tus of wild horses in national parks (Draheim).

47b Endnotes (or notes)

MLA-style papers may contain notes that allow you to comment on your source material, give references to other relevant sources, or provide additional comments about the
text of your paper. Notes should only be used, however,
when they add information crucial for understanding the
main text of your paper.

Number your notes consecutively through the paper. Put
the number at the end of the phrase, clause, or sentence
containing the material you are referring to, after the punctuation. Raise the number above the line, with no punctuation. Leave no extra space before the number.

> The treasure hunt for sixteenth-century pirate loot buried in Nova
> Scotia began in 1927,[1] but hunting was discontinued when the
> treasure seekers found the site flooded at high tide.[2]

You may provide notes in two different ways:

- **Endnotes.** Begin a new page with the heading "Notes,"
  but do not italicize the heading or put it in quotation
  marks. Leave a one-inch margin at the top, center the
  heading, double-space, and then begin listing your notes.

- **Footnotes.** Use the reference tools in your word-processing program to format footnotes on the bottom of relevant pages on your paper. If your word-processing program lacks this function, use endnotes instead unless otherwise specified by your instructor.

For each note in your endnotes or footnotes, indent five spaces, insert the note number and a period, and begin the note. Double-space, and if the note continues on the next line, begin that line at the left-hand margin. In your note, make reference to the author and, if the reference is specific, the page number(s) of the comment. This information should allow the reader to cross-reference to information listed on the Works Cited page. The following example shows how endnotes and a Works Cited page are formatted.

Notes

1. Some historians argue that this widely accepted date is inaccurate. See Flynn 29-43.

2. Greater detail can be found in Jones and Lund.

Works Cited

Flynn, Jerome. *Buried Treasures*. New York: Newport, 1978. Print.

Jones, Avery, and Jessica Lund. "The Nova Scotia Mystery Treasure." *Contemporary History* 9.1 (1985): 81-83. Print.

47c Works Cited list

The list of works cited includes all sources you cite in your paper. Do not include other materials you read but didn't specifically refer to in your paper. Arrange the list alphabetically by the last name of the author; if there is no author, alphabetize by the first word of the title (ignore the articles *A, An*, and *The*).

For the Works Cited section, begin a new page, leave a one-inch margin at the top, center the heading "Works Cited" (with no italicizing or quotation marks), and then double-space before the first entry. For each entry, begin at the left-hand margin for the first line, and indent five spaces (or one-half inch) for additional lines in the entry. Double-space throughout. Place the Works Cited list at the end of your paper after the notes, if you have any. (Also see 47d for a sample Works Cited page.)

MLA

QUICK GUIDE: For an MLA Works Cited page, how do I format . . .

AUTHORS' NAMES
One author: **Cole, James H.**
Two authors: **Cole, James H., and Sue F. Lin.**
Three authors: **Cole, James H., Sue F. Lin, and Sara R. Bola.**
Four or more authors: **Cole, James H., Sue F. Lin, Sara R. Bola, and Dan E. Metz.**
    OR **Cole, James H., et al.**

TITLES (Articles, Webpages, Short Stories, Poems, Songs, Short Works)
Use quotation marks.
"Protecting Yourself."
"The Tyger."
"Rolling in the Deep."

> * In short and long titles, capitalize all words except conjunctions, articles, and prepositions; capitalize them if they appear after a colon.

TITLES (Journals, Magazines, Newspapers) Use italics.
USA Today   *Victorian Studies*   *Vogue*

TITLES (Books, Websites, Databases, Long Works) Use italics and end with a period.
The Hunger Games.   *The Daily Beast.*   *JSTOR.*

PUBLISHER
Give shortened publisher's name, followed by a comma. Shorten the names of publishers by omitting articles at the beginning of a name (*A, An, The*) and business names or descriptive words (*Books, Co., Press*, etc.): **Hyperion,**

If two or more names form part of the company name (e.g. *Prentice Hall, Simon & Schuster,* or *Little, Brown & Co.*), cite only the first name: **Prentice,   Simon,   Little,**

Abbreviate university press as UP: **Yale UP,   U of Utah P,**

If the work is published by an imprint (a smaller publishing house owned by a larger one), give the imprint's name, followed by a hyphen and the larger publisher's name:

Vintage-Random,   Belknap-Harvard UP,

If the company name is commonly known to your readers by an acronym, use the acronym: **GPO,   NCTE,   IBM,**

CITY OF PUBLICATION (for books)	**VOLUME AND ISSUE NUMBERS**
Use the name of the city followed by a colon.	For a book, use *Vol.* for volume: **Vol. 2**.
New York: Chicago: Reston:	For a journal, list volume and issue number: **14.3**

DATES

Year: **2012.**
Month and Year: **Jan. 2012.**
Exact Date: **8 Jan. 2012.**
No Date: **n.d.**
*Abbreviate months except for May, June, and July.

PAGE NUMBERS

8-14.
*Omit second hundredth digit when within the same 100 pages.
108-14.
*Use section letter and page number for newspapers. **A2.**

WEBSITE PUBLISHER

For a website, give the site publisher's name. **NBCNews.com, AOL, Inc.**
If there is "no publisher," indicate this: **N.p.**
* The website publisher's name is often located at the bottom of a webpage or home page, often directly next to the copyright information.

MEDIUM

Include the medium of publication, followed by a period.
Sources in print: **Print.**
Sources on the web: **Web.**
Use the media tag that fits your source. Here are other examples:
Film. **DVD.** **Blu-ray.** **Television.**
iPad app. **Performance.** **Lecture.** **Radio.**
MP3 file. **JPEG file.** *Microsoft PowerPoint* **file.**

Examples of MLA Works Cited Entries

MLA

MLA

Examples of MLA Works Cited

Please note that all entries should be double-spaced on your Works Cited page.

Books and Parts of Books

What is the basic citation format for a book?

Author Names. *Book Title.* City of Publication: Publisher, year of publication. Medium.

(INDENT 5 SPACES)

1. **Book with One Author** To cite books accessed online, see entry 5. To cite books from online library databases, see entry 7.

    > Barnes, Julian. *The Sense of an Ending.* New York: Knopf, 2011. Print.

2. **Book with Two or Three Authors** Reverse the name of the first author only.

    > Friedman, Thomas L., and Michael Mandelbaum. *That Used to Be Us: How America Fell Behind in the World It Invented and How We Can Come Back.* New York: Farrar, 2011. Print.

    > Myers, Jill J., Donna S. McCaw, and Leaunda S. Hemphill. *Responding to Cyber Bullying: An Action Tool for School Leaders.* Thousand Oaks: Corwin, 2011. Print.

3. **Book with More Than Three Authors** For more than three authors, you may list only the first author's name and add *et al.* (for "and others"), or you may give all names in full in the order in which they appear on the title page.

    > Sorenson, Richard D., et al. *The Principal's Guide to Curriculum Leadership.* Thousand Oaks: Corwin, 2011. Print.

    (*or*)

    > Sorenson, Richard D., Lloyd Milton Goldsmith, Zulma Y. Méndez, and Karen Taylor Maxwell. *The Principal's Guide to Curriculum Leadership.* Thousand Oaks: Corwin, 2011. Print.

LATER EDITION OF A BOOK WITH TWO AUTHORS

Title

Edition

Authors
Muriel Harris
Jennifer L. Kunka

From title page

City of Publication

Publisher

Pearson

Boston Columbus Indianapolis New York San Francisco Upper Saddle River
Amsterdam Cape Town Dubai London Madrid Milan Munich Paris
Montreal Toronto Delhi Mexico City Sao Paulo Sydney Hong Kong
Seoul Singapore Taipei Tokyo

Publisher

Copyright © 2013, 2011, 2007 by Pearson Education, Inc.

Publication Date

From copyright page

MLA Works Cited Entry

Harris, Muriel, and Jennifer L. Kunka. *The Writer's FAQs.*

5th ed. Boston: Pearson, 2013. Print.

Medium

MLA In-Text Citation

Harris and Kunka note that writing center consultants "do not just proofread. They want to help you learn how to revise your own work" (13).

See page 13.

Page Number

---

4. **Book by a Corporate or Organizational Author**

> Mayo Clinic. *Mayo Clinic Family Health Book.* 4th ed. New York: Time, 2009. Print.

FAQ

What is the basic citation format for a previously published print book posted online?

Author Names. *Title of Book.* City of Publication: Publisher, Year of publication. *Title of Website.* Web. Date of access.

(INDENT 5 SPACES)

5. **Book Accessed Online** Include the original date of the text, if available. Add the editor's name, publication information, and the date of the edition of the text, if available.

> Christie, Agatha. *The Mysterious Affair at Styles*. 1920. *Project Gutenberg*. Web. 3 Jan. 2012.

> Fitzgerald, F. Scott. *This Side of Paradise*. New York: Scribner, 1920. *Bartleby.com*. Web. 21 Mar. 2012.

6. **E-Book Downloaded for Electronic Book Reader** Cite the source like a print version, but when listing the medium, name the digital format followed by the word *file*.

> Issacson, Walter. *Steve Jobs*. New York: Simon, 2011. iBooks file.

> James, P. D. *Death Comes to Pemberley*. New York: Knopf, 2011. Kindle file.

7. **Book Located in a Library Database or Subscription Service**

> O'Connor, John. *Turning Average Instruction into Great Instruction: School Leadership's Role in Student Achievement*. Lanham: Rowman, 2009. *NetLibrary*. Web. 29 Jan. 2012.

8. **Work with a Publisher's Imprint** Publishers sometimes put books under imprints or special names that usually appear with the publisher's name on the title page. Include the imprint name, a hyphen, and the name of the publisher (e.g., Belknap-Harvard UP, Vintage-Random, or Grove-Atlantic).

> McEwan, Ian. *Solar*. New York: Talese-Doubleday, 2010. Print.

9. **Republished Work** State the original publication date after the title of the book. In the publication information that follows, put the date of publication for the current version.

> Braddon, Mary Elizabeth. *Lady Audley's Secret*. 1862. New York: Oxford UP, 2012. Print.

10. **More Than One Work by the Same Author** Use the author's name in the first entry only. From then on, type three hyphens and a period, and then begin the next title. Alphabetize by title.

> Robinson, Marilynne. *Absence of Mind: The Dispelling of Inwardness from the Modern Myth of the Self*. New Haven: Yale UP, 2010. Print.
> ---. *Home*. New York: Farrar, 2008. Print.

11. **Anthology/Collected Works** An *anthology* is a book that contains several smaller works. If the anthology contains works from several authors, list the editor or editors first. Use the abbreviation *ed.* for one editor and *eds.* for more than one editor. If the anthology contains works by a single author, list the author first and include the editor or editors after the title. When adding the name of an editor or editors after the title of the work, use the abbreviation *Ed.* (which means "Edited by"). To cite one or more works in an anthology, see entries 12 and 13.

> Middleton, Thomas. *Thomas Middleton: The Collected Works*. Ed. Gary Taylor and John Lavagnino. New York: Oxford UP, 2010. Print.

> Aslan, Reza, ed. *Tablet and Pen: Literary Landscapes from the Modern Middle East*. New York: Norton, 2011. Print.

12. **Work in an Anthology/Collected Works** State the author and title of the work first, and then give the title and other information about the anthology, including the pages on which the selection appears. Include the original publication date after the title of the work if it is different from the publication date of the anthology or collected works.

> Hurston, Zora Neale. "Sweat." 1926. *Literature: An Introduction to Fiction, Poetry, and Drama*. 11th ed. Ed. X. J. Kennedy and Dana Gioia. New York: Longman-Pearson, 2010. 530-37. Print.

> Mori, Kyoki. "Between the Forest and the Well: Notes on Death." *The Inevitable: Contemporary Writers Confront Death*. Ed. David Shields and Bradford Morrow. New York: Norton, 2011. 33-49. Print.

13. **Two or More Works in the Same Anthology/Collected Works** If you cite two or more works from the same collection, you can avoid unnecessary repetition by including a complete entry for the collection and then cross-referencing the works to that collection. In the cross-reference, include the author and title of the work, the last name of the editor of the collection, and the page numbers. For previously published material, you may include the original date of publication after the title of the work.

> Forrester, Andrew. "The Unknown Weapon." 1864. Sims 33-102.

Sims, Michael, ed. *The Penguin Book of Victorian Women in Crime*. New York: Penguin, 2011. Print.

Wilkins, Mary E. "The Long Arm." 1895. Sims 133-64.

14. **Scholarly Collection/Work That Names an Editor** Use the abbreviation *ed.* for one editor and *eds.* for more than one editor.

Smith, Jane Bowman, ed. *The Elephant in the Classroom: Race and Writing*. Cresskill: Hampton, 2010. Print.

15. **Article in a Scholarly Collection/Work That Names an Editor** Include the author's name, and add the article title (in quotation marks). Then name the scholarly collection and the editor or editors. If a selection has been published before, give that information and then use *Rpt. in* (for "Reprinted in") with the anthology information.

Doherty, Brian. "Comics Tragedy: Is the Superhero Invulnerable?" *Reason* May 2001: 49-55. Rpt. in *Best American Comics Criticism*. Ed. Ben Schwartz. New York: Fantagraphics, 2010. 24-33. Print.

Herman, David. "Narrative Worldmaking in Graphic Life Writing." *Graphic Subjects: Critical Essays on Autobiography and Graphic Novels*. Ed. Michael A. Chaney. Madison: U of Wisconsin P, 2011. 231-43. Print.

16. **Second or Later Edition**

Corrigan, Timothy. *A Short Guide to Writing about Film*. 7th ed. New York: Longman-Pearson, 2010. Print.

17. **Work That Names a Translator** Use the abbreviation *Trans.* (for "Translated by").

Murakami, Haruki. *1Q84*. Trans. Jay Rubin and Philip Gabriel. New York: Knopf, 2011. Print.

18. **Work with an Author and an Editor** If there is an editor in addition to an author, but it is not an anthology (see entry 11), give the editor's name after the title. Before the editor's name, put the abbreviation *Ed.* (for "Edited by").

James, M. R. *Collected Ghost Stories*. Ed. Darryl Jones. New York: Oxford UP, 2011. Print.

19. **Work That Has More Than One Volume** If you are citing two or more volumes of a work in your paper, put references to volume and page numbers in the parenthetical citations. If

you are citing only one of the volumes in your paper, state the number of that volume in the Works Cited list, and give publication information for that volume alone.

> Hemingway, Ernest. *The Letters of Ernest Hemingway: 1907-1922*. Ed. Sandra Spanier and Robert W. Trogdon. Vol. 1. Cambridge: Cambridge UP, 2011. Print.

> Spodek, Howard. *The World's History*. 4th ed. 2 vols. Upper Saddle River: Prentice-Pearson, 2010. Print.

20. **Poem Accessed Online** Provide the name of the author and text. Include the original date of the text, if available. If print publication information is listed, add the editor's name, publication information, and the date of the edition of the text, if available. If page numbers are not listed, add *N. pag.* after the date of publication.

> Angelou, Maya. "Still I Rise." 1978. *Poetry Foundation*. Poetry Foundation, 2012. Web. 13 Jan. 2012.

> Arnold, Matthew. "Dover Beach." 1867. *A Victorian Anthology, 1837-1895*. Ed. Edmund Clarence Stedman. Cambridge: Riverside, 1895. N. pag. *Bartleby.com*. Web. 18 Feb. 2012.

21. **Graphic Novel** Writers and artists are co-creators of graphic novels. Start your entry with the creator whose work is most central to your project, following it with a label identifying the person's role. If a single person created the entire work, list that person's name at the beginning of the entry.

> Thompson, Craig. *Habibi*. New York: Pantheon-Random, 2011. Print.

> Wolfman, Marv, writer. *The New Teen Titans: Games*. Art by George Pérez. New York: DC, 2011. Print.

> Zezelj, Danijel, artist. *Luna Park*. By Kevin Baker. New York: Vertigo-DC, 2009. Print.

22. **Illustrated Book** Start your entry with the creator whose work is most central to your project. Label the illustrator in the entry. If a single person created the entire work, list that person's name at the beginning of the entry.

> Hill, Laban Carrick. *Dave the Potter: Artist, Poet, Slave*. Illus. Bryan Collier. New York: Little, 2010. Print.

> Stead, Erin, illus. *A Sick Day for Amos McGee*. By Philip C. Stead. New York: Roaring, 2010. Print.

MLA

23. **Introduction, Foreword, Preface, or Afterword** Start the entry with the author of the part you are citing. Then add the information about the book, followed by the page numbers where that part appears. If the author of the part is not the author of the book, use the word *By* and give the book author's full name. If the author of the part and the book are the same, use *By* and the author's last name only.

> Hirsch, E. D., Jr. Preface. *The Making of Americans: Democracy and Our Schools.* By Hirsch. New Haven: Yale UP, 2009. ix-xii. Print.

> West, Cornel. Foreword. *The New Jim Crow: Mass Incarceration in the Age of Colorblindness*. By Michelle Alexander. New York: New, 2012. ix-xi. Print.

24. **Work with a Title Within a Title** If a title that is normally italicized appears within another title, do not italicize it or put it inside quotation marks.

> Epstein, Edmund Lloyd. *A Guide through* Finnegans Wake. Gainesville: UP of Florida, 2010. Print.

25. **Work in a Series** If the title page or a preceding page of the book you are citing indicates that it is part of a series, include the series name, without italicizing or quotation marks, and the series number, following the medium of publication.

> Metzer, David. *Musical Modernism at the Turn of the Twenty-First Century*. Cambridge: Cambridge UP, 2011. Print. Music in the Twentieth Century 26.

26. **Biblical and Other Sacred Texts**

> *The Bible*. Introd. and notes by Robert Carroll and Stephen Prickett. Oxford: Oxford UP, 2008. Print. Oxford World Classics. Authorized King James Vers.

> *The Jewish Study Bible: Tanakh Translation, Torah, Nevi'im, Kethuvim*. Trans. Jewish Publication Society. Ed. Adele Berlin, Marc Zvi Brettle, and Michael Fishbane. Oxford: Oxford UP, 2004. Print.

27. **Online Version of a Biblical or Other Sacred Text**

> *The Bible*. King James Vers. *Blue Letter Bible*. Web. 28 Jan. 2012.

28. **Government Publication** Use the abbreviation *GPO* for publications from the Government Printing Office. If a

specific author is not named, list the country and the government agency issuing the work as the author.

> Farr, Warner, et al., eds. *Special Operations Forces Medical Handbook*. 2nd ed. Washington: GPO, 2009. Print.

> United States. Cong. Congressional Budget Office. *Reducing the Deficit: Spending and Revenue Options*. Washington: GPO, 2011. Print.

29. **Government Publication Online** Use GPO as the acronym for the United States Government Printing Office when listed as a publisher. List the country followed by the office or department.

> Canada. Royal Canadian Navy. "Operation StealthComm: Semaphore Flags." *Royal Canadian Navy*. Dept. of Natl. Defence, Govt. of Canada, 16 July 2011. Web. 5 Mar. 2012.

> United States. Cong. Senate. Committee on Banking, Housing, and Urban Affairs. *Hearings on Examining the State of the Housing Market*. 112th Cong., 1st sess. Washington: GPO, 2011. *United States Government Printing Office*. Web. 18 Sept. 2011.

30. **Article in a Dictionary, Encyclopedia, or Reference Book** Treat an encyclopedia article or a dictionary entry from a well-known reference book like a piece in an anthology, but do not cite the editor of the reference work. If the article is signed, give the author first. If it is unsigned, give the title first. If articles are arranged alphabetically, omit volume and page numbers. When citing familiar reference books, list only the edition and year of publication. For less familiar reference books, especially those that have been published only once, give all publication information, but omit page numbers if arranged alphabetically.

> "Hubris." *New Oxford American Dictionary*. 3rd ed. 2010. Print.

> Quigg, Mark. "Child Maltreatment." *The Corsini Encyclopedia of Psychology*. 4th ed. Ed. Irving B. Weiner and W. Edward Craighead. 4 vols. Hoboken: Wiley, 2010. Print.

31. **Article in an Online Dictionary, Encyclopedia, or Reference Database**

> "Malapropism." *Merriam-Webster Online*. Merriam-Webster, 2012. Web. 1 Jan. 2012.

> "India." *Encyclopaedia Britannica.* Encyclopaedia Britannica, 2012. Web. 12 Feb. 2012.

32. **Pamphlet** Cite a pamphlet like a book. If from a government agency, cite with the appropriate attribution.

> Alberti, P., and P. Noyes. *Sugary Drinks: How Much Do We Consume?* New York: New York City Dept. of Health and Mental Hygiene, 2011. Print.

> Starbucks Coffee Company. *Recycling and Reducing the Environmental Impact of Our Cups.* Seattle: Starbucks, 2010. Print.

33. **Online Pamphlet** Follow the example in entry 32. Then include the website title, *Web.*, and the date of access.

> United States. Dept. of Health and Human Services. Centers for Disease Control and Prevention. *Responding to Influenza: A Toolkit for Prenatal Care Providers.* Washington: CDC, 9 Sept. 2011. *Centers for Disease Control and Prevention.* Web. 12 Mar. 2012.

34. **Published Dissertation Accessed Online**

> Clemons, Amy L. *The Rhetoric of Hope: Kenneth Burke and Dystopian Fiction.* Diss. Purdue U, 2010. Ann Arbor: UMI, 2010. *ProQuest Dissertations and Theses.* Web. 12 Mar. 2012.

35. **Abstract of a Dissertation Accessed Online** Begin with the publication information for the original work, and then add the information for the journal in which the abstract appears. If accessed through a library subscription service, then add the name of the database, *Web.*, and the date of access.

> Duffy, William E. "Towards Consequence and Collaboration in Composition Studies: Theorizing Collaboration after the Social Turn." Diss. U of North Carolina at Greensboro, 2011. *DAI* 72.8 (2012). *ProQuest Dissertations and Theses.* Web. 29 Apr. 2012.

Journal Articles

36. **Scholarly Journal Article** Provide the volume and issue numbers after the title of the journal.

> Deane, Bradley. "Imperial Boyhood: Piracy and the Play Ethic." *Victorian Studies* 53.4 (2011): 689-714. Print.

FAQ

What is the basic citation format for a journal article?

Author Names. "Title of Article." *Journal Name* volume number.
↗ issue number (year of publication): page number(s). Medium.

(INDENT 5 SPACES)

37. **Journal Article Located in a Library Database or Subscription Service**

    Kunka, Andrew J. "Intextuality and the Historical Graphic
    Narrative: Kyle Baker's *Nat Turner* and the Styron
    Controversy." *College Literature* 13.3 (2011): 168-93.
    Project Muse. Web. 2 Mar. 2012.

38. **Article in an Online Journal** Include the journal's volume and issue number, if available. If page numbers are listed, include them in the citation. If page numbers are not listed, add *n. pag.* after the date of publication. Then list *Web.* and the date of access. Treat journal articles located through Google Scholar or other fulltext online databases like sources from library databases (see entry 37).

    Jewell, M. S. "Sustaining Argument: Centralizing the Role
    of the Writing Center in Program Assessment."
    Praxis: A Writing Center Journal 8.2 (2011): n. pag.
    Web. 27 Jan. 2011.

FAQ

What is the basic citation format for a magazine article?

Author Name(s). "Title of Article." *Magazine Name* Day Mo.
↗ year: page number(s). Medium.

(INDENT 5 SPACES)

Magazine Articles

39. **Monthly or Bimonthly Magazine Article** For a magazine published every month or every two months, give the month or months (abbreviated except for May, June,

ARTICLE FROM AN ONLINE MAGAZINE

Website Title — Article Title — Author — Publication Date — Site Publisher

MLA Works Cited Entry

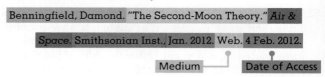

Benningfield, Damond. "The Second-Moon Theory." *Air &
Space.* Smithsonian Inst., Jan. 2012. Web. 4 Feb. 2012.

Medium — Date of Access

MLA In-Text Citation

Some scientists now believe that at one time the Earth
was orbited by two moons (Benningfield).

---

and July) and year, plus the page numbers. Don't add
the volume and issue numbers. If the article does not
appear on consecutive pages, give the first page followed
by a plus sign.

> Bauerleine, Monika, and Clara Jeffrey. "Occupied Washing-
> ton." *Mother Jones* Jan.-Feb. 2012: 18-21. Print.

> Wasik, Bill. "Crowd Control." *Wired* Jan. 2012: 76+. Print.

40. **Weekly or Biweekly Magazine Article** For a magazine
published every week or every two weeks, give the complete date, beginning with the day and abbreviating
the month (except for May, June, or July). If the article does not appear on consecutive pages, give the first
page followed by a plus sign.

> McGrath, Ben. "The Jersey Game." *New Yorker* 2 Jan.
> 2012: 38-53. Print.

FAQ

What is the basic citation format for works that are located on library databases or subscription services?

Author Name(s). "Title of Short Work" (or) *Title of Book* (or) *Periodical*. Print publication information. *Name of Database*. Medium. Date of access.

(INDENT 5 SPACES)

41. **Magazine Article Located in a Library Database or Subscription Service** Add the date you accessed the article at the end of the entry.

    Kahn, Jennifer. "The Visionary." *New Yorker* 11 July 2011: 46+. *Expanded Academic ASAP*. Web. 2 Feb. 2012.

42. **Article in an Online Magazine** Add the date you accessed the article at the end of the entry.

    Doig, Will. "The Bold Urban Future Starts Now." *Salon.com*. Salon Media Group, 31 Dec. 2011. Web. 2 Jan. 2012.

43. **Article on a Magazine App**

    Lehrer, Jonah. "The Forgetting Pill." *Wired* Mar. 2012. iPad app.

Newspaper Articles

FAQ

What is the basic citation format for a newspaper article?

Author Name(s). "Title of Article." *Newspaper Name* day Mo. year, edition: page number(s). Medium.

(INDENT 5 SPACES)

44. **Newspaper Article** Provide the author's name and the title of the article. Then add the name of the newspaper as it appears on the masthead, omitting any introductory article such as *The*. If the city of publication isn't included in the name, add the city in square brackets after the name: *Journal-Courier* [Trenton]. If the paper is nationally

circulated, such as the *Wall Street Journal*, don't add the city of publication. Abbreviate all months except for May, June, and July. Give any information about the edition, and follow it with a colon and page numbers. If the article is not printed on consecutive pages, give only the first page number followed by a plus sign.

> Chang, Kenneth. "To Preserve History on the Moon, Visitors Are Asked to Tread Lightly." *New York Times* 10 Jan. 2012, late ed.: D1+. Print.

> Bensinger, Greg. "Pushing Mobile Payments." *Wall Street Journal* 13 Jan. 2012: B7. Print.

45. **Newspaper Article Located in a Library Database or Subscription Service** Add the date you accessed the article at the end.

> Mariano, Willoughby. "Fewer Jobless Calling It Quits." *Atlanta Journal-Constitution* 1 Jan. 2012: 1B. *LexisNexis*. Web. 29 Jan. 2012.

46. **Article in an Online Newspaper or Newswire** Add the date you accessed the article at the end.

> Gallagher, Kathleen. "Cashing in on the Mobile Revolution." *Milwaukee Journal Sentinel*. Journal Sentinel Inc., 1 Jan. 2012. Web. 19 Feb. 2012.

47. **Article on a Newspaper App**

> Preston, Julia. "Immigration Decreases, But Tensions Remain High." *New York Times* 11 Mar. 2012. iPad app.

Other Periodical Sources

48. **Unsigned Article** Begin the citation with the article title.

> "Protest Could Lead to Rematch." *Atlanta Journal-Constitution* 7 Jan. 2012: C9. Print.

49. **Editorial or Letter to the Editor** If you are citing an editorial, add the word *Editorial* after its title. Use the word *Letter* after the author of a letter to the editor.

> Gooley, Karen. Letter. *Post-Standard* [Syracuse] 6 Mar. 2012: A15. Print.

"A Victory for Equality." Editorial. *Washington Post* 19 Feb. 2012: A22. Print.

50. **Review of a Work** Include the reviewer's name and title of the review, if any, followed by the words *Rev. of* (for "Review of"), the title of the work being reviewed, a comma, the word *by*, and then the author's name. If the work has no title and isn't signed, begin the entry with *Rev. of*, and in your list of works cited, alphabetize under the title of the work being reviewed.

> Braunrot, Bruce. Rev. of *Sculpture and Enlightenment*, by Erika Naginski. *New Perspectives on the Eighteenth Century* 8.1 (2011): 107-08. Print.

> Gleiberman, Owen. "Our Critic's Take." Rev. of *The Girl with the Dragon Tattoo*, dir. David Fincher. *Entertainment Weekly* 6 Jan. 2012: 32. Print.

> Segal, Victoria. Rev. of *El Camino*, by The Black Keys. *Mojo* Jan. 2012: 88. Print.

51. **Published Interview** For interviews published, recorded, or broadcast on television or radio, begin with the name of the person interviewed, the title of the interview in quotation marks (if there is no title, use the word *Interview*), the interviewer's name if known, and any relevant publication information.

> Gettelman, Elizabeth. "Top Gunn." Interview with Tim Gunn. *Mother Jones* Jan.-Feb. 2012: 55-57. Print.

52. **Comic Book (Single Issue)** Writers and artists are co-creators of comic books. Start your entry with the creator whose work is most central to your project, following it with a label identifying the person's role. Italicize the comic title. List the issue number and then cite the publication information as you would cite a book (also see entry 21 for citing graphic novels).

> Azzarello, Brian, writer. *Wonder Woman*. Art by Cliff Chiang. Issue 1. New York: DC, 2011. Print.

Websites and Other Online Sources

53. **Entire Website** Begin with the name of the author or editor, if available. Then list the name of the site (italicized).

MLA

FAQ

What is the basic citation format for a page or article from a website?

Author Names. "Title of Article or Webpage." *Title of Website.* Name of corporate or organizational site publisher, Date of publication, revision or update. Medium. Date of access.

(INDENT 5 SPACES)

NOTE: If there is no corporate or organizational site publisher, insert this where the publisher information belongs: **N.p**.

If there is no date of publication, insert this where the date of publication belongs: **n.d**.

For your date of access, list the day, month, and year: **12 Aug. 2012**.

> *International Spy Museum.* Intl. Spy Museum, 2011. Web. 15 Dec. 2011.
>
> *NBCNews.com.* NBCNews.com, 2012. Web. 21 July 2012.
>
> Mullis, Kary. *KaryMullis.com.* N.p., 2009. Web. 23 Mar. 2010.

54. **Page on a Website** A webpage is a single page on a website. Think of a webpage on a website like a chapter in a book—it is a small part of the entire work. After the author's name (if available), place the name of the webpage in quotation marks.

> Fox, Maggie. "Whooping Cough Epidemic Worst in 50 Years." *NBCNews.com.* NBCNews.com, 19 July 2012. Web. 21 July 2012.
>
> "Language of Espionage." *International Spy Museum.* Intl. Spy Museum, 2011. Web. 15 Dec. 2011.
>
> Mullis, Kary. "Polymerase Chain Reaction." *KaryMullis.com.* N.p., 2009. Web. 23 Mar. 2010.

FAQ

When should a website address be added to a citation?

Most online sources can be easily located by typing relevant information into an online search engine such as Google. Consequently, a website address (also known as a URL) should only be added to your citation for an online source in cases where your instructor requests it or the reader would be unable to find the source without this information. If you need to include a website address in your citation, add it after the date of access. Enclose the entire URL in angle brackets, and end the entry with a period, as shown below. If you must break a long URL on two lines, do so only after a single slash (/) or double slashes (//).

Halperin, Carrie, and Anna Maria Barry-Jester. "Students Design a Better World." *ABC News*. ABC, 17 Dec. 2010. Web. 23 Jan. 2012. <http://abcnews.go.com/Health/students-design-world/story?id=12425101>.

55. **Scholarly Project Accessed Online** If there is an editor, list that persotn first, followed by *ed*. If the site is developed by a group, list the group as the author.

> Center for Contemporary Black History. *The Malcolm X Project at Columbia University*. Columbia U, Center for Contemporary Black History, n.d. Web. 12 Feb. 2012.

> Hollander, Robert, ed. *Dartmouth Dante Project*. Dartmouth College, 2011. Web. 12 Mar. 2012.

56. **Personal Home Page**

> Perry, Katy. Home page. *Katy Perry*. Capitol, 2012. Web. 14 Feb. 2012.

57. **Page on a Social Networking Website**

> Timberlake, Justin. *Facebook: Justin Timberlake*. Facebook, 29 Dec. 2011. Web. 2 Jan. 2012.

58. **Section of a Personal Page on a Social Networking Website** If the cited work is untitled, indicate the type of source it is by using a title (e.g., Comment, Online posting, Introduction, etc.).

> Mamtani, Rakhee. "Let the Robot Drive: The Autonomous Car of the Future Is Here." Comment. *Facebook: Wired*. Facebook, 23 Jan. 2012. Web. 2 Feb. 2012.

59. **Tweet** If you know the author's name, list it and include the username in parentheses if different from the author's name. If you do not know the author's name, list the username. Give the entire tweet in quotation marks. Add the date, time, and *Tweet*.

Booker, Cory. "I don't have allegiance to Charters or District Schools. I have allegiance to kids and I support all public schools that serve them." 5 Mar. 2012. 2:42 p.m. Tweet.

Mitchell, Andrea (mitchellreports). "POTUS: anyone who tells you we can drill our way out of this problem doesnt know what theyre talking about or isnt telling u the truth." 1 Mar. 2012. 1:42 p.m. Tweet.

60. **Entire Blog** List the blog owner as the author. If the blog owner uses a pseudonym or handle, use that name.

Little Professor. *The Little Professor*. Typepad, n.d. Web. 17 Dec. 2011.

McBride, Bill. *Calculated Risk*. CR4RE, 2012. Web. 3 Jan. 2012.

Zúniga, Markos Moulitsas. *Daily Kos: State of the Nation*. Kos Media, n.d. Web. 17 Mar. 2012.

61. **Posting on a Blog** Include the title of the posting in quotation marks after the name of the blog owner. If the posting is from a writer other than the blog owner, list the author of the posting, the title of the posting (in quotation marks), the blog title (italicized), and then *By* and the blog owner.

Gray, Kaili Joy. "Donald Trump Begs Americans to Beg Him to Run for President." *Daily Kos: State of the Nation*. By Markos Moulitsas Zúniga. Kos Media, 2 Jan. 2012. Web. 17 Mar. 2012.

Little Professor. "Rules for Writing Neo-Victorian Novels." *The Little Professor*. Typepad, 15 Mar. 2006. Web. 17 Dec. 2011.

McBride, Bill. "Vehicle Miles Driven Decline: A Possible Contributing Factor." *Calculated Risk*. CR4RE, 1 Jan. 2012. Web. 3 Jan. 2012.

Apps and Software

62. **App** While MLA has not yet provided a specific example of how to cite an app, this model follows MLA's general citation rules. Include the version number, when available. Place the app type at the end of the entry.

StarWalk. Vers. 5.6.2. Vito Technology, 2012. iPad app.

Peterson's Feeder Birds of North America. Vers. 1.0.1. Appweavers, 2011. iPad app.

63. **Article or Short Work on an App** Place the title of the article or short work in quotation marks. Include the version number, when available. Place the app type at the end of the entry.

> "Hubble." *StarWalk*. Vers. 5.6.2. Vito Technology, 2012. iPad app.

> "Red-Bellied Woodpecker." *Peterson's Feeder Birds of North America*. Vers. 1.0.1. Appweavers, 2011. iPad app.

64. **Computer Software/Video Game** Place the medium type or gaming platform at the end of the entry.

> *Just Dance 3*. Ubisoft, 2011. Wii.

> *Sid Meier's Civilization V*. 2K-Firaxis. 2010. DVD-ROM.

Communications

65. **Letter or Memo** For a letter sent to you, name the letter writer, followed by *Letter to the author* and the date. For a letter in an archival collection, include the name of the archive, followed by a period. Add the institution name and city. Cite a published letter like a work in an anthology (see entry 12), but include the date of the letter. Cite the medium of publication as *MS* (for manuscript) or *TS* (for typescript) if the document is unpublished.

> Blumen, Lado. Letter to Lui Han. 14 Oct. 1998. MS. Lado Blumen Papers. Minneapolis Museum of Art Lib., Minneapolis.

> Johnson, Jeffrey. Letter to the author. 11 Jan. 2012. MS.

> Nafman, Theresa. Memo to Narragansett School Board. Narragansett High School, Boston. 3 May 2004. TS.

> Shaw, George Bernard. "To Curt Otto." 20 Mar. 1920. *Bernard Shaw and His Publishers*. Ed. Michel W. Pharand. Toronto: U of Toronto P, 2009. 129-30. Print.

66. **E-Mail Communication**

> Hampton, Hayes. "Poetry Event." Message to the author. 5 Feb. 2012. E-mail.

67. **Real-Time Communication/Instant Messaging (IM)** This format applies to online chat forums and instant messaging programs. Cite the name of the sender, the title of the discussion (if available), recipient of the message, and the date of the communication. Then include the medium of publication.

Campbell, David. Message to Michael Sterling. 29 Nov. 2011. Gmail Chat.

Kehrwald, Kevin. "Oscar Nominations." Message to the author. 20 Feb. 2012. Windows Live Messenger. Facebook Chat.

68. **Personal, Telephone, or E-Mail Interview** If you conducted the interview, start with the name of the person interviewed, the type of interview (*Personal interview, Telephone interview, E-mail interview*), and the date.

Best, Keith. E-mail interview. 9 Jan. 2012.

Flannagan, Rebecca. Telephone interview. 3 Feb. 2012.

Krier, April. Personal interview. 15 Mar. 2012.

For radio and television interviews, see entry 83; for online interviews, see entry 84.

Television, Film, and Radio

69. **Television Program** Include the title of the episode (in quotation marks), the title of the program (italicized), the name of the network, the call letters and city of the local station (if relevant), the broadcast date and *Television*. If pertinent, add information such as the names of the performers, director, or narrator.

"Marine One." *Homeland*. Dir. Michael Cuesta. Perf. Claire Danes and Damian Lewis. Showtime. 18 Dec. 2011. Television.

Horses of the West. Narr. Ali McGraw. PBS. SCETV, Columbia, 14 Mar. 2012. Television.

70. **Online Television Program**

"Loyalty." *Revenge*. Dir. J. Miller Tobin. Perf. Madeleine Stowe, Emily VanCamp, and Gabriel Mann. *ABC.com*. ABC, 4 Dec. 2011. Web. 18 Dec. 2011.

71. **Television Program Viewed on an App**

"Standards and Practices." *30 Rock*. Dir. Beth McCarthy-Miller. Perf. Tina Fey, Alec Baldwin, and Tracy Morgan. NBC, 8 Mar. 2012. *NBC*. iPad app.

72. **Film Viewed in a Theater** Begin a reference to a film with the title (italicized). If based on a book or other

work, list *By* and the creator. Then include the director, distributor, and year. You may also include the names of the screenwriter, performers, and producer. List *Film.* at the end of the entry.

> *The Girl with a Dragon Tattoo.* By Steig Larsson. Dir. David Fincher. Perf. Daniel Craig, Rooney Mara, and Christopher Plummer. MGM, 2011. Film.

73. Film, Emphasis on the Director

> Spielberg, Steven, dir. *War Horse.* Perf. Jeremy Irvine, Emily Watson, and David Thewlis. Dreamworks, 2011. Film.

74. DVD, Blu-ray, or Videocassette Include the original release date, when relevant. List the medium (*Videocassette, DVD, or Blu-ray*) at the end of the entry.

> *The Social Network.* Dir. David Fincher. Perf. Jesse Eisenberg, Andrew Garfield, and Justin Timberlake. 2010. Sony, 2011. DVD.

> *Sweet Smell of Success.* Dir. Alexander Mackendrick. Perf. Burt Lancaster and Tony Curtis. 1957. Criterion, 2011. Blu-ray.

75. Film Viewed on an App Include the original release date, when relevant. List the app name (italicized) and app type at the end of the entry.

> *Game Change.* Dir. Jay Roach. Perf. Julianne Moore, Woody Harrelson, and Ed Harris. HBO Films, 2012. *HBOGo.* iPad app.

76. Video Posted Online List the name or pseudonym of the person who posted the video recording, if available.

> The Ohio Union. "Flash Mob at the Ohio Union 5/3/10 – The Ohio State University." *YouTube.* YouTube, 3 May 2010. Web. 5 May 2010.

77. Video Viewed on an App List the name or pseudonym of the person who posted the video, if available.

> Invisible Children. "KONY 2012." *YouTube.* YouTube, 5 Mar. 2012. iPad app.

ONLINE VIDEO

Website Title

Author

Video Title

Publication Date

MLA Works Cited Entry

Obama, Michelle. "First Lady Michelle Obama Encourages

Families to Get Active in the Great Outdoors." *The White*

House. United States Government, 18 July 2012. Web.

24 July 2012.

Site Publisher

Medium

Date of Access

MLA In-Text Citation

Promoting the health benefits of physical activity, First Lady Michelle Obama encourages Americans to go outside, get active, and have fun: "The great outdoors is America's first and best playground."

---

78. **Sound Recording/CD** Depending on whom you want to emphasize, cite the composer, conductor, or performer first. Then list the song title (in quotation marks), album or CD title (italicized); artist; manufacturer; year of issue (if unknown, write *n.d.* for "no date"); and medium (*CD*, *LP*, or *Audiocassette*). Place a comma between manufacturer and date, with periods following all other items.

> Perlman, Itzhak. *Mozart Violin Concertos nos. 3 and 5.* Wiener Philharmoniker Orch. Cond. James Levine. Deutsche Grammophon, 1983. LP.

> Coldplay. "Paradise." *Mylo Xyloto.* Capitol, 2011. CD.

79. **Sound Recording/MP3/Music Download** For MP3 files and other music downloads, indicate file type at the end of the entry.

> Perry, Katy. "Firework." *Teenage Dream*. Capitol, 2010. MP3 file.

80. **Audio Podcast** If the podcast is downloaded to your computer or other audio device, indicate the file type, such as an *MP3 file*. If the podcast is listened to through an open website, list the podcast as a web source.

> Gompertz, Will. "The Art of Monarchy: Behind the Royal Image." *BBC*. 11 Feb. 2012. MP3 file.

> Tracey, Elizabeth, and Rick Lange. "Week of March 12, 2012." *Johns Hopkins Medicine*. Johns Hopkins Medicine, 12 Mar. 2012. Web. 15 Mar. 2012.

81. **Radio Program**

> "When Machines Do the Work." *On Point*. Narr. Tom Ashbrook. Natl. Public Radio. WBUR, Boston, 2 Nov. 2011. Radio.

82. **Online Radio Program**

> Kelemen, Michele, narr. "South Sudan: Will Oil Lead It Out of Poverty?" *All Things Considered*. Natl. Public Radio, 18 Dec. 2011. Web. 2 Jan. 2012.

83. **Radio or Television Interview** Add the appropriate medium at the end of the entry.

> Jolie, Angelina. Interview with Charlie Rose. *The Charlie Rose Show*. PBS. SCETV, Columbia. 22 Dec. 2011. Television.

84. **Online Radio or Television Interview**

> McFarlane, Seth. Interview with Terry Gross. *Fresh Air with Terry Gross*. NPR.com. Natl. Public Radio, 17 Oct. 2011. Web. 2 Jan. 2012.

Visuals (Art)

85. **Work of Art** Begin with the artist's name, italicize the title of the work, and include the date of the work. Then list the medium of the work, followed by a period. Add the institution that houses the work or the person who owns it, followed by a comma, and the city in which it is located.

> Dalí, Salvador. *Forgotten Horizon*. 1936. Oil on wood. Tate Mod., London.

86. **Work of Art in a Print Source** Follow the information in entry 85, but omit the composition medium. Add the appropriate publication information for your print source, citing the page, slide, figure, or plate number.

> Lichtenstein, Roy. *Drowning Girl.* 1963. Museum of Mod. Art, New York. *Roy Lichtenstein.* By Janis Hendrickson. Berlin: Taschen, 1988. 31. Print.

87. **Online Work of Art** Follow the information in entry 85, but add the appropriate publication information for the website on which an image of the work of art is posted.

> Monet, Claude. *The Houses of Parliament, Sunset.* 1903. National Gallery of Art, Washington. *National Gallery of Art,* 2012. Web. 1 Mar. 2012.

88. **Photograph** Cite a photograph in a museum as a work of art. Cite a published photograph by indicating the name of the photographer and the publication information needed to locate the source (see entry 85).

> Gursky, Andreas. *Times Square, New York.* 1997. Photograph. Museum of Mod. Art, New York.

89. **Online Photograph** Follow the guidelines in entry 88, but add the appropriate publication information for the website on which the image is posted.

> Stillwell, John. *Eyewitness: World's Fastest Man.* Photograph. *Guardian.* Guardian News and Media, 6 Mar. 2012. Web. 1 Apr. 2012.

90. **Personal Photograph** For a personal photograph, name the subject and location of your photo. Then include *Personal photograph by author* and the date of the photo, followed by the medium.

> Rockefeller Center, New York. Personal photograph by author. 15 Mar. 2011. JPEG file.

91. **Map or Chart** Treat a map or chart like a book without an author, but add the descriptive label *Map* or *Chart*.

> *Tennessee.* Map. Chicago: Rand, 2010. Print.

92. **Online Map or Chart** Name the map or chart title, followed by the descriptive label *Map* or *Chart*.

> "Chicago." Map. *Mapquest*. Mapquest, 1 May 2012.
> Web. 1 May 2012.

93. **Cartoon or Comic Strip** Begin with the cartoonist's name, followed by the title of the cartoon or strip (if any) in quotation marks and a descriptive label (*Cartoon* or *Comic strip*).

> Armstrong, Robb. "Jumpstart." Comic strip. *Morning News* [Florence] 12 Mar. 2012: A5. Print.

> Klosner, John. Cartoon. *New Yorker* 12 Mar. 2012: 48. Print.

94. **Online Cartoon or Comic Strip**

> Hambrock, John. "The Brilliant Mind of Edison Lee." Comic Strip. *Milwaukee Journal Sentinel*. Journal Sentinel Inc., 11 Mar. 2012. Web. 12 Mar. 2012.

> Stantis, Scott. "The Frontrunner." Cartoon. *Chicago Tribune*. Chicago Tribune, 6 Mar. 2012. Web. 12 Mar. 2012.

95. **Advertisement** Begin with the name of the product, company, or institution that is the subject of the advertisement, followed by the descriptive label *Advertisement*.

> Apple iCloud. Advertisement. *Apple.com*. Apple Inc., 2012. Web. 18 Feb. 2012.

> Amazon Kindle Fire. Advertisement. CNN. 6 Jan. 2012. Television.

> Toyota Prius V. Advertisement. *Wired* Jan. 2012: 47. Print.

Other Media

96. **Lecture, Speech, or Address** Begin with the speaker's name, followed by the title of the presentation (if available) in quotation marks. Add the meeting and sponsoring organization, location, and date. Add a descriptive label such as *Address* or *Speech* to indicate the medium.

> Villanueva, Victor. "Blind: Talking of the New Racism." Intl. Writing Center Assn. Convention. Minneapolis Hyatt Regency, Minneapolis. 21 Oct. 2005. Address.

McEwan, Ian. Law School Auditorium, U of South Carolina, Columbia. 11 Apr. 2012. Address.

97. **Online Lecture, Speech, or Address** Follow the guidelines in entry 96. Then include the name of the website, corporate or organizational site provider, date of publication, *Web.*, and date of access.

> Eisenhower, Dwight D. "D-Day Invasion Order." 5 June 1944. Speech. History.com. Arts and Entertainment Television Network, 2012. Web. 27 Jan. 2012.

> Richardson, Laura Seargeant. "The Medium Doesn't Matter." Lecture. *MITWorld*. MIT, 19 May 2010. Web. 20 Apr. 2012.

98. **Lecture, Speech, or Address on an App** Follow the guidelines in entry 96. Then include the app name (in italics), version, and app type.

> Conneally, Paul. "Digital Humanitarianism." Nov. 2011. Lecture. *TED*. Vers. 1.6.3. 2011. iPad app.

99. **Live Performance of a Play** Include the theater and city where the performance was given, separated by a comma and followed by a period, and the date of the performance. Add *Performance.* at the end of the entry.

> *Waiting for Godot*. By Samuel Beckett. Dir. Sean Mathias. Perf. Ian McKellen and Patrick Stewart. Theatre Royal Haymarket, London. 10 May 2009. Performance.

100. **Musical Composition** Cite like a book, beginning with the composer's name.

> Mozart, Wolfgang Amadeus. *The Magic Flute*. 1791. London: Faber, 2001. Print.

47d Paper format

Follow the format shown here for the first page and the Works Cited page of an MLA-style research paper.

Paper Format Quick Guide – MLA

Paper format	Set your top, bottom, left, and right margins at one inch. Justify your left margin but not the right unless your instructor requests it.
	Double-space all pages, headers, block quotes, and the Works Cited. Use a standard, easy-to-read font (like Times New Roman, Cambria, Arial, or Calibri) that is 10- or 12-point size.
	Indent the first line of every paragraph ½ inch or five spaces from the left margin. For long quotations, indent one inch or ten spaces from the left margin.
Title and personal information	MLA-style papers do not require a separate title page. In the top left margin of your first page, create a double-spaced list. On separate lines, include your name, your instructor's name, the course number, and the date.
	Then double-space and type the title, centered on the page. Double-space the title if it extends to a second line. Capitalize all words in the title except for articles, conjunctions, and prepositions (unless they are the first word or follow a colon).
Header and page numbers	Beginning on page 1, create a header that is ½ inch from the top of the page and flush with the right margin. Include your last name, a space, and the page number: **Smith 1**
Headings and subheadings	Headings are short titles that break up sections and subsections in long reports and papers. Use consistent phrasing and font style for these.
Tables and figures	Insert tables and figures within the body of the text. Labels for tables appear directly above them. The label and the table title appear on separate lines (double-spaced). **Table 1** **Circulation Statistics for Victorian Sensation Novels** For figures (including graphs, charts, photos, maps, etc.), create a brief label and place it directly below the figure: **Fig. 7. Cruikshank's Illustration for _Oliver Twist_.**
Works Cited	Insert a title called _Works Cited_ and center it on the page. All entries should be double-spaced and organized alphabetically. Format entries in hanging indent style, meaning the second and following lines of an entry are indented .5".

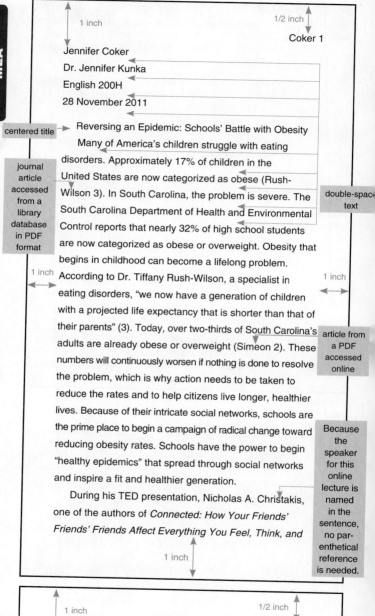

1 inch

1/2 inch
Coker 1

Jennifer Coker

Dr. Jennifer Kunka

English 200H

28 November 2011

centered title → Reversing an Epidemic: Schools' Battle with Obesity

Many of America's children struggle with eating

journal article accessed from a library database in PDF format

disorders. Approximately 17% of children in the United States are now categorized as obese (Rush-Wilson 3). In South Carolina, the problem is severe. The South Carolina Department of Health and Environmental Control reports that nearly 32% of high school students are now categorized as obese or overweight. Obesity that begins in childhood can become a lifelong problem.

double-spaced text

1 inch

According to Dr. Tiffany Rush-Wilson, a specialist in eating disorders, "we now have a generation of children with a projected life expectancy that is shorter than that of their parents" (3). Today, over two-thirds of South Carolina's adults are already obese or overweight (Simeon 2). These numbers will continuously worsen if nothing is done to resolve the problem, which is why action needs to be taken to reduce the rates and to help citizens live longer, healthier lives. Because of their intricate social networks, schools are the prime place to begin a campaign of radical change toward reducing obesity rates. Schools have the power to begin "healthy epidemics" that spread through social networks and inspire a fit and healthier generation.

1 inch

article from a PDF accessed online

During his TED presentation, Nicholas A. Christakis, one of the authors of *Connected: How Your Friends' Friends' Friends Affect Everything You Feel, Think, and*

Because the speaker for this online lecture is named in the sentence, no parenthetical reference is needed.

1 inch

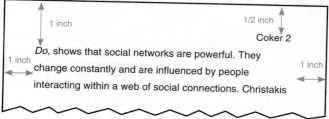

1 inch

1/2 inch
Coker 2

Do, shows that social networks are powerful. They change constantly and are influenced by people interacting within a web of social connections. Christakis

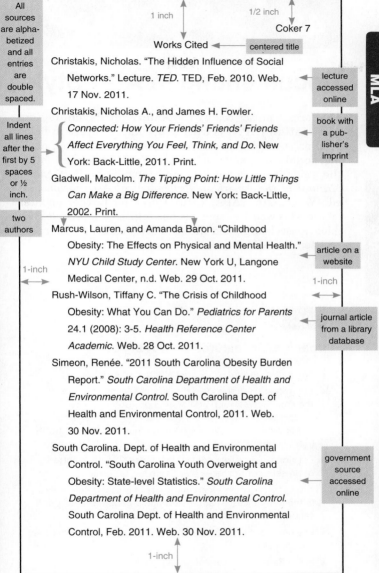

All sources are alphabetized and all entries are double spaced.

1 inch

1/2 inch

Coker 7

Works Cited ← centered title

Christakis, Nicholas. "The Hidden Influence of Social Networks." Lecture. *TED*. TED, Feb. 2010. Web. 17 Nov. 2011. ← lecture accessed online

Indent all lines after the first by 5 spaces or ½ inch.

Christakis, Nicholas A., and James H. Fowler. *Connected: How Your Friends' Friends' Friends Affect Everything You Feel, Think, and Do*. New York: Back-Little, 2011. Print. ← book with a publisher's imprint

Gladwell, Malcolm. *The Tipping Point: How Little Things Can Make a Big Difference*. New York: Back-Little, 2002. Print.

two authors

Marcus, Lauren, and Amanda Baron. "Childhood Obesity: The Effects on Physical and Mental Health." *NYU Child Study Center*. New York U, Langone Medical Center, n.d. Web. 29 Oct. 2011. ← article on a website

1-inch

Rush-Wilson, Tiffany C. "The Crisis of Childhood Obesity: What You Can Do." *Pediatrics for Parents* 24.1 (2008): 3-5. *Health Reference Center Academic*. Web. 28 Oct. 2011. ← journal article from a library database

Simeon, Renée. "2011 South Carolina Obesity Burden Report." *South Carolina Department of Health and Environmental Control*. South Carolina Dept. of Health and Environmental Control, 2011. Web. 30 Nov. 2011.

South Carolina. Dept. of Health and Environmental Control. "South Carolina Youth Overweight and Obesity: State-level Statistics." *South Carolina Department of Health and Environmental Control*. South Carolina Dept. of Health and Environmental Control, Feb. 2011. Web. 30 Nov. 2011. ← government source accessed online

1-inch

MLA

48

Documenting in APA Style

The format prescribed by the **American Psychological Association (APA)** is used to document papers in fields such as psychology, sociology, business, education, nursing, social work, and criminology. For APA format, follow the guidelines offered here and consult the *Publication Manual of the American Psychological Association*, 6th ed. (Washington: APA, 2010). Check for further updates on the APA website (apastyle.apa.org), the APA Style Blog (blog.apastyle.org), and the APA style team's Twitter feed (twitter.com/APA_Style).

APA

FAQ

What are the features of APA style?

- The paper begins with a brief abstract or summary.
- For in-text citations, give the author's last name and the source's year of publication. For quoted material, paraphrases, or other references to specific information in the original source, add a page (*p.*) number or paragraph (*para.*) number to guide readers to the original passage.
- Put signal words (see 46d) in past tense ("Smith reported") or present perfect tense ("as Smith has reported").
- A list of works mentioned in the paper is called References. In the References list at the end of the paper, give full publication information, alphabetized by author.
- Use authors' full last names but only initials for their first and middle names.
- In the References, capitalize only the first word and proper names in book and article titles, but capitalize all major words in journal titles. Italicize book and journal titles. Do not put article titles in quotation marks.
- Use the ampersand (&) instead of the word *and* with authors' names in parenthetical citations, tables, captions, and the References.

48a In-text citations

When you use APA format and refer to sources in your text, include the author's name, a comma, and then date of publication. For direct quotations or specific references to the original source, add another comma after the date. For print sources, include the page number, with *p.* (for page) before the number. For online or electronic sources, include the paragraph number, with *para.* (for paragraph) before the number.

Examples of APA In-Text Citations

1. Author's Name Given in the Text 224
2. Author's Name Not Given in the Text 224
3. Direct Quotations 224
4. Work by Multiple Authors 224
5. Group as Author 225
6. Unknown Author, for Print Source or Webpage 225
7. Authors with the Same Last Name 225
8. Two or More Works in the Same Citation 225
9. Republished Work 225
10. Biblical and Classical Works 226
11. Specific Parts of a Source 226
12. Personal Communications 226
13. Website 227
14. Indirect Source 227

FAQ

Are specific page or paragraph references needed for in-text citations?

In APA style, the author and year are typically included in in-text citations. When the reference provides a summary of a work's general conclusions, no page or paragraph reference is generally included.

> **This conclusion is supported by Gregg (2011) and Legendre and Rogers (2012).**

However, quotations or specific references to the text should contain a page or paragraph number to guide readers to the original passage. For print sources, add *p.* and the page number. For online or electronic sources, add *para.* and the paragraph number.

> **Davis (2012) reported that response times would be affected by the number of available staff members (p. 14). McGee (2012), however, argued that response times would be more affected by the lack of available equipment (para. 6).**

1. **Author's Name Given in the Text** Cite only the year of publication in parentheses. If you refer to the same study again in the paragraph with the source's name, you don't have to cite the year again if it is clear that the same study is being referred to.

    > After the experiment, Wickham (2011) noted an increase in oxygen levels and visibility. Wickham also noted a corresponding decrease in carbon monoxide levels.

2. **Author's Name Not Given in the Text** In parentheses, cite the name and year, separated by a comma.

    > In a recent study of response times (Chung, 2012), no change was noticed.

3. **Direct Quotations** Scientific style tends to favor paraphrased and summarized material over quotations. However, when you need to quote a source, enclose the quote in quotation marks, and then give the author and year. For print sources, add *p.* and the page number. For online or electronic sources, add *para.* and the paragraph number. All quotations or specific references to the text need a page or paragraph number to guide readers to the original passage.

    > Damage costs from recent hurricanes have "forced some insurance companies to reevaluate their portfolios" (Wu, 2010, p. 34). Marlyebone (2009) has reported that many insurers "have simply stopped writing new homeowners' insurance policies in coastal counties" (para. 4).

4. **Work by Multiple Authors** For two authors, cite both names every time you refer to the source. Use *and* in the text, but use an ampersand (&) in parenthetical material, tables, captions, and the References list.

    > Cartagena and Rubio (2008) refuted these results. However, a recent study noted a correlation (Kallen & Marin, 2010).

    For three, four, or five authors, include all authors (and date) the first time you cite the source. For later references to the same work, use only the first author's name and *et al.* (for "and others"), with no underlining or italics.

    > Samuels, Patel, Brownstein, and Eton (2011) noted a significant increase in toxicity. In a later study, Cheng et al.

(2010) examined the levels of radiation and developed indicators to measure the impact on human health.

For six or more authors, cite only the first author and *et al.* and the year for all references.

Benton et al. (2012) noted significant improvement in overall health.

5. **Group as Author** Usually, the name of the group that serves as the author (for example, a government agency or a corporation) is spelled out each time it appears in a citation. However, if the name is long but easily identified by its abbreviation, you can give the abbreviation in parentheses when the entire name first appears and then refer to the group by its abbreviated name in additional references.

In 1992, when the National Institutes of Mental Health (NIMH) prepared its report, no field data on this epidemic were available. However, NIMH agreed that future reports would correct this deficiency.

6. **Unknown Author, for Print Source or Webpage** If no author is indicated, in print or in other media, cite the first words of the article title in quotation marks or the first words of the book title. Then add the year.

One article ("Safe as Houses," 2009) speculated on the collapse of the housing market.

7. **Authors with the Same Last Name** When two or more authors in the References have the same last name, include their initials in text citations.

After R. D. Smith (2012) reviewed the initial study (L. C. Smith, 2010), a new report was issued.

8. **Two or More Works in the Same Citation** When two or more works are cited within the same parentheses, arrange them in the order in which they appear in the References list, and separate them with semicolons.

Several studies (Chalmers, 2012; Gutierrez, 2008; Merevich & Jung, 2011) have reported similar behavior patterns in such cases.

9. **Republished Work** If you are using a version of a source originally published in a different year, include in your in-text citation both the original date of publication and

APA

the publication date from the version you consulted, separated by a slash.

> The evolutionary development of species is a complex process (Darwin, 1859/2009).

10. **Biblical and Classical Works** Reference entries are not necessary for major classical works such as the Bible and ancient Greek and Roman works, but identify the version you used in the first citation in your text. If appropriate, in each citation, include the part (book, chapter, lines).

> When Abraham saw three men passing his tent, he asked them to stop and not pass by him (Gen. 18:3, Revised Standard Version).

> The most recent translation (Homer, trans. 2008) reveals a new perspective on this issue.

11. **Specific Parts of a Source** To cite a specific part of a source, include the page, chapter, figure, or table. Use the abbreviation *p.* (for "page") but no abbreviation for "Chapter."

> Previous research did not consider this factor (Hirosi & Phu, 2011, p. 219), but recently Jones (2011, Chapter 3) investigated this phenomenon.

For an electronic source that contains no page number, use the abbreviation for paragraph (*para.*) followed by the paragraph number. When no paragraph number is given, cite the heading and the number of the paragraph following it.

> The two methods showed a significant difference when repeated with a different sample population (Nesmith, 2010, para. 5). Pietro (2012) indicated that no further study indicated any change in the results (Conclusion section, para. 3).

12. **Personal Communications** Personal communications, such as letters, memos, telephone conversations, and electronic communications, such as e-mail, discussion groups, and messages on electronic bulletin boards, are not archived. Because the data can't be recovered, these are included only in the text, not in the References list. Include the initials and last name of the communicator and as exact a date as possible. (For electronic sources that can be documented, see 48c.)

> According to P. P. Roy (personal communication, July 21, 2012), that outcome is likely.

13. **Website** To include a general reference to a website in the text (but not a specific document), include the web address. See 48c for more information.

> Consult the website for the American Psychological Association (http://apastyle.apa.org) for updates on how to cite Internet sources.

14. **Indirect Source** If you locate a passage in a source but the passage is quoted from or attributed to another original source, you should try to locate that original source and cite it in your paper. If that original source is out of print or not available to you, cite the source you consulted in your References list. Then mention the original source in the text of your paper and make reference to the source you consulted in your in-text citation.

> Massoni's theory (as cited in Nikolodros, 2011, p. 457) discusses the connections between brain cortex activity and social stimuli.

48b Footnotes

In your paper, you may need footnotes to expand on content and to acknowledge copyrighted material. Content footnotes add important information that can't be integrated into the text. Use them only if they strengthen the discussion. Copyright permission footnotes refer to the sources of quotations and other copyrighted materials. Number the footnotes consecutively with superscript Arabic numerals (1, 2, 3, etc.). Include the footnotes at the bottom of the pages on which they appear, or list all footnotes together on a separate page after the References.

48c References list

Arrange all entries in alphabetical order by the author's last name; for several works by one author, arrange by year of publication with the earliest one first (see entry 24 for an example). For each entry in the list, the first line begins at the left margin and all following lines are indented five spaces. Start the References list on a new page, with the word *References* centered at the top of the page, and double-space all entries.

APA

QUICK GUIDE: For an APA References page, how do I format . . .

AUTHORS' NAMES
One author: **Cole, J. H.**
Two authors: **Cole, J. H., & Lin, S. F.**
Three to seven authors: **Cole, J. H., Lin, S. F., & Bola, S. R.**
More than seven authors (list the first six authors, insert an ellipsis, and add the last author): **Cole, J. H., Lin, S. F., Bola, S. R., Metz, D. E., Phu, L. X., Hill, I. M., . . . Kim, T. N.**

DATES
Year: **(2012).**
Month and Year: **(2012, January).**
Exact Date: **(2012, January 8).**
No Date: **(n.d.)**
*Do not abbreviate months.

PAGE NUMBERS
8–14.
108–114.
2108–2114.
Use section letter and page number for newspapers: **A2.**

TITLES (Articles, Webpages, and Short Works)
Do not use quotation marks. Capitalize only the first word, the word after a colon, and proper nouns.
Protecting yourself from flu germs: A protocol for North Dakota.

TITLES (Books and Other Non-Periodicals)   Use italics.
Capitalize only the first word, the word after a colon, and proper nouns.
The tipping point: How little things can make a big difference.

TITLES (Periodicals—Journals, Magazines, Newspapers)   Use italics.
Capitalize all words except for conjunctions, articles, and prepositions, unless they appear after a colon or begin the title.
The Lancet   ***Scientific American***   ***The New York Times***

CITY OF PUBLICATION
List the city and state followed by a colon.   **Chicago, IL:**

VOLUME AND ISSUE NUMBERS
For journals, list just the volume number if the pagination continues from issue to issue. Volume numbers should be italicized: ***25,***
Include the volume and issue number in your entry if each issue of the publication starts with page 1. Italicize the volume number. Enclose the issue number in parentheses and do not italicize it: ***25*(3),**

PUBLISHER
Give the full names of publishers, but omit *Co.* and *Inc.*
University of Chicago Press.   **Farrar, Straus, and Giroux.**

DOIs

Many journal articles, books, and technical reports are now identified by DOI (Digital Object Identifier) numbers. A DOI is a unique code assigned to that publication. If there's a DOI number assigned, include it after the publication information (see entries 1 and 21). If you access the publication online, list the DOI instead of the URL.   **doi:10.1002/jbt.20384**

RETRIEVAL INFORMATION

Retrieval information is needed for sources accessed online. A retrieval line generally includes "Retrieved from" and the URL. In some cases, a retrieval line is not necessary; in other cases, more information may be needed:

- **URL** Include a URL for works accessed online that do not have DOIs. Include just the home page URL (up to the first /) when accessing materials available by search or subscription.
  http://www.cnn.com/   http://www.cdc.gov/

  Give the full URL for pages on sites that are difficult to search. If you have to divide the URL onto two or more lines, break the address before slashes and punctuation marks (except within *http://*), and never add a hyphen. Write the URL like the rest of your text; do not use underlining, italics, angle brackets, or an end period.

- **Date of retrieval** Include the date you accessed the material only if the item is very likely to be updated or changed (see entry 47).

- **Databases** For materials located on widely available databases, including library subscription services, do not include a retrieval line. Include the names of databases in the retrieval line only if the source is rare, a print version is difficult to locate, or the material is available only on a small number of databases (see entries 7, 10, and 16).

APA

Examples of APA References Entries

JOURNAL ARTICLES

MAGAZINE ARTICLES

APA

APA

Examples of APA References

Please note that all entries should be double-spaced on your References page. Start the first line at the left margin, and indent the following lines one half-inch from the left margin.

Journal Articles

1. Journal Article with a DOI—One Author

Cohen, B. B. (2012). Conducting evaluation in contested terrain: Challenges, methodology, and approach in an American context. *Evaluation and Program Planning, 35*, 189–198. doi:10.1016/j.evalprogplan.2010.11.002

2. Journal Article with a DOI—Two to Seven Authors

Bui, A. L., & Fonarow, G. C. (2012). Home monitoring for heart failure management. *Journal of the American College of Cardiology, 59*, 97–104. doi:10.1016/j.jacc.2011.09.044

JOURNAL ARTICLE WITH A DOI

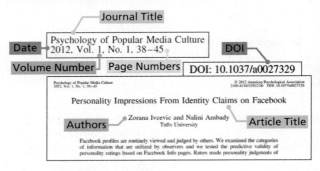

Journal Title

Date — Psychology of Popular Media Culture
2012, Vol. 1, No. 1, 38–45 — DOI

Volume Number — Page Numbers — DOI: 10.1037/a0027329

Personality Impressions From Identity Claims on Facebook

Authors — Zorana Ivcevic and Nalini Ambady
Tufts University — Article Title

Facebook profiles are routinely viewed and judged by others. We examined the categories
of information that are utilized by observers and we tested the predictive validity of
personality ratings based on Facebook Info pages. Raters made personality judgments of

APA References Entry

Ivcevic, Z., & Ambady, N. (2012). Personality impressions

from identity claims on Facebook. *Psychology of*

Popular Media Culture, 1, 38–45. doi:10.1037/a0027329

APA In-Text Citation
According to Ivcevic and Ambady (2012), viewers'
assessments of individuals' Facebook profile
pictures correlated strongly to those same individuals' self-reported levels of extraversion (p. 42).

North, C. S., Abbacchi, A., & Cloninger, C. R. (2012). Personality and posttraumatic stress disorder among
directly exposed survivors of the Oklahoma City
bombing. *Comprehensive Psychiatry, 53,* 1–8.
doi:10.1016/j.comppsych.2011.02.005

3. **Journal Article with a DOI—More Than Seven Authors** List
the first six authors followed by an ellipsis (three spaced
periods) and the final author's name.

Shikotra, A., Choy, D. F., Ohri, C. M., Doran, E., Butler,
C., Hargadon, B., . . . Bradding, P. (2012). Increased
expression of immunoreactive thymic stromal lym-
phopoietin in patients with severe asthma. *Journal
of Allergy and Clinical Immunology, 129,* 104–111.
doi:10.1016/j.jaci.2011.08.031

4. **Article in a Journal Paginated Continuously—No DOI** If
the journal is paginated continuously from issue to

issue, include the volume number but do not add the issue number.

Portal, E. L., Suck, A. T., & Hinkle, J. S. (2010). Counseling in Mexico: History, current identity, and future trends. *Journal of Counseling and Development, 88*, 33–37.

5. **Article in a Journal Paginated Separately by Issue—No DOI** If each of the journal issues is paginated beginning with 1, include the issue number in parentheses after the volume number.

Rush-Wilson, T. C. (2008). The crisis of childhood obesity: What you can do. *Pediatrics for Parents, 24*(1), 3–5.

6. **Article from an Online Journal—No DOI** Add a retrieval line with the web address (URL) for the article. List just the home page URL if the site has a search function.

Banwell, S. (2011). Women, violence, and gray zones: Resolving the paradox of the female victim-perpetrator. *Internet Journal of Criminology, 11*. Retrieved from http://www.internetjournalofcriminology.com

7. **Journal Article with No DOI from an Online Database, Library Database, or Subscription Service** If the article does not have a DOI but is widely available through library databases and subscription services, cite it like a print journal article and do not name the database. Name the database *only* if the source is rare or is available on a small number of databases.

Dowling, J. (2012). The very model of a better mousetrap. *American History, 46*, 56–61.

Wright, W. K. (1916). Psychology and the war. *Psychological Bulletin, 13*(12), 462–466. Retrieved from PsycINFO database.

Magazine Articles

8. **Article in a Monthly or Bimonthly Magazine** Include the publication month after the year. Include the volume number in italics after the magazine title. If each issue of the magazine begins with page 1, add the issue number in parentheses after the volume number.

Lubow, A. (2012, January). An eye for genius. *Smithsonian, 42*(9), 50–62.

9. **Article in a Weekly or Biweekly Magazine** Include the publication month and day after the year. Include the

volume number in italics after the magazine title. If each issue of the magazine begins with page 1, add the issue number in parentheses after the volume number.

> Levy, A. (2012, January 2). Drug test. *The New Yorker,*
> *87*(42), 30–36.

10. **Magazine Article from an Online Database, Library Database, or Subscription Service** Follow the same citation format you would use for a print magazine. Add a retrieval line that names the database *only* if the source is rare or available on a small number of databases.

> Powell, B. (2011, December 26). When supply chains
> break. *Fortune, 164*(10), 29–32.

> Trollope, A. (1861). The civil service as a profession. *The*
> *Cornhill Magazine, 3,* 214–228. Retrieved from the
> Wellesley Index of Victorian Periodicals.

11. **Article in an Online Magazine** If a volume and issue number are available, add them after the online magazine title.

> Albanesius, C. (2012, January 1). Proposed hacker satel-
> lite system would fight web censorship. *PCMag.com.*
> Retrieved from http://www.pcmag.com

12. **Exclusive Online Magazine Content** Use this format for online content not available in the print version of a magazine.

> Levy, S. (2010, February 22). How Google's algorithm rules
> the web [Online exclusive]. *Wired, 18*(3). Retrieved
> from http://www.wired.com/magazine/2010/02
> /ff_google_algorithm/

Newspaper Articles

13. **Article in a Newspaper** For newspaper articles, use *p.* (for a single page) or *pp.* (for multiple pages) before the page numbers. If the article appears on multiple disconnected pages, list each page number separated by a comma.

> Gugliotta, G. (2012, January 10). Finding a way to put a zebra
> in your gas tank. *The New York Times,* pp. D1, D4.

14. **Unsigned Article** Place the title of the article before the date of publication.

> Ex-envoy to U.S. testifies in probe. (2012, January 10). *The*
> *Washington Post,* p. A8.

15. **Article in an Online Newspaper** Include the URL for the newspaper's home page.

> Huppke, R. W. (2012, January 1). Incorporating happiness into the workplace. *Chicago Tribune*. Retrieved from http://www.chicagotribune.com

16. **Newspaper Article from an Online Database, Library Database, or Subscription Service** Follow the same citation format you would use for a newspaper article. Add a retrieval line that names the database *only* if the source is rare or available on a small number of databases.

> McCullough, M. (2012, March 8). Penn, Wistar researchers thwart HIV without antiviral drugs. *Philadelphia Inquirer*, p. A1.

> Smith, C. S. (1898, July 3). Wartime prosperity. *The New York Times*, p. 18. Retrieved from The Historical New York Times database.

17. **Editorial** Insert the word *Editorial* in brackets after the title of the article.

> Editorial: The greatest Olympian [Editorial]. (2012, August 2). *The New York Times*, p. A18.

18. **Letter to the Editor** Insert *Letter to the editor* in brackets after the title.

> Zutis, C. (2012, March 7). Rover no threat to your health [Letter to the editor]. *San Francisco Chronicle*, p. A11.

Other Periodical Sources

19. **Review of a Work** If the review is untitled, use the material in brackets as the title and indicate whether the review is of a book, film, or video; the brackets indicate the material is a description of form and content, not a title.

> Shah, S. (2011). [Review of the motion picture *Contagion*]. *The Lancet, 378*, 1211.

20. **Published Interview** Cite published interviews like articles in journals, newspapers, or magazines, and list the interviewer as the author.

> Worth, J. (2006, November). Punk rock capitalism? *New Internationalist, 395*, 16–17.

BOOK

APA References Entry

Pollan, M. (2008). *In defense of food: An eater's manifesto.*

New York, NY: Penguin Press.

APA In-Text Citation

Pollan (2008) recommends that Americans avoid eating on the go: "Gas stations have become processed-corn stations: ethanol outside for your car and high-fructose corn syrup inside for you" (p. 192).

Books, Parts of Books, and Reports

21. **Book with a DOI** If the book has been assigned a digital object identifier (DOI), omit the publication city and publisher and add the DOI after the book title.

> Bianchi, D. W., Crombleholme, T. M., D'Alton, M. E., & Malone, F. (2010). *Fetology: Diagnosis and management of the fetal patient.* doi:10.1036/0071442014

22. Book with No DOI

> Lewis, M. (2010). *The big short: Inside the doomsday machine.* New York, NY: Norton.

23. Book Accessed Online If the book has a DOI, use the format for entry 21 instead.

> James, W. (1907). *Pragmatism.* Retrieved from http://www.gutenberg.org

24. More Than One Work by the Same Author Include the author's name in each reference and arrange by year of publication, the earliest first.

> Gladwell, M. (2005). *Blink: The power of thinking without thinking.* New York, NY: Little, Brown.

> Gladwell, M. (2008). *Outliers: The story of success.* New York, NY: Little, Brown.

25. Republished Work

> Darwin, C. (2009). *On the origin of species* (W. Bynum, Ed.). New York, NY: Penguin. (Original work published 1859)

26. Anthology, Scholarly Collection, or Work That Names an Editor

> Brettell, C. B., & Sargent, C. F. (Eds.). (2009). *Gender in cross-cultural perspective* (5th ed.). Upper Saddle River, NJ: Prentice Hall.

27. Article or Chapter in an Anthology, Scholarly Collection, or Work That Names an Editor

> Mehrad, B. (2010). Natural killer cells in the respiratory tract. In M. T. Lotze & A. W. Thomson (Eds.), *Natural killer cells: Basic science and clinical application* (pp. 321–329). Burlington, MA: Academic Press.

28. Second or Later Edition Place the number of the edition in parentheses after the book title. If the book is a revised edition, instead of a number, place *Rev. ed.* in parentheses after the book title.

> Bauman, R. W. (2012). *Microbiology with diseases by body system* (3rd ed.). Boston, MA: Benjamin Cummings.

29. Work That Names a Translator

> Bourdieu, P. (1984). *Distinction: A social critique on the judgement of taste* (R. Nice, Trans.). Cambridge, MA:

Harvard University Press. (Original work published 1979)

30. **Work by a Group or Corporate Author** If the group or corporate author published the work, list *Author* as the publisher.

> American Medical Association. (2009). *Principles of CPT coding* (6th ed). Chicago, IL: Author.

31. **Work That Has More Than One Volume**

> Narlikar, A. V., and Fu, Y. Y. (2010). *Oxford handbook of nanoscience and technology* (Vols. 1–3). New York, NY: Oxford University Press.

32. **Introduction, Foreword, Preface, or Afterword** List the author of the section first. Include the page numbers after the title of the book.

> West, C. (2012). Foreword. In M. Alexander, *The new Jim Crow: Mass incarceration in the age of colorblindness* (pp. ix–xi). New York, NY: New Press.

33. **Biblical and Classical Works** Major classical works, such as the Bible and ancient Greek and Roman works, are not listed in the References. Instead, they are cited in the paper when referred to. See 48a for in-text citation format and examples.

34. **Technical or Research Report** If there is a report number, include it in parentheses after the title. If the report has been assigned a digital object identifier (DOI), omit the publication city and publisher and add the DOI at the end of the entry.

> Reda, I. (2010, March). *Solar eclipse monitoring for solar energy applications using solar and moon position algorithms* (Report No. NREL/TP-3B0-47681). doi:10.2172/974908

35. **Technical or Research Report Accessed Online** If there is a report number, include it in parentheses after the title. After "Retrieved from," include the name of the publisher unless the publisher is also the corporate or organizational author of the report. If there is a DOI number, include this instead of the retrieval line.

> Greenberg, M. D., & McGovern, G. (2012). An early assessment of the civil justice system after the financial crisis: Something wicked this way comes? (Report No. OP-353-ICJ). Retrieved from Rand: http://www.rand.org/

36. Government Publication

> Office of the President. (2012). *Budget of the United States government, fiscal year 2013*. Washington, DC: U.S. Government Printing Office.

37. U.S. Government Report Available Online

> U.S. Government Accountability Office. (2011, December 23). *Homeless women veterans: Actions needed to ensure safe and appropriate housing* (Publication No. GAO-12-182). Retrieved from http://www.gao.gov/

38. Signed Article in a Dictionary, Encyclopedia, or Reference Book

> Reibman, J. E. (2010). Fredric Wertham. In M. Keith Booker (Ed.), *Encyclopedia of comic books and graphic novels* (Vol. 2, pp. 683–685). Santa Barbara, CA: Greenwood.

39. Unsigned Article in a Dictionary, Encyclopedia, or Reference Book If using a multivolume work, add the volume number after the book title (see entry 31).

> Whizzbang. (2008). In *Webster's new college dictionary* (3rd ed., p. 1290). Boston, MA: Houghton Mifflin Harcourt.

40. Online Dictionary, Encyclopedia, or Reference Book Article

> Biofuel. (2011). In *Encyclopaedia Britannica online*. Retrieved from http://www.britannica.com

41. Print Brochure

> Starbucks Coffee Company. (2010). Recycling and reducing the environmental impact of our cups [Brochure]. Seattle, WA: Author.

42. Online Brochure

> World Health Organization. (2011). Combat drug resistance [Brochure]. Retrieved from http://www.emro.who.int

43. Published Dissertation Accessed from a Database Add the dissertation file number at the end of the entry.

> Senk, P. A. (2011). *A nursing domain model: Prevention of pressure ulcers* (Doctoral dissertation). Retrieved from ProQuest Dissertations and Theses. (UMI No. 3462814)

APA

Websites and Electronic Communications

44. **Page on a Website** Add the date of access to the retrieval line only if the URL or content is likely to change. APA does not always require the title of the website for citations of non-periodical sources. Include the website title (in italics) when it would help your reader to locate your web source, especially when the source has a different name than the author of the site. Include the URL for only the home page if the site has a search function.

> Goodman, B. (2011, December 28). Study finds bacteria in unused paper towels. Retrieved from http://www .webmd.com

45. **Chapter or Section of an Internet Document**

> National Commission on the Causes of the Financial and Economic Crisis in the United States. (2011, January). Shadow banking. In *The Financial Crisis Inquiry Report* (chap. 2). Retrieved from http://www.gpo.gov

46. **Blog Posting**

> McBride, B. (2012, January 1). Some housing forecasts [Web log post]. Retrieved from http://www .calculatedriskblog.com

47. **Wiki Article** Wikis are websites that are written and edited by many people. Assess the credibility of such sources before including them in your work. Wikis are likely to be updated, so include the retrieval date in your entry.

> Effective demand. (2011, December 9). Retrieved January 2, 2012, from The Economics Wiki: http://economics .wikia.com/wiki/Effective_Demand

48. **Tweet** Include the full tweet in your entry.

> CoryBooker. (2012, March 5). I don't have allegiance to Charters or District Schools. I have allegiance to kids and I support all public schools that serve them [Twitter post]. Retrieved from http://twitter.com/#!/corybooker

49. **Post on a Social Networking Site** Include the full post in your entry.

> Zuckerberg, M. (2012, January 18). The internet is the most powerful tool we have for creating a more open

and connected world [Facebook update]. Retrieved from http://www.facebook.com/#!/zuck

50. **E-Mail and Instant Messaging (IM)** Personal e-mail, instant messaging, and other electronic communications that are not archived are identified as personal communications in the paper and are not listed in the References. See example 12 in Chapter 48a.

Apps and Computer Software

51. **Computer Program or Software** Reference entries are unnecessary for most popular software programs. This citation format applies only to specialized software programs.

> Stardock. (2011). WindowBlinds (Version 7.3) [Computer software]. Retrieved from http://www.stardock.com

52. **App** Follow the format for citing computer software.

> Vito Technology. (2012). Starwalk (Version 5.6.2) [iPad app]. Retrieved from http://itunes.apple.com/

Audio and Visual Sources

53. **Television Series** Start with the creator's name and then, in parentheses, the person's function (for example, *Producer*). After the title, insert *Television series* enclosed in brackets, followed by a period. Add the place the broadcast originated from, a colon, and the broadcasting network.

> Wolf, D. (Creator/Executive producer). (1999–2012). *Law and order: Special victims unit* [Television series]. New York, NY: NBC.

54. **Episode from a Television Series**

> Fellowes, J. (Creator/Writer), & Pearce, A. (Director). (2012, January 8). Episode 2.1 [Television series episode]. In R. Eaton, J. Fellowes, & G. Neame (Executive producers), *Masterpiece classic: Downton Abbey*. Boston, MA: WGBH.

55. **Television Series Episode Online**

> Edge, D. (Writer/Director/Producer). (2012, February 28). Inside Japan's nuclear meltdown [Television series episode]. In D. Fanning & M. Sullivan (Executive producers), *Frontline*. Retrieved from http://www.pbs.org

56. Motion Picture Released Theatrically

Soderbergh, S. (Director), Jacobs, G., Shamberg, M., & Sher, S. (Producers). (2011). *Contagion* [Motion picture]. United States: Warner Brothers.

57. DVD

Fuller, S. (Writer/Director/Producer). (2010). *Shock corridor* [DVD]. United States: Criterion. (Original release date 1963)

58. Online Video Recording

Voltz, S., & Grobe, F. (2006). The Diet Coke and Mentos experiments [Video file]. Retrieved from http://www.eepybird.com/dcm1.html

59. Audio Recording on CD

Tosh, D. (Speaker). (2011, March 8). *Happy thoughts* [CD]. New York, NY: Comedy Central.

60. Music Recording on CD or MP3 List the songwriter(s) first. If the songwriter and the performer are the same person, list the person's name only at the beginning of the entry.

Brown, B., Kelly, C., Lawrence, P., Levine, A., Mars, B., & Wyatt, A. (2010). Grenade [Recorded by B. Mars]. On *Doo-wops & hooligans* [MP3 file]. New York, NY: Atlantic.

Swift, T. (2010). Mean. On *Speak now* [CD]. Nashville, TN: Big Machine Records.

61. Podcast

Inskeep, S., & Montagne, R. (Hosts). (2012, January 2). Up close and personal: Introducing intimate theater [Audio podcast]. *Morning Edition.* Retrieved from http://www.npr.org

Ryssdal, K. (Host). (2011, December 19). *Marketplace* [Audio podcast]. Available from iTunes.

62. Radio Broadcast

Shiffman, K. (Senior Producer). (2011, December 22). *On point with Tom Ashbrook* [Radio program]. Boston, MA: WBUR.

63. Print Map

Greater Atlanta [Map]. (2010). Skokie, IL: Rand McNally.

AUDIO PODCAST

APA References Entry

Gellerman, B. (2012, January 20). China in the Arctic? [Audio

podcast]. *Living on Earth.* Retrieved from http://www

.loe.org   URL

APA In-Text Citation

Depleted Arctic ice beds have stoked the interests of
several nations looking for new shipping lanes and
sources of oil (Gellerman, 2012).

Author

64. Online Map

San Diego [Map]. (2012). Retrieved from http://www
.mapquest.com

65. Print Advertisement

Toyota. (2012, January). Prius V [Advertisement]. Wired,
20(1), 47.

66. Online Advertisement

Apple. (2011). iCloud [Advertisement]. Retrieved from
http://www.apple.com

67. Commercial

Amazon. (2012, January 6). Kindle Fire [Advertisement].
New York, NY: NBC.

Other Media

68. Personal, Telephone, and E-Mail Interviews Personal,
telephone, and e-mail interviews are not included in
the References. Instead, use a parenthetical citation in
the text. See entry 20 for citing a published interview.

69. Lecture Notes or Multimedia Slides

National Diabetes Education Program. (2011, March 3).
The science: Type 2 diabetes prevention [PowerPoint
slides]. Retrieved from http://www.ndep.nih.gov

70. Online Lecture, Speech, or Address

Cator, K. (2011, April 28). Learning 3.0: Why technology
belongs in every classroom. Lecture at MIT. Cambridge, MA. Retrieved from http://mitworld.mit.edu

48d Paper format

Follow the format shown here for a title page, abstract, first
page of the paper, and first page of the References list.

Paper Format Quick Guide—APA

Paper format	Set your top, bottom, left, and right margins at one inch. Double-space all pages, headers, block quotes, notes, and the References. Use a standard, easy-to-read font (like Times New Roman, Cambria, Arial, or Calibri) that is 10- or 12-point size.
	Indent the first line of paragraphs and footnotes ½ inch or five spaces from the left margin. Indent long quotations ½ inch or five spaces from the left margin.
	Order your pages as follows:
	1. Title page
	2. Abstract
	3. Text of paper
	4. References (start on a separate page)
	5. Footnotes (optional; list them together, starting on a separate page)
	6. Appendices (optional; start each on a separate page)
	7. Tables (optional; start each on a separate page)
	8. Figures and figure captions (optional; place each figure with its caption on a separate page)
Title page and titles	Include a title page (all double-spaced) with the title centered between left and right margins and positioned in the upper half of the page. Include your name and college on separate lines. Your instructor may request more information, such as the instructor's name, course, and date. Center all lines.
	Capitalize all words in the title except for articles, conjunctions, and short prepositions (unless they are the first word or follow a colon).
Running head and page numbers	In the upper left margin of the header on the title page, begin a running head. This is an abbreviated version of the title that appears on each page of your document. On the first page, include *Running head*, followed by a colon, and an abbreviated version of the title in all capital letters. On the rest of the pages, just include the abbreviated title.
	Page numbers should be placed in the header at the right margin, beginning with the title page.
Abstract	An abstract is a short summary about the major conclusions of your work. At the top of the second page, center the word *Abstract*. Then double-space and provide your summary.

APA

Headings and subheadings	Headings and subheadings are short titles that define sections and subsections in long reports and papers. Only one level of heading is recommended for short papers, centered on each page in bold font, with each word (except short prepositions, articles, and conjunctions) capitalized. If multiple levels of headings are needed, follow this format as a guide. **Level 1:** **Bold, Centered Title** **Level 2:** **Bold Title on Left Margin** **Level 3:** **Indented title in bold.** **Level 4:** ***Indented title in bold and italics.*** **Level 5:** *Indented title in italics.*
Tables and figures	Labels for tables appear directly above them. The label and the table title (italicized) appear on separate lines (double-spaced). **Table 1** ***Ninth-Grade Science Performance Scores among G-20 Nations*** For figures (including graphs, charts, photos, maps, etc.), create a brief label and place it directly below the figure. Italicize *Figure* and lowercase all words except the first and proper nouns: ***Figure 7.*** **Variance of ninth-grade science performance scores from 1962–2012.**
Footnotes	You may use your word-processing software to insert footnotes. In the text, insert a superscript number (small and raised above the text) to expand on content or indicate a source citation. You may include footnotes on the bottom of each page in which they appear. You may also choose to create a separate page after the References. Insert a title called *Footnotes* and center it on the page. Notes should appear double-spaced. See Chapter 48b.
Bibliography	Insert a title called *References* and center it on the page. All entries should be double-spaced and organized alphabetically. Format entries in hanging indent style, meaning the second and following lines of an entry are indented .5".

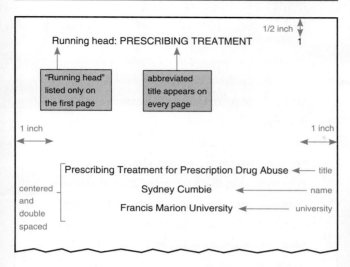

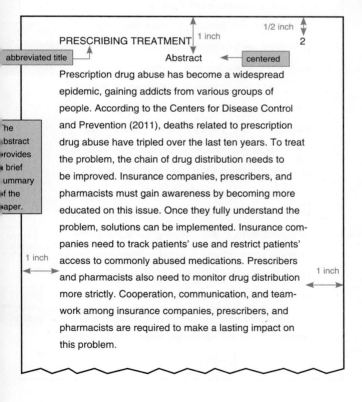

PRESCRIBING TREATMENT 2

Abstract

Prescription drug abuse has become a widespread epidemic, gaining addicts from various groups of people. According to the Centers for Disease Control and Prevention (2011), deaths related to prescription drug abuse have tripled over the last ten years. To treat the problem, the chain of drug distribution needs to be improved. Insurance companies, prescribers, and pharmacists must gain awareness by becoming more educated on this issue. Once they fully understand the problem, solutions can be implemented. Insurance companies need to track patients' use and restrict patients' access to commonly abused medications. Prescribers and pharmacists also need to monitor drug distribution more strictly. Cooperation, communication, and teamwork among insurance companies, prescribers, and pharmacists are required to make a lasting impact on this problem.

APA

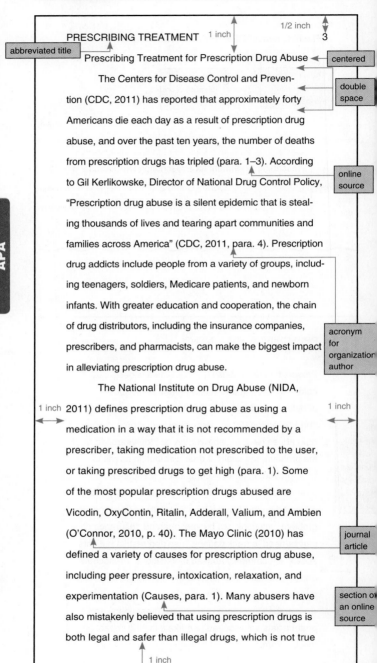

PRESCRIBING TREATMENT — *abbreviated title*

1/2 inch · 3

Prescribing Treatment for Prescription Drug Abuse — *centered*

The Centers for Disease Control and Preven- — *double space*
tion (CDC, 2011) has reported that approximately forty
Americans die each day as a result of prescription drug
abuse, and over the past ten years, the number of deaths
from prescription drugs has tripled (para. 1–3). According — *online source*
to Gil Kerlikowske, Director of National Drug Control Policy,
"Prescription drug abuse is a silent epidemic that is stealing thousands of lives and tearing apart communities and
families across America" (CDC, 2011, para. 4). Prescription
drug addicts include people from a variety of groups, including teenagers, soldiers, Medicare patients, and newborn
infants. With greater education and cooperation, the chain
of drug distributors, including the insurance companies, — *acronym for organization author*
prescribers, and pharmacists, can make the biggest impact
in alleviating prescription drug abuse.

The National Institute on Drug Abuse (NIDA,
2011) defines prescription drug abuse as using a
medication in a way that it is not recommended by a
prescriber, taking medication not prescribed to the user,
or taking prescribed drugs to get high (para. 1). Some
of the most popular prescription drugs abused are
Vicodin, OxyContin, Ritalin, Adderall, Valium, and Ambien
(O'Connor, 2010, p. 40). The Mayo Clinic (2010) has — *journal article*
defined a variety of causes for prescription drug abuse,
including peer pressure, intoxication, relaxation, and
experimentation (Causes, para. 1). Many abusers have — *section of an online source*
also mistakenly believed that using prescription drugs is
both legal and safer than illegal drugs, which is not true

1 inch

References

abbreviated title

centered

All sources are alphabetized and all entries are double spaced

Anderson, C. (2011, April 19). US targets "pill mills,"

prescription drug abuses. *Miami Herald*. Retrieved

from http://www.miamiherald.com/

double space

Andrews, M. (2011, April 5). Some doctors ask patients to

sign "pain contracts" to get prescriptions. *Kaiser Health

News*. Retrieved from http://www.kaiserhealthnews.org/

Back, S. E., Lawson, K. M., Singleton, L. M., & Brady,

K. T. (2011). Characteristics and correlates of men

and women with prescription opioid dependence.

Addictive Behaviors, 36, 829–834. doi://10.1016/j

.addbeh.2011.03.013

journal article with a DOI

APA

Centers for Disease Control and Prevention. (2011,

November 1). Prescription painkiller overdoses at epi-

demic levels. Retrieved from http://www.cdc.gov/

article on a website

Davis, H. L. (2011, March 23). Controlling pain without

creating addicts. *Buffalo News*, p. A1.

article from a newspaper

Mayo Clinic. (2010, June 25). Prescription drug abuse.

Retrieved from http://www.mayoclinic.com/

National Institute on Drug Abuse. (2011, May). Prescrip-

tion drug abuse. Retrieved from http://www

.drugabuse.gov/

O'Connor, G. (2010). Doctors' role in the prescription

abuse crisis. *Addiction Professional, 8*(4), 40–41.

article from journal with nonconsecutive pagination

Pear, R. (2011, October 3). Report on Medicare cites pre-

scription drug abuse. *The New York Times*. Retrieved

from http://www.nytimes.com/

newspaper article online

U.S. Drug Enforcement Administration. (2011, October

19). DEA to hold its third nationwide Prescription Drug

Take-Back Day this month. Retrieved http://www

.justice.gov/dea/

1 inch

1 inch

1 inch

49

Chicago Manual of Style (CMOS)

In disciplines such as history and other humanities, the preferred style is that of *The Chicago Manual of Style* (16th ed., 2010), which is also explained in the *Student's Guide to Writing College Papers* (4th ed., 2010).

When you use CMOS style, you may use notes or endnotes to acknowledge sources in the text, or you may use in-text citations that refer the reader to a bibliography at the end of the paper.

49a In-text citations

When using *Chicago Manual* style, you can opt to use numbered notes or the author-date citation format.

Numbered notes

- **Numbering in the text.** Numbered notes indicate publication information and add explanations and other material that would otherwise interrupt the main text. Number citations consecutively with superscript numbers ([1]). Put the note number at the end of the sentence or end of a clause immediately following the punctuation mark. Don't insert a space between the punctuation mark and the superscript number.

  > Appropriate government regulation may be the key to turning resource-rich countries into successful, profitable economies for its citizens.[6] Peter Maass has noted that "countries dependent on resource exports . . . are susceptible to lower growth, higher corruption, less freedom, and more warfare."[7]

- **Placing notes.** List notes at the bottom of the page as footnotes or at the end of the essay as endnotes.

- **Spacing notes.** Single-space each note. Indent the first line of each note the same space that you indent paragraphs. Use your word-processing software to format this section of your paper.

- **Ordering the parts of notes.** Begin with the author's first and last names, add the title, and then include the publishing information and page numbers.

- **Punctuating, capitalizing, and abbreviating.** Use commas between elements, and put publishing information within parentheses. Include the page number, but omit the abbreviation *p.* or *pp.* Italicize titles of books and periodicals. Capitalize titles of articles, books, and journals. Use quotation marks around titles of periodical articles and sections of books.

- **Using a bibliography page.** A bibliography page is usually added to a paper containing notes.

- **Adapting the style to the source material.** *Chicago Manual* style allows for some flexibility in creating bibliography entries, particularly for works accessed online. In bibliography and notes entries, include all relevant source materials needed to retrieve the source.

Ordering Notes in a Paper The first time you cite a source, include the authors' full names, followed by a comma; the full title; publication information, enclosed in parentheses; a comma; and the page or pages being cited, omitting *p.* or *pp.* Later citations include authors' last names, a shortened version of the title, and page numbers.

Use *Ibid.* to refer to the work in the directly preceding note or, if the page is different, use *Ibid.* followed by a comma and the page number.

> 6. Paul Collier, *The Plundered Planet: Why We Must—and How We Can—Manage Nature for Global Prosperity* (New York: Oxford University Press, 2010), 5.
> 7. Peter Maass, *Crude World: The Violent Twilight of Oil* (New York: Knopf, 2009), 6.
> 8. Collier, *Plundered Planet*, 132–33.
> 9. Ibid., 122.
> 10. Maass, *Crude World*, 7.

Author-date citation format

The author-date citation format requires both in-text citations and a bibliography page. For in-text citations:

- Up to three authors are cited by last name. If there are four or more authors, list only the first author's last name, followed by *et al.*

- The date of publication is given next, with no intervening punctuation.

- If a page number is required, it is given following a comma.

  (Newhouse and Zuzu 1889)   (Baez et al. 2011, 244)

  (Patel 2012, 18)   As explained by Patel (2012, 18), . . .

For online or electronic works without page numbers, indicate the section title (if available) under which the specific reference can be located:

  (Quinn 2010, under "Espionage")

49b Bibliography entries

Title your list "Bibliography," "Works Cited," or "References." In the bibliography, list authors with last name first. Elements in the bibliography are separated by periods.

Start the first line of each entry at the left margin, and indent all other lines in the entry. Double-space all entries. Italicize titles of books and periodicals. Use quotation marks around titles of periodicals and sections of books.

CMOS

CMOS

References Examples

In the following examples, *N* stands for note format and *B* stands for bibliography format.

Books, Parts of Books, and Reports

1. One Author

N: 1. Nicholas A. Lambert, *Planning Armageddon: British Economic Warfare and the First World War* (Cambridge: Harvard University Press, 2012), 62.

B: Lambert, Nicholas A. *Planning Armageddon: British Economic Warfare and the First World War*. Cambridge: Harvard University Press, 2012.

2. **Two Authors**

N: 2. Theda Skocpol and Vanessa Williamson, *The Tea Party and the Remaking of Republican Conservatism* (New York: Oxford University Press, 2012), 12.

B: Skocpol, Theda, and Vanessa Williamson. *The Tea Party and the Remaking of Republican Conservatism*. New York: Oxford University Press, 2012.

3. **Three Authors**

N: 3. Philippa Gregory, David Baldwin, and Michael Jones, *The Women of the Cousins' War: The Duchess, the Queen, and the King's Mother* (New York: Simon & Schuster, 2011), 20–21.

B: Gregory, Philippa, David Baldwin, and Michael Jones. *The Women of the Cousins' War: The Duchess, the Queen, and the King's Mother*. New York: Simon & Schuster, 2011.

4. **Four or More Authors** In the notes format, list the first author and add *et al.* or *and others* with no intervening punctuation.

N: 4. James A. Baker III et al., *The Iraq Study Group Report: The Way Forward—a New Approach* (New York: Vintage, 2006), 27.

In the bibliography format, list all authors for a work with between four and ten authors. If the work has eleven or more authors, list the first seven authors and add *et al.*

B: Baker, James A., III, Lee H. Hamilton, Lawrence S. Eagleburger, Vernon E. Jordan Jr., Edwin Meese III, Sandra Day O'Connor, Leon E. Panetta, William J. Perry, Charles S. Robb, and Alan K. Simpson. *The Iraq Study Group Report: The Way Forward—a New Approach*. New York: Vintage, 2006.

CMOS

FAQ

What types of extra information do I need to cite online sources?

When citing sources you accessed online, additional information may be needed in your notes and bibliography entries.

Digital Object Identifier (DOI) Number—A DOI number is a unique code a publisher assigns to a book, journal article, or other source. If a DOI number is available for your source, list it at the end of your entry. (See entries 20 and 23.)

URL—If no DOI is available for your online source, include the full URL (or online address) at the end of your entry. (See entries 20 and 23.)

Date of Access—If your online source does not contain a date of publication or update, or if your instructor requests it, include the date you accessed your source. In notes entries, after the source title, include *accessed* and the date, followed by a comma. In bibliography entries, after the source title, include *Accessed* and the date, followed by a period.

5. **Online Book** When accessing a book online, include the book's Digital Object Identifier (DOI) number at the end of the entry. If no DOI is available, provide the book's URL at the end of the citation. For an older book that has been edited for online reproduction, give the original year of publication, and then add the name of the website and year of online publication.

N: 5. William Caferro, *Contesting the Renaissance* (Malden, MA: Wiley/Blackwell, 2011), 62, doi:10.1002/9781444324501

B: Caferro, William. *Contesting the Renaissance*. Malden, MA: Wiley/Blackwell, 2011. doi:10.1002/9781444324501

6. **Book for an Electronic Reader** Name the edition type at the end of the citation.

N: 6. Daniel Kahneman, *Thinking, Fast and Slow* (New York: Farrar, Straus and Giroux, 2011), Kindle edition.

B: Kahneman, Daniel. *Thinking, Fast and Slow*. New York: Farrar, Straus and Giroux, 2011. Kindle edition.

7. **Book with an Editor**
N: 7. George Ritzer and Zeynep Atalay, eds., *Readings in Globalization: Key Concepts and Major Debates* (Malden, MA: Wiley-Blackwell, 2010), 1.

B: Ritzer, George, and Zeynep Atalay, eds. *Readings in Globalization: Key Concepts and Major Debates*. Malden, MA: Wiley-Blackwell, 2010.

8. **Second or Later Edition**
N: 8. John Mack Faragher, Mari Jo Buhle, Daniel H. Czitrom, and Susan H. Armitage, *Out of Many: A History of the American People*, 7th ed. (Upper Saddle River, NJ: Prentice Hall, 2012), 139–41.

CMOS

B: Faragher, John Mack, Mari Jo Buhle, Daniel H. Czitrom, and
Susan H. Armitage. *Out of Many: A History of the American
People*. 7th ed. Upper Saddle River, NJ: Prentice Hall, 2012.

9. Reprinted Book

N: 9. Edith Wharton, *House of Mirth* (1905; repr., London: Vintage, 2011), 64–65.

B: Wharton, Edith. *House of Mirth*. 1905. Reprint, London:
Vintage, 2011.

10. Online Reprinted Book For an older book edited for online reproduction, give the original year of publication, and then add the name of the website and year of online publication. Add a URL at the end.

N: 10. Edith Wharton, *The Age of Innocence* (1920; Bartleby,
2000), 64, http://www.bartleby.com/1005/.

B: Wharton, Edith. *The Age of Innocence*. Reprint of the 1920
New York edition, Bartleby, 2000. http://www.bartleby
.com/1005/

11. Selection or Book Chapter in an Anthology/Scholarly Collection

N: 11. Robert E. Wright, "Capitalism and the Rise of the
Corporation Nation," in *Capitalism Takes Command: The Social
Transformation of Nineteenth-Century America*, ed. Michael
Zakim and Gary J. Kornbluth (Chicago: University of Chicago
Press, 2012), 146.

B: Wright, Robert E. "Capitalism and the Rise of the Corporation
Nation." In *Capitalism Takes Command: The Social Transformation of Nineteenth-Century America*, edited by Michael
Zakim and Gary J. Kornbluth, 145–68. Chicago: University
of Chicago Press, 2012.

12. Multivolume Book In the notes format, when citing a book without an individual volume title, omit the volume number after the book title. Instead, after the facts of publication, insert the volume number, followed by a colon, and the page numbers (e.g., 2:45–96).

N: 12. Spielvogel, Jackson J., *Western Civilization*, vol. 1, *To
1715*, 8th ed. (New York: Wadsworth, 2011), 134–35.

B: Spielvogel, Jackson J. *Western Civilization*. Vol. 1, *To 1715*.
8th ed. New York: Wadsworth, 2011.

CMOS

13. Online Government Document

N: 13. Federal Trade Commission, *Annual Report 2011: Fair Debt Collection Practices Act* (Washington, DC: Federal Trade Commission, March 14, 2011), 6, http://www.ftc.gov/os/2011/03/110321fairdebtcollectreport.pdf

B: Federal Trade Commission. *Annual Report 2011: Fair Debt Collection Practices Act*. Washington, DC: Federal Trade Commission, March 14, 2011. http://www.ftc.gov/os/2011/03/110321fairdebtcollectreport.pdf

14. Article in a Reference Book Don't include the volume or page number. Instead, cite the term in the reference book under which the information is contained. Use the abbreviation *s.v.* for *sub verbo*, meaning "under the word," and place the term in quotation marks. Well-known reference books are not listed in the bibliography.

N: 14. *Encyclopaedia Britannica*, 15th ed., s.v. "Parks, Rosa."

15. Article in an Online Reference Book Follow the example in entry 14 but omit the edition number. Add an access date and the URL.

N: 15. *Encyclopaedia Britannica Online*, s.v. "Parks, Rosa," accessed February 4, 2012, http://www.britannica.com/EBchecked/topic/444180/Rosa-Parks

16. Source Quoted from Another Source Quotations from secondary sources should ordinarily be avoided. If, however, the original source is unavailable, list both sources in the entry.

N: 16. H. H. Dubs, "An Ancient Chinese Mystery Cult," *Harvard Theological Review* 35 (1942): 223, quoted in Susan Naquin, *Millenarian Rebellion in China: The Eight Trigrams Uprising of 1813* (New Haven, CT: Yale University Press, 1976), 288.

B: Dubs, H. H. "An Ancient Chinese Mystery Cult." *Harvard Theological Review* 35 (1942): 223. Quoted in Susan Naquin, *Millenarian Rebellion in China: The Eight Trigrams Uprising of 1813*. New Haven, CT: Yale University Press, 1976, 288.

17. Biblical or Other Scriptural Reference Include the book (abbreviated with no underlining or italics), chapter, and verse, but no page number. Scriptural references are usually cited in the notes or in the parenthetical citation.

N: 17. Gen. 21:14–18.

CMOS

Journal Articles

18. Article in a Journal

N: 18. Donald A. Zinman, "The Heir Apparent Presidency of James Madison," *Presidential Studies Quarterly* 41, no. 4 (2011): 714.

B: Zinman, Donald A. "The Heir Apparent Presidency of James Madison." *Presidential Studies Quarterly* 41, no. 4 (2011): 712–26.

TRY THIS

Citing Articles Located in a Library Database or Subscription Service

Start your notes or bibliography entry by following the citation format for the print version of the source.

- Include an access date only if a publication date is not available. **accessed May 1, 2012**

- For sources available by subscription (as in a library database) or for material that does not contain a stable URL or DOI, name the database at the end of the entry, followed by a period. **LexisNexis.   Newsbank.**

- If the source contains a stable URL or a Digital Object Identifier (DOI) number, list it instead of the URL that appears in your Internet browser.

  http://0-www.jstor.org.libcatalog.fmarion.edu/stable/30030042

  doi:10.1111/j.1540-5907.2010.00472.x

---

19. Journal Article Located in a Library Database or Subscription Service If the article has numbered pages (including those you can see in a PDF file), include them after the year of publication. Name the article's Digital Object Identifier (DOI) number at the end of the entry. If no DOI is available, name the database in which you located the article.

N: 19. David Lewis, "High Times on the Silk Road: The Central Asian Paradox," *World Policy Journal* 27, no. 1 (2010), 39–49, Project Muse.

N: 20. Marc F. Plattner, "Populism, Pluralism, and Liberal Democracy," *Journal of Democracy* 21, no. 1 (2010), 81–92, doi:10.1353/jod.0.0154.

B: Lewis, David. "High Times on the Silk Road: The Central Asian Paradox." *World Policy Journal* 27, no. 1 (2010): 39–49. Project Muse.

B: Plattner, Marc F. "Populism, Pluralism, and Liberal Democracy."

Journal of Democracy 21, no. 1 (2010): 81–92. doi:10.1353

/jod.0.0154.

20. **Article from an Online Journal with a DOI or URL** If the article has numbered pages (including those you can see in a PDF file), include them after the year of publication. Name the article's Digital Object Identifier (DOI) number at the end of the entry. If no DOI is available, provide the full URL for the article.

N: 21. Robert M. Haberle and Melinda A. Kahre, "Detecting Secular Climate Change on Mars," MARS: The International Journal of Mars Science and Exploration 5 (August 2010): 69, doi:10.1555/mars.2010.0003.

N: 22. Irene Watson, "Aboriginality and the Violence of Colonialism," Borderlands 8, no. 1 (May 2009): 6, http://www .borderlandsejournal.adelaide.edu.au/vol8no1_2009 /iwatson_aboriginality.pdf.

B: Haberle, Robert M., and Melinda A. Kahre. "Detecting Secular

Climate Change on Mars." MARS: The International Journal

of Mars Science and Exploration 5 (August 2010): 68–75.

doi:10.1555/mars.2010.0003.

B: Watson, Irene. "Aboriginality and the Violence of Colonialism."

Borderlands 8, no. 1 (May 2009): 1–8. http://www

.borderlandsejournal.adelaide.edu.au/vol8no1_2009

/iwatson_aboriginality.pdf (accessed March 2, 2010).

Magazine Articles

21. **Article in a Magazine** While referenced page numbers should be included in the notes entry, omit page numbers for the bibliographic entry.

N: 23. Michael Specter, "The Deadliest Virus," New Yorker, March 12, 2012, 33.

B: Specter, Michael. "The Deadliest Virus." New Yorker, March

12, 2012.

22. **Magazine Article Located in a Library Database or Subscription Service** If the magazine has numbered pages, provide a page reference in the notes. Otherwise, provide a reference to headings or numbered paragraphs, if available, in the notes. Name the article's Digital Object Identifier (DOI) number at the end of the entry. If no DOI is available, name the database in which you located the article.

N: 24. Sean McLachlan, "Roman History: Hiking Across History on the Hadrian's Wall Path," *British Heritage*, May 2010, 38, Academic OneFile.

B: McLachlan, Sean. "Roman History: Hiking Across History on the Hadrian's Wall Path." *British Heritage*, May 2010. Academic OneFile.

23. **Article from an Online Magazine** If the magazine has numbered pages, provide a page reference in the notes. Otherwise, provide a reference to headings or numbered paragraphs, if available, in the notes. Name the article's Digital Object Identifier (DOI) number at the end of the entry. If no DOI is available, provide the full URL for the article.

N: 25. Jonah Lehrer, "The Forgetting Pill Erases Painful Memories Forever," *Wired*, February 17, 2012, http://www.wired.com/magazine/2012/02/ff_forgettingpill/.

B: Lehrer, Jonah. "The Forgetting Pill Erases Painful Memories Forever." *Wired*, February 17, 2012. http://www.wired.com/magazine /2012/02/ff_forgettingpill/.

Newspaper Articles

24. **Article in a Newspaper** No page numbers are listed. If you are citing a specific edition of the paper, you may add a comma after the year and list the edition (e.g., late edition, Southeast edition), followed by a period.

N: 26. Kenneth Chang, "For Space Mess, Scientists Seek Celestial Boom," *New York Times*, February 19, 2012.

B: Chang, Kenneth. "For Space Mess, Scientists Seek Celestial Boom." *New York Times*, February 29, 2012.

25. **Newspaper Article Located in a Library Database or Subscription Service**

N: 27. Elizabeth A. Harris, "Alone in Public Housing, with a Spare Bedroom," *New York Times*, March 12, 2012, Lexis-Nexis Academic.

B: Harris, Elizabeth A. "Alone in Public Housing, with a Spare Bedroom." *New York Times*, March 12, 2012. LexisNexis Academic.

26. **Article from an Online Newspaper**
N: 28. David Perlman, "Chorus Frog Carries Killer Fungus," *San Francisco Chronicle*, March 13, 2012, http://www.sfgate .com/cgi-bin/article.cgi?file=/c/a/2012/03/13/MNKO1NJKED .DTL

B: Perlman, David. "Chorus Frog Carries Killer Fungus." *San Francisco Chronicle*, March 13, 2012. http://www.sfgate .com/cgi-bin/article.cgi?file=/c/a/2012/03/13 /MNKO1NJKED.DTL

Other Periodical Sources

27. **Book Review**
N: 29. Evan Rhodes, review of *Fight Pictures: A History of Boxing and Early Cinema*, by Dan Streible, *Modernism/Modernity* 17, no. 1 (2010): 264–66.

B: Rhodes, Evan. Review of *Fight Pictures: A History of Boxing and Early Cinema*, by Dan Streible. *Modernism/Modernity* 17, no. 1 (2010): 264–66.

28. **Published Interview** Follow the basic format for an article in a periodical or on a website. List the name of the person or people being interviewed first.

N: 30. Daniel Craig and Harrison Ford, "Close Encounter," by Benjamin Svetkey, *Entertainment Weekly*, July 29, 2011, 3.

B: Craig, Daniel, and Harrison Ford. "Close Encounter." By Benjamin Svetkey. *Entertainment Weekly*, July 29, 2011.

Websites and Electronic Communications

29. **Page on a Website**
N: 31. "Plants: Native Seed Gene Bank," *San Diego Zoo*, Zoological Society of San Diego, accessed November 13, 2011, http://www.sandiegozoo.org/CF/plants/seed_bank.html

N: 32. Andrew Hollinger, "United States Holocaust Memorial Museum Lauds New International Tracing Service Agreement," *United States Holocaust Memorial Museum*, December 9, 2011, http://www.ushmm.org/museum/press/archives/detail .php?category=07-general&content=2011-12-09

B: *San Diego Zoo*. Zoological Society of San Diego. Accessed November 13, 2011, http://www.sandiegozoo.org/.

B: *United States Holocaust Memorial Museum*. Accessed December 15, 2011, http://www.ushmm.org/.

CMOS

CMOS

30. **Blog Entry** Start the entry with the name or pseudonym of the writer. Add the word *blog* in parentheses after the title of the blog. Provide specific citation information for the notes, but only give information about the blog's home page in the bibliography.

N: 33. The Little Professor, "Authorial Intent," *The Little Professor* (blog), April 23, 2010, accessed May 2, 2010, http://littleprofessor.typepad.com/the_little_professor/2010/04/authorial-intent.html

N: 34. McBride, Bill, "Mortgage Settlement Filed with Court," *Calculated Risk* (blog), March 12, 2012, accessed April 1, 2012, http://www.calculatedriskblog.com/2012/03/mortgage-settlement-filed-with-court.html

B: The Little Professor. *The Little Professor* (blog). http://littleprofessor.typepad.com.

B: McBride, Bill. *Calculated Risk* (blog). http://www.calculatedriskblog.com.

31. **Comment on a Blog or Website** Start the notes entry with the name or pseudonym of the commenter. Add the word *blog* or *website* in parentheses after the site title. Provide specific citation information for the notes, but only give information about the blog or website's home page in the bibliography.

N: 35. Zhiv, April 27, 2010 (7:08 p.m.), comment on Little Professor, "Authorial Intent," *The Little Professor* (blog), April 23, 2010, accessed May 2, 2010, http://littleprofessor.typepad.com/the_little_professor/2010/04/authorial-intent.html#comments.

N: 36. Firemane, March 12, 2012 (1:25 p.m.), comment on Bill McBride, "Mortgage Settlement Filed with Court," *Calculated Risk* (blog), March 12, 2012, accessed April 1, 2012, http://www.hoocoodanode.org/node/15349.

B: The Little Professor. *The Little Professor* (blog). http://littleprofessor.typepad.com.

B: McBride, Bill. *Calculated Risk* (blog). http://www.calculatedriskblog.com.

32. **Tweet** Information about tweets usually appears only in the notes or parenthetical citations, not in the bibliography. Add an electronic address and access date and time at the end of the entry.

N: 37. Cory Booker, Twitter post, March 5, 2012. 2:42 p.m., http://twitter.com/#!/corybooker

33. **E-Mail Message or Posting to a Mailing List** E-mail messages and postings to mailing lists usually appear only in the notes or parenthetical citations, not in the bibliography. Add an electronic address and access date at the end of the entry if the posting is archived on a website.

N: 38. Dora Dodger-Gilbert, e-mail message to Veterinary Questions and Viewpoints mailing list, January 3, 2012.
    39. Daniel Kaplan, e-mail message to author, February 23, 2012.

APPS

34. **App** The *Chicago Manual* does not yet provide explicit instructions for citing an app. These guidelines follow the manual's recommendations about multimedia sources.

N: 40. "Hubble," *StarWalk*, Version 5.6.2, iPad app, Vito Technology, 2012.

B: "Hubble." *StarWalk*. Version 5.6.2. iPad app. Vito Technology, 2012.

Audio and Visual Sources

35. **Television Episode**
N: 41. *Game of Thrones*, Episode no. 1.10, directed by Alan Taylor and written by David Benioff and D. B. Weiss, HBO, June 19, 2011.

B: *Game of Thrones*. Episode no. 1.10. Directed by Alan Taylor and written by David Benioff and D. B. Weiss. HBO. June 19, 2011.

36. **Television Interview**
N: 42. Hillary Clinton, interview by David Gregory, *Meet the Press*, NBC, October 23, 2011.

B: Clinton, Hillary. Interview by David Gregory. *Meet the Press*. NBC. October 23, 2011.

37. **Film on Videotape or DVD**
N: 43. *The Young Victoria*, DVD, directed by Jean-Marc Vallée (2009; Culver City, CA: Sony Pictures, 2010).

B: *The Young Victoria*. DVD. Directed by Jean-Marc Vallée. 2009. Culver City, CA: Sony Pictures, 2010.

38. **Online Video** Add the provider and file format at the end of the entry.

N: 44. Bryan Stevenson, "We Need to Talk About an Injustice," March 2012, TED video, 23:41 (Posted March 2012), http://www.ted.com/talks/bryan_stevenson_we_need_to_talk _about_an_injustice.html.

B: Stevenson, Bryan. "We Need to Talk About an Injustice." Filmed March 2012. TED video, 23:41. Posted March 2012. http://www.ted.com/talks/bryan_stevenson_we_need_to _talk_about_an_injustice.html.

39. **Sound Recording** Include the product number (often located on the spine of a CD) at the end of the entry.

N: 45. Johann Sebastian Bach, *Four Concerti for Various Instruments*, Orchestra of St. Luke's, dir. Michael Feldman, Musical Heritage Society, CD 512268T.

B: Bach, Johann Sebastian. *Four Concerti for Various Instruments*. Orchestra of St. Luke's, dir. Michael Feldman. Musical Heritage Society, CD 512268T.

40. **Podcast, MP3, or Other Downloaded Material** Add the provider and file format at the end of the entry.

N: 46. Melvyn Bragg, Carolin Crawford, Paul Murdin, and Michael Rowan-Robinson, "The Cool Universe," *BBC Radio 4: In Our Time* (May 6, 2010), iTunes MP3.

N: 47. Ellie Goulding, *Lights* (New York: Interscope, 2011), iTunes MP3.

B: Bragg, Melvyn, Carolin Crawford, Paul Murdin, and Michael Rowan-Robinson. "The Cool Universe." *BBC Radio 4: In Our Time*. May 6, 2010. iTunes MP3.

B: Goulding, Ellie. *Lights*. New York: Interscope, 2011. iTunes MP3.

Other Media

41. **Advertisement** List advertisements in the bibliography only if they are retrievable.

N: 48. H&R Block, "Greenback," television advertisement, Fallon Minneapolis, directed by Mark Romanek, 2011.

B: H&R Block. "Greenback." Television advertisement. Fallon Minneapolis, directed by Mark Romanek, 2011.

42. **Personal or Telephone Interview** In the author-date format, personal communications are acknowledged in the text but not in the bibliography.

N: 49. Kenneth Autrey, interview by the author, May 12, 2012, Florence, South Carolina.

N: 50. John Sutton, telephone interview by the author, January 12, 2012.

49c   Paper format

Follow the format shown here for a title page, first and second pages of the paper, and the bibliography. Also refer to the *Student's Guide to Writing College Papers* (4th ed., 2010) for additional guidelines.

Paper Format Quick Guide—CMOS	
Paper format	Use 12-point serif font (like Times New Roman or Cambria) throughout your paper. Set margins between 1 and 1.5 inches.
Title page and titles	Include a title page for papers with five or more pages. Place the title 1/3 down the page, and insert your personal information (name, class, instructor, and date) 2/3 down the page. Center all lines. For papers with less than five pages, insert your title at the top center of the page. Insert four blank lines and then insert your information (name, class, instructor, and date). Insert four blank lines and begin the first paragraph. Capitalize all words in the title except for articles, conjunctions, and short prepositions (unless they are the first word, last word, or follow a colon). If you have a subtitle, include the title and a colon, and then place the subtitle on the line immediately below it.
Header and page numbers	If you have a title page, count the title page as page 0 and the first page of the paper as page 1. Begin the header on page 2. If you don't have a title page, begin the paper on page 1 and begin the header on page 2. Place the header on the right margin in 10-point font. Include your name, a hyphen, and the page number, as shown: **Smith-2**
Tables and figures	Insert tables and figures within the body of the text. For a table, create a brief label and place it directly above the table: **Table 1: Unemployment rates by state in 2012**

CMOS

	For figures, create a brief label and place it directly below the figure: **Figure 7: Average per capita income for counties in Arkansas**
Notes	Use your word-processing software to insert the notes. In the text, insert a superscript number (small and raised above the text) to indicate a source citation.
	For footnotes, the note information should appear at the bottom of the page, single-spaced, and in 10-point font.
	If you use endnotes instead, create a new page before the bibliography and center *Endnotes* at the top. Single-space notes with a blank line between each.
Bibliography	Insert a title called *Bibliography* and center it on the page. Double-space and alphabetize entries in hanging-indent style.

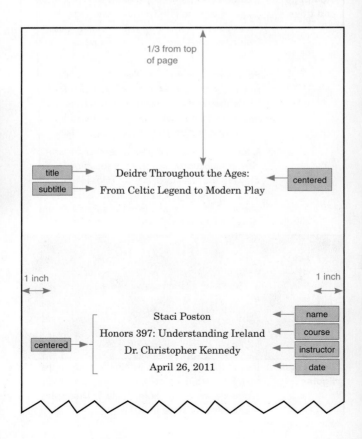

1/3 from top of page

title ——▶ Deidre Throughout the Ages: ◀—— centered
subtitle ——▶ From Celtic Legend to Modern Play

1 inch

1 inch

Staci Poston ◀—— name
centered ——▶ Honors 397: Understanding Ireland ◀—— course
Dr. Christopher Kennedy ◀—— instructor
April 26, 2011 ◀—— date

1 inch

Mythological stories contain universal themes and archetypes that recur throughout their telling and retelling. As Joseph Campbell explains, "The themes are timeless, and the inflection is to the culture."[1] The story of Deirdre, a well-known Irish legend, contains similarities to other stories and fairy tales because of this function of mythology. Besides existing in Irish history as far back as the Ulster Cycle, the story has continued to be reproduced and used by modern storytellers, such as playwright J. M. Synge's *Deirdre of the Sorrows* (1910). Though the ideas, themes, and archetypes remain constant, the story itself changes and adapts over time, depending on the context, culture, and medium in which it is told.

The legend of Deirdre is told in *The Tragic Death of the Sons of Usnech*, which is estimated to have been first composed in the 8th or 9th century. However, the oldest extant version of the legend is preserved in the *The Book of Leinster* (c. 1160), a part of the Ulster Cycle.[2] *The Book of Leinster* is a compilation of both sacred and secular Irish verse and prose from manuscripts and oral traditions that was written and completed in the mid-12th century.[3]

The original legend of Deirdre begins with a prophecy. At a feast, a druid named Cathbad tells Deirdre's parents of the beauty and danger that their child will have: "A fair woman is she, for whom heroes that fight / In their chariots for Ulster, to death shall be dight."[4] Though the men of Ulster protest this and request that the infant be killed, her father, Fedlimid, arranges for her to be raised in

1. Joseph Campbell, *The Power of Myth*, ed. Betty Sue Flowers (New York: Anchor Books, 1988), 13.

2. *Encyclopaedia Britannica Online*, s.v. "Deirdre," accessed March 3, 2011, http://www.britannica.com/EBchecked/topic/156147/Deirdre.

3. *Encyclopaedia Britannica Online*, s.v. "The Book of Leinster," accessed March 3, 2011, http://www.britannica.com/EBchecked/topic/335440/The-Book-of-Leinster.

4. "Deirdre—or, The Exile of the Sons of Usnech," in *The Book of Leinster* (1160; Celtic Literature Collective, 2011), http://www.maryjones.us/ctexts/usnech.html.

1 inch

CMOS

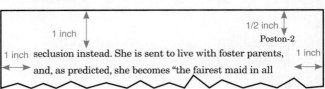

seclusion instead. She is sent to live with foster parents, and, as predicted, she becomes "the fairest maid in all

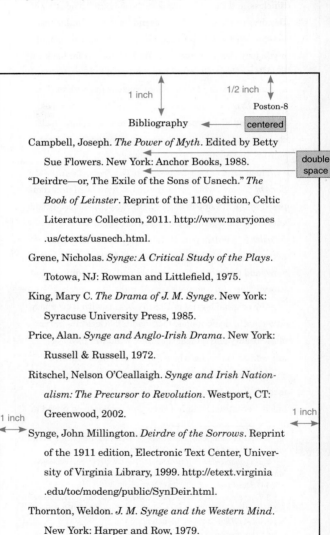

Bibliography ← centered

Campbell, Joseph. *The Power of Myth*. Edited by Betty Sue Flowers. New York: Anchor Books, 1988.

"Deirdre—or, The Exile of the Sons of Usnech." *The Book of Leinster*. Reprint of the 1160 edition, Celtic Literature Collection, 2011. http://www.maryjones .us/ctexts/usnech.html.

Grene, Nicholas. *Synge: A Critical Study of the Plays*. Totowa, NJ: Rowman and Littlefield, 1975.

King, Mary C. *The Drama of J. M. Synge*. New York: Syracuse University Press, 1985.

Price, Alan. *Synge and Anglo-Irish Drama*. New York: Russell & Russell, 1972.

Ritschel, Nelson O'Ceallaigh. *Synge and Irish Nationalism: The Precursor to Revolution*. Westport, CT: Greenwood, 2002.

Synge, John Millington. *Deirdre of the Sorrows*. Reprint of the 1911 edition, Electronic Text Center, University of Virginia Library, 1999. http://etext.virginia .edu/toc/modeng/public/SynDeir.html.

Thornton, Weldon. *J. M. Synge and the Western Mind*. New York: Harper and Row, 1979.

CMOS

50

Council of Science Editors (CSE) Style

Writers in the physical and life sciences follow Council of Science Editors (CSE) style, found in *Scientific Style and Format: The CSE Manual for Authors, Editors, and Publishers* (7th ed., 2006). The *CSE Manual* offers three documentation styles: *name-year*, *citation-sequence*, and *citation-name*.

50a In-text citations

1. **Name-Year Format** Authors' names and publication dates are included in parenthetical citations in the text, closely resembling *Chicago Manual* name-date style (see Chapter 49a).

   In-Text Citation

   H1N1 influenza, which comprises elements of human sea-sonal, porcine, and avian influenza viruses (Gatherer 2009), evolved quickly and spread rapidly. Studies on emerging zoonotic influenza strains (Charlton et al. 2009; Gatherer 2009) show that the development of rapid-testing diagnostic tools is essential for monitoring pandemics like H1N1 influenza.

   In the list of references at the end of the paper, list names alphabetically with the date after the name. Journal titles are abbreviated, without periods.

   Reference List Entries

   Charlton B, Crossley B, Hietala S. 2009. Conventional and future diagnostics for avian influenza. Comp Immunol Microbiol Infec Dis. 32(4):341–50.

   Gatherer D. 2009. The 2009 H1N1 influenza outbreak in its historical context. J Clin Virol. 45(3):174–78.

2. **Citation-Sequence Style** References may instead be cited by means of in-text superscript numbers (numbers set above the line, such as [1] and [2]) that refer to a

CSE

list of numbered references at the end of the paper. The references are numbered in the order in which they are cited in the text, and later references to the same work use the original number. When you have two or more sources cited at once, put the numbers in sequence, separated with commas but no spaces.

In-Text Citation

Studies of influenza viruses [1,4,9] show humans can become doubly infected with seasonal and zoonotic influenza strains. The mixture of strains can lead to new variants that require new testing procedures [1,2] and new vaccines [3–6] to detect and control pandemic outbreaks.

Reference List Entries

1. Gatherer, D. The 2009 H1N1 influenza outbreak in its historical context. J Clin Virol. 2009;45(3):174–78.

2. Charlton B, Crossley B, Hietala S. Conventional and future diagnostics for avian influenza. Comp Immunol Microbiol Infec Dis. 2009;32(4):341–50.

3. **Citation-Name Style** In this style, all sources are first listed on the References page in alphabetical order by authors' names and then assigned a number in sequence. These numbers correspond to in-text superscript numbers. Other than the change in numbering, the in-text and the reference list citation formats are the same as that used for the citation-sequence style.

50b References list

At the end of the paper, include a list titled "References" or "Cited References." The placement of the date depends on which style you use.

- **Name-year style.** Put the date after the author's name. Arrange the list alphabetically by last names. Do not indent any lines in the entries.

- **Citation-sequence and citation-name styles.** For books, put the date after the publisher's name. For periodicals, put the date after the periodical name. Arrange the list by number. Put the number at the left margin, followed by a period and a space and then the authors' names.

References in CSE style

Use periods between major divisions of the entry.

Author	Start with the last name first, no comma, and initials without periods for first and middle names. Separate authors' names with commas. End the list of authors' names with a period.
Title	For books and article titles, capitalize only the first word and proper nouns. Do not underline, italicize, or use quotation marks. For journals, abbreviate titles and capitalize all major words.
City of publication (state abbreviation): publisher; publication date	Include a semicolon and a space between the name of the publisher and the date. Use a semicolon with no space between the date and volume number of the journal. Abbreviate months. End with a period.
Pages	End the entry with a period. For journal articles, show the page numbers and end with a period. For books, you may include the total number of pages, with *p.* after the number, but this is optional.

Examples of CSE Format for a Reference List

BOOKS, PARTS OF BOOKS, AND REPORTS

JOURNAL ARTICLES

MAGAZINE ARTICLES

CSE

Notes: In the following examples, NY stands for name-year
format and CS/CN stands for citation-sequence and citation-
name format. References should be single-spaced, with a blank
line between each entry.

Books, Parts of Books, and Reports

1. **Book with One Author**

CS/CN: 1. Burnett DG. The sounding of the whale: science and
         cetaceans in the twentieth century. Chicago (IL): Univer-
         sity of Chicago Press; 2012.

NY: Burnett DG. 2012. The sounding of the whale: science and
        cetaceans in the twentieth century. Chicago (IL): University of
        Chicago Press.

2. **Book with More Than One Author** If there are more than
   ten authors, list the first ten and add *et al.*

CS/CN: 2. Joachain CJ, Kylstra NJ, Potvliege RM. Atoms in intense laser
         fields. New York (NY): Cambridge University Press; 2012.

NY: Joachain CJ, Kylstra NJ, Potvliege RM. 2012. Atoms in intense
        laser fields. New York (NY): Cambridge University Press.

3. **Anthology, Scholarly Collection, or Work That Names an
   Editor**

CS/CN: 3. Preedy VR, Watson RR, editors. Olives and olive oil in
         health and disease prevention. Burlington (MA): Aca-
         demic Press; 2010.

NY: Preedy VR, Watson RR, editors. 2010. Olives and olive oil
        in health and disease prevention. Burlington (MA): Aca-
        demic Press.

4. **Article or Chapter in an Anthology, Scholarly Collection, or Work That Names an Editor**

CS/CN: 4. Griffin PJ. Nuclear technologies. In: Marshall M, Oxley J, editors. Aspects of explosives detection. Amsterdam: Elsevier; 2009. p. 59–87.

NY: Griffin PJ. 2009. Nuclear technologies. In: Marshall M, Oxley J, editors. Aspects of explosives detection. Amsterdam: Elsevier; p. 59–87.

5. **Second or Later Edition**

CS/CN: 5. Lutgens FK, Tarbuck EJ, Tasa D. Essentials of geology. 11th ed. Upper Saddle River (NJ): Prentice Hall; 2012.

NY: Lutgens FK, Tarbuck EJ, Tasa D. 2012. Essentials of geology. 11th ed. Upper Saddle River (NJ): Prentice Hall.

6. **Work by a Group or Corporate Author** Begin the name-year entry with the group's acronym, placed in square brackets.

CS/CN: 6. Council of Science Editors, Style Manual Committee. Scientific style and format: the CSE manual for authors, editors, and publishers. 7th ed. Reston (VA): The Council; 2006.

NY: [CSE] Council of Science Editors, Style Manual Committee. 2006. Scientific style and format: the CSE manual for authors, editors, and publishers. 7th ed. Reston (VA): The Council.

7. **Book Accessed Online**

CS/CN: 7. Kansagara D, Gleitsmann K, Gillingham M, Freeman M, Quiñones A. Nutritional supplements for age-related macular degeneration: a systematic review [Internet]. Washington (DC): Dept of Veterans Affairs; 2012 [cited 2012 May 7]. Available from: http://www.ncbi.nlm.nih.gov/books/NBK84269/

NY: Kansagara D, Gleitsmann K, Gillingham M, Freeman M, Quiñones A. 2012. Nutritional supplements for age-related macular degeneration: a systematic review [Internet]. Washington (DC): Dept of Veterans Affairs; [cited 2012 May 7]. Available from: http://www.ncbi.nlm.nih.gov/books/NBK84269/

8. **Government Publication Accessed Online**

CS/CN: 8. National Aeronautics and Space Administration. Inadequate security practices expose key NASA network to cyber attack [Internet]. Washington (DC): National Aeronautics and Space Administration. 2011 Mar 28. Report No. IG-11-017. Available from: http://oig.nasa.gov/audits/reports/FY11/IG-11-017.pdf

CSE

NY: [NASA] National Aeronautics and Space Administration. 2011 Mar 28. Inadequate security practices expose key NASA network to cyber attack [Internet]. Washington (DC): National Aeronautics and Space Administration. Report No. IG-11-017. Available from: http://oig.nasa.gov/audits/reports/FY11/IG-11-017.pdf

Journal Articles

9. Article in a Journal

CS/CN: 9. Rodima-Taylor D, Olwig MF, Chhetri N. Adaptation as innovation, innovation as adaptation: an institutional approach to climate change. App Geog. 2012;33(2):107–11.

NY: Rodima-Taylor D, Olwig MF, Chhetri N. 2012. Adaptation as innovation, innovation as adaptation: an institutional approach to climate change. App Geog. 33(2):107–11.

10. Journal Article Located in a Library Database or Subscription Service

CS/CN: 10. Qi H, Lu H, Qiu HJ, Petrenko V, Liu A. Phagemid vectors for phage display: properties, characteristics, and construction. J Mol Biol [Internet]. 2012 [cited 2012 May 4];417(3):129–43. Science Direct. Available from: http://www.sciencedirect.com/ by subscription.

NY: Qi H, Lu H, Qiu HJ, Petrenko V, Liu A. 2012. Phagemid vectors for phage display: properties, characteristics, and construction. J Mol Biol [Internet]. [cited 2012 May 4];417(3):129–43. Science Direct. Available from: http://www.sciencedirect.com/ by subscription.

11. Article in an Online Journal

CS/CN: 11. Fike DS, Raehl CL, McCall KL, Burgoon SC, Schwarzlose SJ, Lockman PR. Improving community college student learning outcomes in biology. Elec J of Sci Ed [Internet]. 2011 [cited 2012 Jan 4];15(1). Available from: http://ejse.southwestern.edu/article/download/7358/6476

NY: Fike DS, Raehl CL, McCall KL, Burgoon SC, Schwarzlose SJ, Lockman PR. 2011. Improving community college student learning outcomes in biology. Elec J of Sci Ed [Internet]. [cited 2012 Jan 4];15(1). Available from: http://ejse.southwestern.edu/article/download/7358/6476

Magazine Articles

12. Article in a Magazine

CS/CN: 12. Castelvecchi D. The compass within. Sci Am. 2012 Jan;48–53.

NY: Castelvecchi D. 2012 Jan. The compass within. Sci Am. 48–53.

13. Magazine Article Located in a Library Database or Subscription Service

CS/CN: 13. Sepkowitz K. Achoo? The curious case of the non-flu season. Newsweek. 2012 Jan 30;12.

NY: Sepkowitz K. 2012 Jan 30. Achoo? The curious case of the non-flu season. Newsweek.12.

14. Article in an Online Magazine

CS/CN: 14. Keim B. Starling flocks behave like flying magnets. Wired [Internet]. 2012 Mar 13 [cited 2012 Apr 19]; [14 paragraphs]. Available from: http://www.wired.com/wiredscience/2012/03/starling-flock-dynamics

NY: Keim B. 2012 Mar 13. Starling flocks behave like flying magnets. Wired [Internet]. [cited 2012 Apr 19]; [14 paragraphs]. Available from: http://www.wired.com/wiredscience/2012/03/starling-flock-dynamics

Newspaper Articles

15. Article in a Newspaper Provide the page number and column number of the beginning of the article.

CS/CN: 15. Barringer F. Scientists find new dangers in tiny but pervasive particles in air pollution. New York Times (National Ed.). 2012 Feb 17;Sect. A:17 (col.1–6).

NY: Barringer F. 2012 Feb 17. Scientists find new dangers in tiny but pervasive particles in air pollution. New York Times (National Ed.). Sect. A:17 (col.1–6).

16. Newspaper Article Located in a Library Database or Subscription Service Provide the page number and column number of the beginning of the article.

CS/CN: 16. Borenstein S. Solar storm strikes again. Toronto Star [Internet]. 2012 Mar 10 [cited 2012 Apr 5]. Sect. A:21. Custom Newspapers. Available from: http://infotrac.galegroup.com/ by subscription.

NY: Borenstein S. 2012 Mar 10. Solar storm strikes again. Toronto Star [Internet]. [cited 2012 Apr 5];Sect. A:21. Custom Newspapers. Available from: http://infotrac.galegroup.com/ by subscription.

17. Article in an Online Newspaper Provide the page number and column number of the beginning of the article.

CSE

CS/CN: 17. Perlman D. Chorus frog carries killer fungus. San Francisco Chronicle [Internet]. 2012 Mar 12; [27 paragraphs]. Available from: http://www.sfgate.com/cgi-bin/article.cgi?f=/c/a/2012/03/13/MNKO1NJKED.DTL

NY: Perlman D. 2012 Mar 12. Chorus frog carries killer fungus. San Francisco Chronicle [Internet]. [27 paragraphs]. Available from: http://www.sfgate.com/cgi-bin/article.cgi?f=/c/a/2012/03/13/MNKO1NJKED.DTL

18. **Unsigned Newspaper Article** Begin the entry with the article title.

CS/CN: 18. Japan marks year since quake, tsunami disaster. Florence Morning News. 2012 Feb 17;Sect. A:4 (col. 2–4).

NY: Japan marks year since quake, tsunami disaster. 2012 Feb 17. Florence Morning News. Sect. A:4 (col. 2–4).

19. **Editorial** After the title, add [editorial].

CS/CN: 19. Reilly WK, Cayten MR. Preventing a Deepwater Horizon redux [editorial]. Washington Post, 2012 Feb 19;Sect. A:21 (col. 2–4).

NY: Reilly WK, Cayten MR. 2012 Feb 19. Preventing a Deepwater Horizon redux [editorial]. Washington Post. Sect. A:21 (col. 2–4).

Online, Audio, and Visual Media

20. **Website Home Page**

CS/CN: 20. Southern California earthquake data center [Internet]. Pasadena (CA): Cal Tech; c1992–2012 [cited 2012 Mar 15]. Available from: http://www.data.scec.org/

NY: Southern California earthquake data center [Internet]. c1992–2012. Pasadena (CA): Cal Tech; [cited 2012 Mar 15]. Available from: http://www.data.scec.org/

21. **Page or Article on a Website**

CS/CN: 21. Pew Research Center [Internet]. Washington (DC): Pew Research Center; c2012. Oil spill seen as ecological disaster; 2010 May 11 [cited 2012 May 15]. Available from: http://pewresearch.org/pubs/1590/poll-gulf-oil-disaster-obama-bp-support-for-drilling

NY: Pew Research Center [Internet]. c2012. Washington (DC): Pew Research Center. Oil spill seen as ecological disaster; 2010 May 11 [cited 2012 May 15]. Available from: http://pewresearch.org/pubs/1590/poll-gulf-oil-disaster-obama-bp-support-for-drilling

22. DVD, Blu-ray, or Videocassette

CS/CN: 22. Frontline: Inside Japan's nuclear meltdown [DVD]. Edge
D, director; Fanning D, Sullivan M, executive producers.
Arlington (VA): PBS; 2012. 1 DVD: 60 min., sound, color

NY: Frontline: Inside Japan's nuclear meltdown [DVD]. 2012.
Edge D, director; Fanning D, Sullivan M, executive producers. Arlington (VA): PBS. 1 DVD: 60 min., sound, color

23. Online Video

CS/CN: 23. Fortress of the bears [Internet video]. Kaufman F, exec-
utive producer; Murphy B, series producer. New York
(NY): PBS; 2012 Jan 25 [cited 2012 Mar 22]. 50:09 min.
Available from: http://video.pbs.org/video/2187882295

NY: Fortress of the bears [Internet video]. Kaufman F, executive
producer; Murphy B, series producer. New York (NY): PBS;
2012 Jan 25 [cited 2012 Mar 22]. 50:09 min. Available from:
http://video.pbs.org/video/2187882295

24. Audio Podcast

CS/CN: 24. Gorilla genome sheds light on human evolution [Internet
podcast]. Flatow I, host; Scally A, interviewee. New
York: Science Friday; 2012 Mar 9; [cited 2012 Apr 2].
3:34 min. Available from: http://www.sciencefriday.com/
program/archives/201203091

NY: Gorilla genome sheds light on human evolution [Internet
podcast]. 2012 Mar 9. Flatow I, host; Scally A, interviewee.
New York: Science Friday; [cited 2012 Apr 2]. 3:34 min.
Available from: http://www.sciencefriday.com/program/
archives/201203091

25. **E-Mail and Instant Messaging (IM)** Personal e-mail,
instant messaging, and other personal communications
are identified in the body of the paper and are not listed
in the References.

50c Paper format

The CSE Manual does not provide explicit directions for
formatting student papers. The information provided here,
however, follows CSE protocols for formatting written work.

CSE

Paper Format Quick Guide—CSE	
Paper format	Set paper margins of at least one inch on all sides. Double-space the main text of your paper, but single-space block quotations and your notes. Use single space for your bibliography entries, but leave a blank line between items.
Title page and titles	Include a title page. Place the title 1/3 down the page, and insert name, class, and date 2/3 down the page. Center all lines.
Header and page numbers	Place page numbers in a consistent location throughout your paper, either flush with the right margin, centered in the header, or centered in the footer.
Abstract, headings, and subheadings	Many CSE papers include an abstract, which is a short summary of your work. At the top of the second page, center the word *Abstract* and double-space summary.
	Use a consistent style for headings and subheadings. Following scientific style, the paper may include headings such as *Introduction*, *Methods*, *Results*, and *Discussion*.
Tables and figures	Insert tables and figures within the body of the text. For a table, create a brief label and place it directly above the table: **Table 1: Average July temperature for Mexico, 1950–2010**
	For figures, create a brief label and place it directly below the figure: **Figure 7: Structure of a Multiple Vortex Tornado**
Notes	In the text, insert a superscript number (small and raised above the text) to indicate a source citation.
	For the citation-sequence style, number the references at the end of your paper in the order they appear in your paper. For the citation-name style, at the end of your paper, organize entries alphabetically and assign each a number. Use these numbers for your superscript in-text citations.
References	Insert a title called *References* and center it on the page. Use single space for your entries, but leave a blank line between items. For the name-year style, indent entries under the first word.

Glossary of Usage

A, An   Use *a* before words beginning with a consonant and before words beginning with a vowel that sounds like a consonant:

> a cat   a house   a one-way street   a union   a history

Use *an* before words that begin with a vowel and before words with a silent *h*.

> an egg   an ice cube   an hour   an honor

Accept, Except   *Accept* means *to agree to, to believe*, or *to receive*.

> The detective **accepted** his account of the event.

Except, a verb, means *to exclude or leave out*, and *except*, a preposition, means *leaving out*.

> Because he did not know the answers, he was **excepted** from the list of contestants and asked to leave.

> **Except** for brussels sprouts, I eat most vegetables.

Advice, Advise   *Advice* is a noun, and *advise* is a verb.

> She always offers too much **advice**.

> Would you **advise** me about choosing the right course?

Ain't   This is a nonstandard way of saying *am not, is not, has not, have not*, and so on.

All Ready, Already   *All ready* means *prepared; already* means *before* or *by this time*.

> The courses for the meal are **all ready** to be served.

> When I got home, she was **already** there.

All Right, Alright   *All right* is two words, not one. *Alright* is an incorrect form.

Alot, A Lot   *Alot* is an incorrect form of *a lot*.

Among, Between   Use *among* when referring to three or more things and *between* when referring to two things.

> The decision was discussed **among** all the members of the committee.

> I had to decide **between** the chocolate pie and the almond ice cream.

Amount, Number   Use *amount* for things or ideas that are general or abstract and cannot be counted. For example, *furniture* is a general term and cannot be counted. That is, we cannot say *one furniture* or *two furnitures*. Use *number* for things that can be counted (for example, *four chairs* or *three tables*).

> He had a huge **amount** of work to finish before the deadline.

> A **number** of people saw the accident.

An   See the entry for **a, an**.

And   Although some discourage using *and* as the first word in a sentence, it is an acceptable word with which to begin a sentence.

Anybody, Any Body   See the entry for **anyone, any one**.

Anyone, Any One   *Anyone* means *any person at all*. *Any one* refers to a specific person or thing in a group. There are similar distinctions for other words ending in -*body* and -*one* (for example, *everybody, every body, anybody, any body, someone*, and *some one*).

> The teacher asked if **anyone** knew the answer.

> **Any one** of those children could have taken the ball.

As, As If, As Though, Like   Use *as* in a comparison (not *like*) when equality is intended or when the meaning is *in the function of.*

> Celia acted **as** (not *like*) the leader when the group was getting organized. (Celia = leader)

Use *as if* or *as though* for the subjunctive.

> He spent his money **as if** (*or* **as though**) he were rich.

Use *like* in a comparison (not *as*) when the meaning is *in the manner of* or *to the same degree as.*

> The boy swam **like** a fish.

Awhile, A While   *Awhile* is an adverb meaning *a short time* and modifies a verb:

> He talked **awhile** and then left.

A while is an article with the noun *while* and means *a period of time:*

> I'll be there in **a while**.

Bad, Badly   *Bad* is an adjective and is used after linking verbs. *Badly* is an adverb. (See 20b.)

> The wheat crop looked **bad** (not *badly*) because of lack of rain.

> There was a **bad** flood last summer.

> The building was **badly** constructed and unable to withstand strong winds.

Beside, Besides   *Beside* is a preposition meaning *at the side of, compared with,* or *having nothing to do with. Besides* is a preposition meaning *in addition to* or *other than. Besides* as an adverb means *also* or *moreover.*

> That is **beside** the point.

> **Besides** the radio, they had no contact with the outside world.

> **Besides**, I enjoyed the concert.

Between, Among   See the entry for **among, between**.

Breath, Breathe   *Breath* is a noun, and *breathe* is a verb.

> She held her **breath** when she dived into the water.

> Learn to **breathe** deeply when you swim.

But   Although some people discourage the use of *but* as the first word in a sentence, it can be used to begin a sentence.

Can, May   *Can* expresses ability, knowledge, or capacity:

> He **can** play both the violin and the cello.

May is a verb that expresses possibility or permission. Careful writers avoid using *can* to mean *permission:*

> **May** [not *can*] I sit here?

Choose, Chose   *Choose* is the present tense of the verb, and *chose* is the past tense:

> Jennie should **choose** strawberry ice cream.

> Yesterday, she **chose** strawberry-flavored popcorn.

Cite, Site   *Cite* is a verb that means *to quote an authority or source; site* is a noun referring to *a place.*

> Be sure to **cite** your sources in the paper.

> That is the **site** of the new city swimming pool.

Could of   This is incorrect. Instead use *could have.*

Different from, Different than   *Different from* is always correct, but some writers use *different than* if a clause follows this phrase.

> This program is **different from** the others.

> That is a **different** result **than** they predicted.

Done   The past tense forms of the verb *do* are *did* and *done*. *Did* is the simple form that needs no additional verb as a helper. *Done* is the past form that requires the helper *have*. Some writers make the mistake of interchanging *did* and *done*.

They ~~done~~ it again. (*or*) They ~~done~~ it again.
  did   *have done*

Etc.   This is an abbreviation of the Latin *et cetera*, meaning *and the rest*. It should be used sparingly if at all in formal academic writing. Use instead phrases such as *and so forth* or *and so on*.

Everybody, Every Body   See the entry for **anyone, any one**.

Everyone, Every One   See the entry for **anyone, any one**.

Except, Accept   See the entry for **accept, except**.

Farther, Further   *Farther* is used when actual distance is involved, and *further* is used to mean *to a greater extent, more*.

The house is **farther** from the road than I realized.

That was **furthest** from my thoughts at the time.

Fewer, Less   *Fewer* is used for things that can be counted (*fewer trees, fewer people*), and *less* is used for ideas, abstractions, things that are thought of collectively rather than separately (*less trouble, less furniture*), and things that are measured by amount, not number (*less milk, less fuel*).

Gone, Went   Past tense forms of the verb *go*. *Went* is the simple form that needs no additional verb as a helper. *Gone* is the past form that requires the helper *have*. Some writers make the mistake of interchanging *went* and *gone*. (See section 18b.)

They ~~gone~~ away yesterday.
  went (*or*) *have gone*

Good, Well   *Good* is an adjective and therefore describes only nouns. *Well* is an adverb and therefore describes adjectives, other adverbs, and verbs. The word *well* is used as an adjective only in the sense of *in good health*. (See 20b.)

The stereo works ~~good~~. I feel ~~good~~.
  well   *well*

She is a **good** driver.

Got, Have   *Got* is the past tense of *get* and should not be used in place of *have*. Similarly, *got to* should not be used as a substitute for *must*. *Have got to* is an informal substitute for *must*.

Do you ~~got~~ any pennies for the meter?
  have

I ~~got~~ to go now.
  must

Informal: You **have got to** see that movie.

Have, Got   See the entry for **got, have**.

Have, Of   *Have*, not *of*, should follow verbs such as *could, might, must,* and *should*.

They should ~~of~~ called by now.
  have

I   Although some people discourage the use of *I* in formal essays, it is acceptable. If you wish to eliminate the use of *I*, see Chapter 11 on passive verbs.

Is When, Is Why, Is Where, Is Because   These are incorrect forms for definitions. See 8f on faulty predication.

Its, It's   *Its* is a personal pronoun in the possessive case. *It's* is a contraction for *it is*.

The kitten licked **its** paw.   **It's** a good time for a vacation.

Lay, Lie   *Lay* is a verb that needs an object and should not be used in place of *lie*, a verb that takes no direct object. (See 18c.)

He should ~~lay~~ down and rest awhile.
  lie

You can ~~lie~~ that package on the front table.
  lay

Less, Fewer   See the entry for **fewer, less**.

Like, As   See the entry for **as, as if, as though, like**.

Like for   The phrase "I'd like for you to do that" is incorrect. Omit *for*.

May, Can   See the entry for **can, may**.

Number, Amount   See the entry for **amount, number**.

Of, Have   See the entry for **have, of**.

O.K., OK, Okay   These can be used informally but should not be used in formal or academic writing.

Reason. . . Because   This is redundant. Instead of *because*, use *that*.

The reason she dropped the course is ~~because~~ *that* she couldn't keep up with the homework.

> **Less wordy revision:**   She dropped the course **because** she couldn't keep up with the homework.

Reason Why   Using *why* is redundant. Drop the word *why*.

The reason ~~why~~ I called is to remind you of your promise.

Saw, Seen   Past tense forms of the verb *see*. *Saw* is the simple form that needs no additional verb as a helper. *Seen* is the past form that requires the helper *have*. Some writers make the mistake of interchanging *saw* and *seen*. (See 18b.)

They ~~seen~~ *saw* it happen. (*or*) They ~~seen~~ *have seen* it happen.

Set, Sit   *Set* means *to place* and is followed by a direct object. *Sit* means *to be seated*. It is incorrect to substitute *set* for *sit*.

Come in and ~~set~~ *sit* down.

~~Sit~~ *Set* the flowers on the table.

Should of   This is incorrect. Instead use *should have*.

Sit, Set   See the entry for **set, sit**.

Site, Cite   See the entry for **cite, site**.

Somebody, Some Body   See the entry for **anyone, any one**.

Someone, Some One   See the entry for **anyone, any one**.

Suppose to, Use to   These are nonstandard forms for *supposed to* and *used to*.

Than, Then   *Than* introduces the second element in a comparison. *Then* means *at that time, next, after that*, or *in that case*.

She is taller **than** I am.

He picked up the ticket and **then** left the house.

That There, This Here, These Here, Those There   These are incorrect forms for *that, this, these, those*.

That, Which   Use *that* for essential clauses and *which* for nonessential clauses. Some writers, however, also use *which* for essential clauses. (See 25c.)

Their, There, They're   *Their* is a possessive pronoun; *there* means *in, at*, or *to that place*; and *they're* is a contraction for *they are*.

Their house has been sold.

There is the parking lot.

They're both good swimmers.

Theirself, Theirselves, Themself   These are all incorrect forms for *themselves*.

Them   It is incorrect to use *them* in place of either the pronoun *these* or *those*.

Look at ~~them~~ *those* apples.

Then, Than See the entry for **than, then**.

To, Too, Two *To* is a preposition, *too* is an adverb meaning *very* or *also*, and *two* is a number.

> He brought his bass guitar **to** the party.

> He brought his drums **too**.

> He had **two** music stands.

Use to, Suppose to See the entry for **suppose to, use to**.

Want for Omit the incorrect *for* in phrases such as "I want *for* you to come here."

Well, Good See the entry for **good, well**.

Went, Gone See the entry for **gone, went**.

Where It is incorrect to use *where* to mean *when* or *that*.

> The Fourth of July is a holiday ~~where~~ _{when} people watch fireworks.

> I see ~~where~~ _{that} there is now a ban on shooting panthers.

Where. . . at This is a redundant form. Omit *at*.

> This is where the picnic is ~~at~~.

Which, That See the entry for **that, which**.

While, Awhile See the entry for **awhile, a while**.

Who, Whom Use *who* for the subjective case; use *whom* for the objective case.

> He is the person **who** signs that form.

> He is the person **whom** I asked for help.

Who's, Whose *Who's* is a contraction for *who is; whose* is a possessive pronoun.

> **Who's** included on that list?

> **Whose** wristwatch is this?

Your, You're *Your* is a possessive pronoun; *you're* is a contraction for *you are*.

> **Your** hands are cold.

> **You're** a great success.

Glossary of Grammatical Terms

Abstract Nouns See Chapter 37.

Active Voice See Chapter 11.

Adjective and Adverb Clauses See **Dependent Clauses**.

Adjectives See 20a.

Adverbs See 20b.

Agreement See 18a.

Antecedents Words or groups of words to which pronouns refer.

When the **bell** was rung, **it** sounded very loudly.

(*Bell* is the antecedent of *it*.)

Articles See Chapter 38.

Auxiliary Verbs Verbs used with main verbs in verb phrases.

should be going
(auxiliary verb)

has taken
(auxiliary verb)

Case See 19a.

Clauses Groups of related words that contain both subjects and predicates and function either as sentences or as parts of sentences. Clauses are either independent (or main) or dependent (or subordinate). (See Chapter 17 and 25a, b, and c.)

Collective Nouns Nouns that refer to groups of people or things, such as a *committee, team*, or *jury*. (See 18a.)

Comma Splices Punctuation errors in which two or more independent clauses in compound sentences are separated only by commas and no coordinating conjunctions. (See 17a.)

but (or);
Jessie said he could not help,ˌthat was his usual response.

Common Nouns See Chapter 37.

Comparative See 20c.

Complement When linking verbs link subjects to adjectives or nouns, the adjectives or nouns are complements.

Phyllis was **tired**.
(complement)
She became a **musician**.
(complement)

Complex Sentences Sentences with at least one independent clause and at least one dependent clause arranged in any order.

Compound-Complex Sentences Sentences with at least two independent clauses and at least one dependent clause arranged in any order.

Compound Nouns Words such as *swimming pool, dropout, roommate*, and *stepmother*, formed of more than one word that could stand on its own.

Compound Sentences Sentences with two or more independent clauses and no dependent clauses. (See Chapter 17.)

Conjunctions Words that connect other words, phrases, and clauses in sentences. *Coordinating conjunctions* connect independent clauses; *subordinating conjunctions* connect dependent or subordinating clauses with independent or main clauses.

Coordinating
conjunctions:

and, but, for, or, nor, so, yet

Some subordinating
conjunctions:

after, although, because, if, since,
until, while

Conjunctive Adverbs Words that begin or join independent clauses. (See Chapter 25.)

consequently, however, therefore, thus, moreover

Connotation The attitudes and emotional overtones beyond the direct definition of a word. For example, the words *plump* and *fat* both mean *fleshy*, but *plump* has a more positive connotation than *fat*. (See 12d.)

Coordination Equal importance. Two independent clauses in the same sentence are coordinate because they have equal importance and the same emphasis.

Dangling Modifiers See 21a.

Demonstrative Pronouns Pronouns that refer to things.

Denotation The explicit dictionary definition of a word, as opposed to the connotation of a word. (See 12d.)

Dependent Clauses (Subordinate Clauses)   Clauses that cannot stand alone as complete sentences. (See Chapters 24, 25.)

Direct Discourse   See 28a.

Direct/Indirect Quotations   See 28a.

Direct Objects   Nouns or pronouns that follow a transitive verb and complete the meaning or receive the action of the verb. The direct object answers the question *what?* or *whom?*

Essential and Nonessential Clauses and Phrases   See 25c.

Faulty Parallelism   See 23b.

Faulty Predication   See 8f.

Fragments   Groups of words punctuated as sentences that either do not have both a subject and a complete verb or that are dependent clauses. (See Chapter 16.)

> Whenever we wanted to pick fresh fruit while we were staying on my
> , we would head for the orchard with buckets
> grandmother's farm.

Fused Sentences   Punctuation errors (also called *run-ons*) in which there is no punctuation between independent clauses in the sentence. (See 17b.)

> Jennifer never learned how to ask politely she just took what she wanted.

Gerunds   Verbal forms ending in *-ing* that function as nouns or as parts of verb forms. (See 36e.)

> Arnon enjoys **cooking**.
>   (gerund)
>   **Jogging** is another of his pastimes.
> (gerund)

Homonyms   Words that sound alike but are spelled differently and have different meanings. (hear/here, passed/past, buy/by, etc.) (See 34c.)

Idioms   Expressions meaning something beyond the simple definition or literal translation into another language. See Chapter 41.

Independent Clauses   Clauses that can stand alone as complete sentences because they do not depend on other clauses to complete their meanings. (See 25a.)

Indirect Discourse   See 28a.

Infinitives   Phrases made up of the present form of the verb preceded by *to*. Infinitives can have subjects, objects, complements, or modifiers.

> Everyone wanted **to swim** in the new pool.
>   (infinitive)

Irregular Verbs   See 18b.

Jargon   See 12a.

Linking Verbs   See 18a.

Misplaced Modifiers   See 21b.

Modal Verbs   See 36c.

Modifiers   See Chapter 21.

Nonessential (or Nonrestrictive) Clauses and Phrases   See 25c.

Nouns   Words that name people, places, things, and ideas and have plural or possessive endings. Nouns function as subjects, direct objects, predicate nominatives, objects of prepositions, and indirect objects.

Object of the Preposition   The noun following the preposition. The preposition, its object, and any modifiers make up the prepositional phrase.

> For **Daniel**
> (object of the preposition *for*)
> She knocked twice **on the big wooden door**.
>   (prepositional phrase)

Parallel Construction   See Chapter 23.

Participles Verb forms that may be part of the complete verb or function as adjectives or adverbs. The present participle ends in *-ing*, and the past participle usually ends in *-ed*, *-d*, *-n*, or *-t*. (See **Phrases**.)

Present participles: *running, sleeping, digging*

She is **running** for mayor in this campaign.
(*present participle*)

Past participles: *walked, deleted, chosen*

The candidate **elected** will take office in January.
(*past participle*)

Parts of Speech The eight classes into which words are grouped according to their function, place, meaning, and use in a sentence: nouns, pronouns, verbs, adjectives, adverbs, prepositions, conjunctions, and interjections.

Passive Voice See Chapter 11.

Person See 19a.

Personal Pronouns See 19a.

Phrases Groups of related words without subjects and predicates.

Verb phrases function as verbs.

She **has been eating** too much sugar.
(*verb phrase*)

Noun phrases function as nouns.

A major winter storm hit **the eastern coast of Maine**.
(*noun phrase*)   (*noun phrase*)

Prepositional phrases usually function as modifiers.

That book **of hers** is overdue at the library.
(*prepositional phrase*)

Possessive Pronouns See 19a.

Predication Words or groups of words that express action or state of beginning in a sentence and consist of one or more verbs, plus any complements or modifiers.

Prepositions Words that link and relate their objects (usually nouns or pronouns) to some other word or words in a sentence. Prepositions usually precede their objects but may follow the objects and appear at the end of the sentence.

The server gave the check **to my date** by mistake.
(*prepositional phrase*)

I wonder **what** she is asking **for**.
(*object of the preposition*) (*preposition*)

Pronoun Case See 19a.

Pronouns Words that substitute for nouns. (See 19a.) Pronouns should refer to previously stated nouns, called *antecedents*.

When **Josh** came in, **he** brought some firewood.
(*antecedent*)   (*pronoun*)

There are seven forms of pronouns: personal, possessive, reflexive, interrogative, demonstrative, indefinite, and relative.

Proper Nouns See 30a.

Relative Pronouns Pronouns that show the relationship of a dependent clause to a noun in the sentence. Relative pronouns substitute for nouns already mentioned in sentences; introduce adjective or noun clauses; and include *that, which, who, whom,* and *whose*.

This was the movie **that** won the Academy Award.

Restrictive Clauses and Phrases See 25c.

Run-On Sentences See **Fused Sentences** and 17b.

Sentence Fragment See **Fragments**.

Sentences Groups of words that have at least one independent clause (a complete unit of thought with a subject and predicate). Sentences can be classified by their structure as simple, compound, complex, and compound-complex.

Simple: one independent clause

Compound: two or more independent clauses

Complex:	one or more independent clauses and one or more dependent clauses
Compound-complex:	two or more independent clauses and one or more dependent clauses

Split Infinitives Phrases in which modifiers are inserted between *to* and the verb. Some people object to split infinitives, but others consider them grammatically acceptable.

to quickly turn   to easily reach   to forcefully enter

Subject The word or words in a sentence that act or are acted on by the verb or are linked by the verb to another word or words in the sentence. The *simple subject* includes only the noun or other main word or words, and the *complete subject* includes all the modifiers with the subject.

Harvey objected to his roommate's alarm going off at 9:00 a.m.
(Harvey is the subject.)

Every single one of the people in the room heard her giggle.
(The simple subject is *one*; the complete subject is the whole phrase.)

Subjunctive Mood See 18e.

Subordinating Conjunctions Words such as *although, if, until*, and *when* that join two clauses and subordinate one to the other.

She is late. She overslept.

She is late **because** she overslept.

Subordination The act of placing one clause in a subordinate or dependent relationship to another in a sentence because it is less important and is dependent for its meaning on the other clause.

Suffixes Word parts added to the ends of words (-ful, -less, etc.).

Superlative Forms of Adjectives and Adverbs See 20c.

Synonyms Words with similar meanings (damp/moist, pretty/attractive, etc.).

Tense See **Verb Tenses**.

Tone See Chapter 12.

Transitions Words in sentences that show relationships between sentences and paragraphs. (See Chapter 15.)

Transitive Verbs See **Verbs**.

Verbals Words that are derived from verbs but do not act as verbs in sentences. Three types of verbals are infinitives, participles, and gerunds.

Infinitives:	*to* + verb
	to say to wind
Participles:	Words used as modifiers or with helping verbs. The present participle ends in *-ing*, and many past participles end in *-ed*.
	The dog is **panting**. (present participle) He bought only **used** clothing. (past participle)
Gerunds:	Present participles used as nouns.
	Smiling was not a natural act for her. (gerund)

Verb Conjugations The forms of verbs in various tenses. (See Chapter 36 and 18b.)

Verbs Words or groups of words (verb phrases) in predicates that express action, show a state of being, or act as a link between the subject and the rest of the predicate. Verbs change form to show time (tense), mood, and voice and are classified as transitive, intransitive, and linking verbs. (See 18b and Chapter 36.)

Transitive verbs:	Require objects to complete the predicate.
	He **cut** the cardboard **box** with his knife. (transitive verb) (object)

Intransitive verbs: Do not require objects.

My ancient cat often **lies** on the porch.
(*intransitive verb*)

Linking verbs: Link the subject to the following noun or
adjective.

The trees **are** bare.
(*linking verb*)

Verb Tenses   The times indicated by the verb forms in the past, present, or future. (See 18b and 36a.)

Voice   Verbs are either in the *active* or *passive* voice. (See Chapter 11.) Voice can also refer to levels of formality used in writing. (See Chapter 12).

Credits

Text Credits: Christakis, Nicholas A., and James H. Fowler. Connected: The Surprising Power of Social Networks and How They Shape Our Lives—How Your Friends' Friends' Friends Affect Everything You Feel, Think, and Do. New York: Back Bay-Little, 2011. Print; © 2012 Living on Earth. Used with permission of Living on Earth and World Media Foundation. www.loe.org Living on Earth is the weekly environmental news and information program distributed by Public Radio International. Use of material does not imply endorsement; Damond Benningfield, "The Second-Moon Theory," Air & Space, January, 2012, http://www.airspacemag.com/space-exploration/The-Second-Moon-Theory.html; Harris, Muriel G.; Kunka, Jennifer. Prentice Hall Reference Guide, 8th Ed., © 2012. Reprinted and Electronically reproduced by permission of Pearson Education, Inc., Upper Saddle River, New Jersey; Ivcevic, Z., & Ambady, N. (2012). Personality impressions from identity claims on Facebook. Psychology of Popular Media Culture, 1, 38–45. doi:10.1037/a0027329. Javers, Eamon. "Levin Probe Faults Washington Mutual for Risky Loans." Politico. Capital News Co., 14 Apr. 2010. Web. 1 Mar. 2012; Jennifer Coker; Levin, Carl. "Opening Statement of Senator Carl Levin, U.S. Senate Permanent Subcommittee on Investigations Hearing on Wall Street and the Financial Crisis." Carl Levin: United States Senator. United States Senate, 13 Apr. 2010. Web. 1 Mar. 2012; Lowenstein, Kate. Health Oct. 2011: 86+; Ma, Julie. "A 'Vertical Greenhouse' Could Make a Swedish City Self-Sufficient." GOOD. GOOD Worldwide, 12 Mar. 2012. Web. 14 Mar. 2012; Obama, Michelle. "First Lady Michelle Obama Encourages Families to Get Active in the Great Outdoors." WhiteHouse.gov. 18 Jul. 2012. White House. Specter, Michael. "The Deadliest Virus." New Yorker 12 Mar. 2012: 32–37. Print; Staci Poston; Sydney Cumbie; Twenge, Jean M., and W. Keith Campbell. The Narcissism Epidemic: Living in the Age of Entitlement. New York: Free Press, 2009. Print; Webber, Michael E. "More Food, Less Energy." Scientific American Jan. 2012: 74–79. Print; U.S. Geological Survey.

Photo Credits: Page 16: Oregon Humane Society/Leopold Ketel + Partner; **Page 21:** Department of the Interior/USGS; **Page 26 left:** Brasil2/iStockphoto; **Page 26 right:** Greg Thompson/USFWS; **Page 236:** From *In Defense of Food* by Michael Pollan, copyright © 2008 by Michael Pollan/The Penguin Press, a division of Penguin Group (USA) Inc.

Index

293

Correction Symbols

Symbol	Problem	Section
abbr	abbreviation error	33
adj	adjective error	20
adv	adverb error	20
agr	agreement error	18a, 19b
art	article error	38
awk	awkward construction	8, 22
ca	case error	19a
cap(s)	capitalization error	30
cit	citation missing/format error	47–50
coh	coherence needed	1, 8
cs	comma splice	17a
dm	dangling modifier	21a
frag	fragment	16
fs	fused/run-on sentence	17b
hyph	hyphenation error	29a
ital	italics error	31
lc	use lowercase	30
log	logic	1a-e, 3, 8f
mm	misplaced modifier	21b
¶/no¶	new paragraph/do not begin new paragraph	1e-f
num	number	32
//	parallelism error	23
pass	unneeded passive voice	11
pl	plural needed	34b, 37
pred	predication error	8f
prep	preposition error	39
p	punctuation error	29
.	period error	29c
?	question mark error	29c
!	exclamation mark error	29c
,	comma error	24, 25
;	semicolon error	27
:	colon error	29b
'	apostrophe error	26
""	quotation marks error	28
—	dash error	29d
( )	parentheses error	29f
ref	reference error	19b
shft	shift error	22
sp	spelling error	34
sxt	sexist language	14
trans	transition needed	1g, 15
usage	usage error	Glossary of Usage
var	variety needed	9
v	verb error	18b, 36
vt	verb tense error	36a
w	wordy	10
wc	word choice/wrong word	12, 13, 14
x	obvious error	
^	insert	
∿/tr	transpose	
ℐ	delete	